READING VICTORIAN
SCHOOLROOMS

Children's Literature and Culture
Jack Zipes, *Series Editor*

READING VICTORIAN SCHOOLROOMS

Childhood and Education in Nineteenth-Century Fiction

ELIZABETH GARGANO

Routledge
Taylor & Francis Group
New York   London

Routledge
Taylor & Francis Group
270 Madison Avenue
New York, NY 10016

Routledge
Taylor & Francis Group
2 Park Square
Milton Park, Abingdon
Oxon OX14 4RN

Printed in the United States of America on acid-free paper
10 9 8 7 6 5 4 3 2 1

International Standard Book Number-13: 978-0-415-98034-0 (Hardcover)

Library of Congress Cataloging-in-Publication Data

Gargano, Elizabeth.
    Reading Victorian schoolrooms : childhood and education in nineteenth-century fiction / Elizabeth Gargano.
        p. cm. -- (Children's literature and culture ; 44)
    Includes bibliographical references and index.
    ISBN 978-0-415-98034-0 (hardback : alk. paper)
    1. Education in literature. 2. English fiction--19th century--History and criticism. 3. Children's stories, English--History and criticism. 4. Children in literature. I. Title.

PR878.E38G37 2007
823'.8093557--dc22   2006101157

Visit the Taylor & Francis Web site at
http://www.taylorandfrancis.com

and the Routledge Web site at
http://www.routledge.com

For Peter and Joe

CONTENTS

LIST OF ILLUSTRATIONS

SERIES EDITOR'S FOREWORD

Dedicated to furthering original research in children's literature and culture, the Children's Literature and Culture series includes monographs on individual authors and illustrators, historical examinations of different periods, literary analyses of genres, and comparative studies on literature and the mass media. The series is international in scope and is intended to encourage innovative research in children's literature with a focus on interdisciplinary methodology.

Children's literature and culture are understood in the broadest sense of the term *children* to encompass the period of childhood up through adolescence. Owing to the fact that the notion of childhood has changed so much since the origination of children's literature, this Routledge series is particularly concerned with transformations in children's culture and how they have affected the representation and socialization of children. While the emphasis of the series is on children's literature, all types of studies that deal with children's radio, film, television, and art are included in an endeavor to grasp the aesthetics and values of children's culture. Not only have there been momentous changes in children's culture in the last fifty years, but there have been radical shifts in the scholarship that deals with these changes. In this regard, the goal of the Children's Literature and Culture series is to enhance research in this field and, at the same time, point to new directions that bring together the best scholarly work throughout the world.

Jack Zipes

ACKNOWLEDGMENTS

A portion of Chapter 4 appeared previously as "Death by Learning: Zymosis and the Perils of School in E. J. May's *Dashwood Priory*," an essay in *Children's Literature* 33 (2005).

Because *Reading Victorian Schoolrooms* explores the intimate, flexible, and often conversational mode of instruction that the Victorians celebrated as "domestic education," I can't help reflecting on the good fortune that sent me so many wonderful teachers and mentors. I am especially grateful to Karen Chase and Michael Levenson for reading this manuscript many times in its initial stages, for offering invaluable editorial advice, and for continuing to encourage me as the project grew and developed. Another early reader of this project when I was pursuing graduate studies at the University of Virginia, Rita Felski also offered careful readings, incisive comments, and suggestions for further research. I am particularly indebted to my colleague Mark West for his unstinting support and wise suggestions regarding the manuscript. Conversing with him about children's literature and culture was an education in itself. Paula Connolly, Jennifer Munroe, and Tony Jackson, colleagues and members of an insightful, supportive, and challenging writing group, also read portions of the manuscript and inspired me to reshape it. The suggestions of my editor Jack Zipes helped me look at the project through new eyes, enabling me to trace a more complex and engaging narrative. Finally, I want to thank my husband Peter Blair and our son Joseph for their encouragement, patience, and inspiration, which I can never repay.

INTRODUCTION

"I have heard strange things of schools," muses the wise Fanny Williams in Frederic Farrar's classic schoolboy narrative, *Eric: or Little by Little* (1858). She goes on to reflect that school may well ruin her young cousin Eric—as indeed it does (12). As the novel's title indicates, exposure to hardened, older schoolboys wears away Eric's moral character "little by little"; eventually, guilt-ridden because of his misadventures at school, he runs away, falls ill, and dies at home, redeemed by and reconciled to his family circle. Quaint and dated as her words appear today, Fanny spoke for many Victorians. As education became increasingly institutionalized throughout the century, numerous Victorian school narratives portrayed harsh, excessively regimented classrooms, contrasting the looming specter of educational standardization with a supposedly nurturing tradition of domestic instruction that dated back to Rousseau's *Émile* (1762). In practice, individual novelists often accepted a degree of educational standardization as a social necessity. Yet as this book argues, during the Victorian era, fictive schoolroom scenes ritualistically dramatize a perceived imbalance between the rapid institutionalization of education and the shrinking realm of domestic instruction. This contest between institutional and domestic spheres involved high stakes, as writers and the reading public grappled with the questions of who had the right to define and shape the experience of childhood, and where that process of definition would take place. As adults with competing agendas strove to reenvision the space, nature, and status of childhood, journalists, novelists, and educational reformers resorted to vivid spatial metaphors to define emotionally freighted choices. Depicting the space of school as a divisive, segmented, and conflicted site, numerous novelists also portrayed this problematic territory as analogous to the culturally defined terrain of modern childhood.

Today in England and America, with the spaces of a vast national school system cemented in rules and regulations as well as in brick and mortar, Victorian school narratives help us recover the "strangeness" that the fictional Fanny Williams associated with the emergence of a rigorously defined school space. At the beginning of the century, England had no national system of schools, no mandatory primary education, and few assumptions about what constituted a standardized curriculum—a body of knowledge that all children should study. By the end of the century all three elements were in place. This dramatic story of educational, historical, and cultural change resonated through a diverse array of nineteenth-century school narratives, including mainstream novels and those designed specifically for child readers.

The journey toward a nationally funded school system was slow and circuitous, marked by a series of legislative milestones. In the 1830s and 1840s, the state authorized limited funding to selected schools. In 1862, the Revised Code mandated inspections for a mixed bag of government-affiliated schools. Finally, the 1870 Education Act extended and consolidated the tentatively defined system already in place. In fact, the growth of a national school system was only one component, albeit a major one, of the proliferation of schools across the English landscape. Increasingly, Victorian children attended an assortment of day schools, private boarding schools, factory schools, parish schools, and academies for dissenters sponsored by the British and Foreign School Society, not to mention the illustrious public schools reserved for social elites. Class loyalties and tensions worked in complex ways to valorize schooling outside the home. Inspired in part by conservative fears about extending the franchise to artisans and working-class voters, legislators gradually carved out a national school system to educate the new pool of potential voters in middle- and upper-class values, while simultaneously teaching them to be content with their current economic and social status. This conflicted project opened avenues for upward mobility while often overtly discouraging it. A concurrent expansion of the elite public and private schools, which offered a classical education in Latin and Greek, presented a similarly confused picture. If classical education represented the social marker of the "gentleman," its expansion problematized class boundaries even as the elite schools served as bastions of exclusivity and privilege. As schooling outside the home both reinforced and blurred class differences, it also challenged traditional assumptions about the primacy of domestic education and parental control.

In fact, the proliferation of Victorian schools inspired an initially powerful but gradually diminishing resistance toward institutionalized education, embodied in a variety of fictive school narratives. To consider first the rich and conflicted genre of school stories written primarily for children, *Eric,* published at mid-century, harshly and unapologetically critiques school life; by the end of the century, however, Evelyn Sharp's *The Making of a Schoolgirl* (1897) describes the world of school in glowing terms, as a gateway to passionate friendships and intellectual and emotional independence. Though often portrayed by later readers as an example of mindless school boosterism, Thomas Hughes's *Tom Brown's Schooldays* (1857) in fact offers a much more mixed portrait of school life than is generally allowed. To isolate such tales from mainstream literary works for adult readers would be, for my purposes, a critical misstep. Charles Dickens, Charlotte Brontë, and George Eliot not only grappled with the same issues, images, and themes central to the work of Farrar and Hughes, but the boundaries between literature for children and adults remained shifting and permeable during this period, allowing for rich mutual exchanges between children's tales and mainstream novels.

Although the novel's increasingly positive depiction of school life reflects society's rising level of comfort with education outside the home, the Victorians' abiding suspicion of institutionalized schooling should not be underestimated. The many fictive and journalistic attacks on institutionalized schooling critiqued not only the expanding national schools, but also an array of church and charity-sponsored schools, as well as schools established by private individuals as commercial ventures. For many Victorians, the institutionalization of education represented a wrenching, inspiring, and terrifying sea change that would alter not only social and familial relations, but the very notion of childhood itself.

The genre of the novel was in fact in a unique position to dramatize Victorian fears about education outside the home. As many critics have maintained, both the theme of education and the educative project have been central to the novel's development. A dramatic example is the international influence of Rousseau's groundbreaking *Émile*, widely accepted in its day as both a novel and an educational treatise. *Émile* serves as an early example of the *bildungsroman,* which strove to educate readers experientially rather than through didactic injunctions, as they vicariously suffered through the ordeals and rejoiced at the rewards of the fictive protagonists with whom they identified. This aspect of the *bildungsroman*—and the *bildungsromanic* component within many mainstream Victorian novels—allowed novelists to cast their work (whether accurately or not) as a form of *domestic education*, a jeopardized bulwark against a rising tide of institutionalization. Thus, as I will argue, the education debates and the vivid schoolroom scenes that mesmerized readers of Victorian fictions are far more central to understanding the nineteenth-century English novel than has been generally acknowledged. Conceptions of childhood, schooling, and the nature of novel reading converge in some of the most dramatic and influential schoolroom scenes in the work of Dickens, Brontë, Eliot, and others.

Harriet Martineau's *The Crofton Boys* (1841), a children's novel relatively neglected today, depicts a school where boys torment and torture each other under the distant supervision of relatively disengaged schoolmasters. Martineau's schoolboy hero pays a high price for his education: his foot must be amputated after a vicious attack by older schoolboys. The highly educated George Eliot, who wept over *The Crofton Boys*, shared a similar suspicion of institutionalized education. Strikingly, she affirmed "the superiority of the home education" over institutionalized schooling, in part because it promoted "personal responsibility and activity," developing not only the intellect but also the "emotions in connection with the common needs of life."[1] In novels for both adults and children, images of the schoolroom mediate institutional and domestic space and consequently foreground the tensions within Victorian assumptions about the private and the public realms. Easily recognized by its sterile rows of benches and its pared-down, functionalist, rectilinear spaces, the standardized classroom also evokes an increasingly regimented and codified pedagogy, which depicted the child's mind as a simple container waiting to be filled with adult knowledge. To probe, satirize, and combat this model of a hyperrational pedagogy, which appeared to develop the mind at the expense of the heart, body, and spirit, novelists not only critiqued the schoolroom itself; they also turned to other semi-domesticated spaces within the school but outside the classroom proper. Often invoked in contemporary educational discourse, these spaces furthered the fictive critique of standardized education. Along with the new standardized classroom, the locus and emblem of institutionalized learning, such domesticated pedagogical spaces constitute the major focus of this book. They include the common phenomenon of the *teacher's room*, a site adjacent to the schoolroom that embodied a traditional link between teaching and parenting; the *school garden*, which allegedly fostered the natural modes of learning endorsed by Rousseau and his influential pedagogical descendants Pestalozzi and Froebel;[2] and the curative *school sickroom*, which strove to heal a mind and body overburdened by a narrow intellectual regimen. In each case, these competing educational sites embodied varied ways of reintegrating domesticity into the space of school, aiming to correct what increasingly seemed a dangerously standardized and regimented pedagogy.[3]

In my narrative of a rich fictive discourse engaging with cultural change, schoolroom depictions serve as persuasive vehicles of social critique, even though that critique may be conflicted, halting, and ambivalent, confused by middle-class blind spots and didacticism. As practitioners of the middle-class genre of school narratives, Victorian novelists sometimes attempt to defend working-class children from what they see as a soulless standardized pedagogy, in part because they recognize such standardization as an implicit threat to middle-class children as well. Yet when they actually come to envision alternative educational spaces such as the domesticated teacher's room, the "natural" school garden, and the curative school sickroom, they are most likely to stage these redemptive spaces as the locus of middle-class education. Like Rousseau, who doubted that the laboring classes could benefit from an individualized domestic instruction, middle-class novelists generally allow the boundaries of class to limit their horizon.

Nevertheless, the mixed motives and conflicting agendas that novelists bring to bear on the subject of school open spaces for insight, interrogation, and reform. Even when explicitly engaged in reshaping the psychological and social spaces of childhood experience, novelists often evoke layered images that undermine their overt agendas. Henri Lefebvre usefully sums up this dynamic, arguing that socially mandated "representations of space" (space as it is conceived in a legal or official document, for instance) repeatedly come into conflict with the metaphorical, imagistic, and emotionally freighted spaces depicted by artists and writers (images of space as it is lived through the senses and emotions).[4] No wonder, then, that the Victorians relished the emotionally fraught school scenes in novels. As novelists shaped schools out of words instead of brick and mortar, their words nevertheless had direct consequences on actual material structures. The public's horror at Dickens's portrait of Dotheboys Hall, where half-starved boys sank into imbecility, forced numerous Yorkshire boarding schools to close. Similarly, debates raged about the conditions at the Cowan Bridge School, which was seen as the model for Lowood in Brontë's *Jane Eyre* (1847), where orphaned girls suffered through famine, fear, and fever.[5]

Given the broad range of diverse texts that my study seeks to integrate, I must add a few words about my critical methodology and aims. In the effort to recoup the too-often neglected genre of the school novel, critics and scholars understandably draw sharp distinctions between school stories for child readers and mainstream Victorian fictions. As I have already suggested, however, the Victorians found such distinctions less necessary. Clearly, adult readers relished such widely discussed texts as *Alice's Adventures in Wonderland* (1865) and *Tom Brown's Schooldays*

(1857), and in a literary culture that emphasized reading aloud, children could experience mainstream novels along with other family members. Dickens, who plays a major role in my analysis, exemplifies the difficulty of drawing hard and fast distinctions between writers based on their projected audiences. If his bleak school portraits in novels like *Nicholas Nickleby* (1838–1839) and *Dombey and Son* (1846–1848) aim to alert adult readers to the dangers of miseducating their children, Dickens was also a children's author when he wrote his educational *Child's History of England* (1851-1853), and a journalist when he published his popular school visits in *Household Words*, the journal he edited from 1850 through 1859. Thus, *Dombey, The Child's History,* and the school visits in *Household Words* engage with pedagogical agendas in clearly related ways, albeit inflected by generic differences. Recent critics, such as Sandra L. Beckett and Katharine Capshaw Smith, emphasize the rich cross-fertilization between adult and children's fiction, "unsettling lines between adult and child audiences, appropriating adult texts into children's culture and vice versa."[6] In novels for adult and child readers alike, then, fictive images of the schoolroom staked out ideological positions within the education debates, conjuring up instructional sites that were by turns utopian or coercive, inspiring or deadening. My project places so-called mainstream novelists and children's authors in mutual dialogue, interrogating the sometimes tacit implication that children's literature developed in isolation from other forms of fiction.

Further, I situate a diverse array of novelists, including Charlotte Brontë, Farrar, Hughes, Dickens, Martineau, May, and Carroll, within what Thomas Huxley in 1868 called the "chorus of voices" attempting to define education according to often contradictory ends and purposes. Celebrating education as "the great panacea for human troubles," the chorus remains divided about what a good education is, what it might be, and what it ought to accomplish ("Liberal Education" 27). Victorian fictions, school logbooks, educational treatises, and texts on classroom management share in what Gallagher and Greenblatt describe as the "dense networks of meaning" embedded in any given culture (26); to vary the metaphor, such fictions articulate crucial "lines of force" in the web of associations, ideas, and images that make up the nineteenth-century debate on education in England. As agonistic sites where the young protagonists are divested of childhood and groomed for adulthood, school scenes bring together the most intimate and personal experiences with the broadest of social vistas. They build bridges between the pupil's private interior spaces and the public face of a society in transition.

Following a site-based approach, I examine seminal locations within and adjacent to the schoolroom. As Chapter 1 documents, the professionalization of pedagogy in the nineteenth century required a site, a system, and a theory: the rectilinear and functionalist space of the new standardized classroom is reproduced, theoretically at least, all across England in the national school system, as pedagogical theory increasingly insists that children's mental development fits a standard pattern. Drawing on the work of recent theorists of space, including Michel de Certeau and Henri Lefebvre, I explore Dickens's ambivalent depictions of schoolroom space, contextualizing them within contemporary arguments about school architecture and pedagogy. Dickens suggests that the loss or diminution of domesticity warps the child pupil's sensibility, and that standardized schooling may well threaten the very nature of childhood itself as it is traditionally understood.

Chapters 2 and 3 venture outside the classroom proper to examine, respectively, the marginalized place of domesticity at school and the role of the school garden. Both chapters incorporate an analysis of Rousseau's *Émile*, which dramatically influenced the Victorians' view of domesticity and nature at school. Chapter 2 examines a territory supposedly antithetical to the regulated, standardized classroom, the shifting and flexible space of domestic education imaged in the teacher's private room. Brontë's *Jane Eyre* and Dickens's *David Copperfield* deftly deploy images of domestic education within institutionalized settings as a means of cultural critique. In their work, however, the strict division between institutional and domestic education is also a problematic distinction, often in danger of collapsing because the germs of institutionality are revealed within the idealizing rhetoric of domesticity.

Chapter 3 explores the school garden, often portrayed as a corrective for the excesses of the intellectual classroom regimen. An emblem of child-nature, the school garden implicitly links the cultivation of children's minds and bodies with the conversion of raw nature into domesticated property. Constructed in nineteenth-century schools and novels as a gendered space, the school garden cultivates the sensibilities of boys and girls in oppositional ways. *David Copperfield* (1849–1850), *The Crofton Boys*, and *Tom Brown's Schooldays* depict the boys' garden as a level playing field in which boys learn to claim a rugged individualism suitable for future property owners; in striking contrast, in *Jane Eyre* and *Alice's Adventures in Wonderland*, girls learn to envision their own bodies as property that must be cultivated and controlled.

Chapter 4 locates in the school sickroom a last chance to balance institutional and domestic impulses, retuning both body and mind after the rigors of school life. In the perilous space of the sickroom, domesticity and institutionality are difficult to reconcile. Portraits of the sickroom in *Nicholas Nickleby, Dombey and Son, Jane Eyre, Tom Brown's Schooldays, The Crofton Boys*, and E. J. May's *Dashwood Priory, or Mortimer's College Life* (1856) draw on the contemporary zymotic paradigm of illness to evoke a bleak picture of school life, establishing a tension between healthy growth and intellectual development. Incorporating the contemporary Victorian discourse linking overeducation and illness, as well as Michel Foucault's analysis of the developing space of scientific medicine in *The Birth of the Clinic* (1963), the chapter integrates varied theoretical and historical perspectives.

Because my examination of Victorian fictive schoolrooms involves theorizing space, like the novelists who have inspired my project, I find myself constructing discursive schoolrooms—a series of schools built out of words—in order to explore public and private, institutional and individual conceptions of school space. The ancillary pedagogical sites that I map—the teacher's room, the school garden, and the school sickroom—recede incrementally from the standardized classroom; at the same time, they become more problematic and culturally marginalized spaces, allowing for increasingly defiant attacks on the regimented rigors of school. My site-based analysis aims to remind readers that Victorian school scenes existed within a cluster of assumptions about competing school spaces. For Victorian readers, then, the regimented classroom necessarily evoked the oppositional image of a jeopardized domestic instruction, just as any common object conjures up its own shadow.

My work is indebted to Beverly Lyon Clark's *Regendering the School Story* (1996) and Claudia Nelson's *Boys Will Be Girls* (1991), which recouped previously neglected school narratives, exploring the school novel's role in fostering assumptions about the limits and possibilities of gender. My admiration for these critical examinations prompts me to draw on their insights and analyses within the cultural context of Victorian education debates. Finally, my study, which aims to chart a fictive conversation inspired in part by the development of a standardized, increasingly regulated school system, must position itself in relation to Foucauldian arguments explicating the realm of bureaucratic surveillance and its expanding reach throughout the modern era. In recent years, such literary critics as Nancy Armstrong, Joseph Litvak, and D. A. Miller have illuminated the purview of surveillance in Victorian fiction, evoking a landscape very much like Paul Dombey's "last view" of his coercive (and ultimately fatal) school, which the dying boy recalls as "always a dream, full of eyes" (Dickens, *Dombey* 204).[7] In *Discipline and Punish* (1975), many of Foucault's most telling arguments revolve around space. Modern discipline, he emphasizes, requires both the "enclosure" (141) and "partitioning" of space: "Discipline organizes an analytical space," assigning individuals to their proper place within an architecture of inspective supervision (143).

Arguably, the territory of school is defined by varieties of inspection, from the limpid gaze of *Émile's* all-seeing tutor Jean-Jacques to the coercive inspective visits of *Jane Eyre's* Brocklehurst, or the dutiful and wistful school reports of a Matthew Arnold (1889), dispirited by what he regards as unimaginative teaching.[8] Yet this very catalog of inspective acts surely hints at difficulties with Foucault's unified and totalizing vision of educational developments. As varieties of inspection proliferate, they become less a figure than a ground, less a story to be told than a blank page still waiting for an inscription. Inspective agendas are not necessarily equivalent, and the dense inspective atmosphere of a schoolroom, whether Rousseau's or Brocklehurst's, nevertheless reveals blind spots, gaps, and hidden corners, along with (to vary the metaphor) silences, miscommunications, and other failures of speech. As Michel de Certeau argues in *The Practice of Everyday Life* (1980), "Foucault's analysis of the structures of power" also illuminates an alternative "pathway" that may be "inscribed" as either its "consequence" or its "reciprocal": "one can follow the swarming activity of these procedures that, far from being regulated or eliminated by panoptic administration, have reinforced themselves in a proliferating illegitimacy, developed and insinuated themselves into the networks of surveillance" (96).

Such a reading, which entails examining the ground on which the Foucauldian narrative inscribes its figure, allows Certeau to acknowledge the "unreadable but stable tactics," which carve a space for the "surreptitious creativities" that are "merely concealed by the frantic mechanisms and discourses of the observational organization" (96).

Admittedly, Certeau's delineation of the shifting and fluid movements of urban life primarily emphasizes the randomness that circulates through unenclosed spaces, in contrast to the walled-in spaces of a school. Yet even within the partitioned experience of school, such random or unexpected groupings exist, often dramatized by novelists as gaps in the structure of a metaphorical, institutional architecture— spaces that permit transgressions and secrets.

Drawing on Foucauldian arguments when they illuminate specific images and agendas, I nevertheless aim to chart not a broad highway toward standardization and inspective interactions, but rather a series of circuitous engagements between domesticity and institutionality, as defined and circumscribed by distinct yet mutually supportive school sites. In Victorian fiction, institutional and domestic spaces appear not as static entities, but rather as provisional, shifting realms engaged in a dynamic and dialectical relationship. Institutionality is frequently defined by means of its supposed opposite, domesticity; similarly, domesticity may be seen as a powerful and positive force or conversely as a *residuum*—what is left when the realms of institutional space have been walled in (or out). As they creatively challenge each other, the two realms nevertheless enjoy a mutually reinforcing commerce. If the boundary between them shifts according to one's perspective, their oppositionality is nevertheless useful as the two realms are configured and reconfigured to achieve specific social ends.

As institutional and domestic sites are partitioned off from each other within the school, the child protagonist's sensibility reflects such partitioning. While the institutional classroom cultivates the child's mind, domestic pedagogy supposedly nurtures the child's heart. At the same time, the vigorous activity of the school garden and the healing potential of the school sickroom imprint themselves on the child's jeopardized body. If the schoolroom enters the modern world through a complex mapping of spatial partitioning and subordination, the modern child's sensibility is dramatized as similarly divided and regulated. In this sense, Victorian fictions increasingly cast the space of school as analogous to the experiential spaces of modern childhood.

Within the complex spatial partitioning of school experience, the mid-nineteenth-century novel tends to ally itself with the tradition of domestic education, suggesting that the institutionalization of childhood through standardized education jeopardizes specifically "novelistic" ways of learning, knowing, and processing experience. It is no accident that institutional schooling and modern children's literature appear to grow and flower together during the modern era. Frequently appearing at odds (as numerous Victorian tales relish depictions of children who flout authority), they are nevertheless intimately linked. At the same time, the flexible conception of a relatively unregulated childhood experience (standing in contradistinction to coercive schooling) is central to paradigmatic plot structures within the mainstream novel as well.

1

"THE IDEA OF A WALL"
Toward a New Architecture of School and Mind

The best shape for the school-room is an oblong, about twice as
long as it is broad.

**—James Currie, *The Principles and Practice
of Common School Education***

In Dickens's *Martin Chuzzlewit* (1843–1844), Pecksniff, that famously
incompetent instructor of architecture, advises his pupil Martin to try
his hand at designing a school: "Come! as you're ambitious, and are a very
neat draughtsman, you shall—ha ha! —you shall try your hand on these
proposals for a grammar-school: regulating your plan, of course, by the
printed particulars" (87). Unlike the other more pedestrian projects that
Pecksniff has suggested, this one instantly fires Martin's imagination. In
fact, not only would-be architects like Martin, but a diverse array of persons and organizations dreamed of drafting a plan for the ideal school.
For a society facing the prospect of national education for the first time,
the invocation of a standardized pedagogy, embodied in a new professionalized schoolroom, seemed both visionary and supremely practical. E. R. Robson, the official architect for the London Board Schools,
celebrated the "great change" taking place in English education and
strove to construct efficient, functionalist school spaces that reflected
the scientific principles of the new pedagogy (321). Like Robson, numerous nineteenth-century observers of an increasingly inclusive system
of education felt themselves to be standing at the threshold of a new
world—one that might turn out to be a paradise or a fallen Eden. The

prospect of a universal pedagogical method, then, demanded a reevaluation of the past and a wish for a specific kind of future.

In this chapter I explore the dream of a scientific pedagogy that might radically reshape Victorian childhood. Focusing on the debate over implementing a national, governmentally regulated school system, I examine how supposedly scientific teaching methods and changing conceptions of school architecture meshed with a new idea of the child's mind. Proponents (and opponents) of the new pedagogy built their case not just with logical arguments, but also through emotionally freighted images of school space.

Underlying the call for modern educational structures and an innovative pedagogy was a novel conception of the child's developing mind; building on Hume's theory of mental associations, nineteenth-century association psychology painted a linear, highly schematized picture of childhood learning, and of the human mind in general. This chapter points up connections among three phenomena that might at first appear distinct and isolated: a new scientific pedagogy with characteristic spatial practices, innovative, functionalist architectural spaces, and an increasingly schematized and rational conception of mental space.

In the discourse of educational professionalism, the fraught territory of school serves as a nexus connecting these three spatial dimensions. A site, a system, and a theory were necessary to reconstruct elementary and secondary teaching as a profession combining clear and measurable goals with scientific methods. Furthermore, the contest between the new scientific education and more traditional educational approaches became linked with the Victorians' century-long debate about the relative values of *utility* versus *ornament* in art, architecture, and daily life. Thus, proponents of the new pedagogy cast their arguments in terms of efficiency and functionalism, deploring the useless ornamentation associated with older educational sites. In contrast, defenders of a traditional liberal arts education often allied themselves with the Gothic structures of the past.

Foregrounding the centrality of space within the education debates, Dickens's controversial *Hard Times* (1854) draws on, and seeks to answer, contemporary assumptions about school architecture and classroom management, as well as philosophical arguments for a modern pedagogy. Written before the 1870 Education Act codified a sometimes-conflicting set of government regulations, *Hard Times* presents standardized education as an unsettling and even dangerous prospect, giving voice to widespread fears that schooling would forever alter the supposedly untrammeled territory of childhood experience. Ultimately, however, the novel's virtuoso accomplishment is to deconstruct oppositional arguments about utility and ornament, showing how utilitarianism itself is simply yet another *style*, partaking of its own ornamental pleasures. Clearly, Dickens positions his fictions as key texts in the defense of an imperiled view of childhood under attack in an increasingly standardized society. Yet my aim here is not to celebrate Dickens as the protector of an essentialized view of childhood, but rather to show how his rearguard attack on institutionalized education is central to his conception of his fiction's cultural work.

Finally, in explicating the connections among pedagogy, architecture, and psychology, which Victorians largely took for granted, I aim not merely to recover historical and rhetorical assumptions, illuminating as these may be. Instead, my goal is to highlight sociohistorical, cultural practices that helped to change the social construction of childhood, in small and subtle ways as well as on the large scale. To take a down-to-earth example: as schoolchildren were organized into forms or standards on the basis of age and accomplishment (a division not taken for granted in the early nineteenth century), the very trajectory of childhood development was regularized and normalized. Childhood could no longer be viewed as an erratic, mysterious period whose contours were relatively undefined, metaphorically misty around the edges. Instead, childhood itself became spatialized as a series of discrete sequences, orderly in a new and radical way. As Foucault asserts in *Discipline and Punish*, "The normal is established as a principle of coercion in teaching with the introduction of a standardized education" (184). Foucault analyzes four aspects of disciplinary space that would increasingly shape our collective experience: (1) enclosure, (2) partitioning, (3) the development of useful or functional sites within public and private structures, and (4) the increasing tendency to hierarchize and rank spatial components. Such disciplinary spatial practices exist to train and restrain the "docile" bodies that inhabit them, and school space would increasingly manifest all these elements as it strove to partition childhood experience.[1] The appeal of the Dickensian narrative line is that it allows the docile body to push back against this constricting architecture of modernity, staging a contest in which the child-pupils sometimes win, if only within the consolatory structures of school fictions.

CARLYLE'S QUESTION: TOWARD AN ARCHITECTURE OF EDUCATION

Lamenting the dismal state of contemporary education in *Sartor Resartus* (1836), Carlyle's Teufelsdröchk, original genius and founder of a philosophy both profound and absurd, cries out that society needs a new architect of the spirit: "Alas, so it is everywhere, so it will ever be; till the Hodman is discharged, or reduced to Hodbearing; and an Architect is hired, and on all hands fitly encouraged" (82). The unimaginative teachers who attempt to mold Teufelsdröchk—first in secondary school and later at his representative but nameless university—aspire to be architects of the intellect; the narrative of Teufeldrochk's education, however, unmasks them as hodmen, menial workers who cart stones to a building site with no sense of how such building materials might fit together. In Teufelsdröchk's narrative, the conventional school architecture perpetrated by unimaginative hodmen is an oppressively limiting enterprise. Described as "a square enclosure" that "wall[s] in" over a thousand "striplings," the ironically described "High Seminary" allows its immured pupils to "tumble about as they listed, from three to seven years" (85). Within such an educational architecture, chaotic adolescent energies find no fitting home, but are merely temporarily constrained.

Published during a period of extensive school building, and of fierce debates about the form and function of new school structures, Carlyle's meditation on educational architecture takes on even greater resonance. If, as Carlyle suggests, school architecture is a problem that calls for a new solution and new builders, who is to be the new architect? There was certainly no shortage of applicants for the position, understood both literally and metaphorically. The British and Foreign School Society, founded by Joseph Lancaster in the early 1800s, rushed to create schools where religious dissenters would feel at home. The early history of the society is a chronicle of ferocious building.[2] Lancaster trained young schoolmasters, who then proceeded to organize schools on the Lancastrian plan, erecting vast, barnlike schoolrooms where a single master sometimes instructed as many as four hundred pupils with the help of student monitors. An 1811 article from *Allen's Philanthropist* describes the progress of one of Lancaster's protégés in glowing terms: "in the space of only eight months a boy scarcely seventeen has lately organized schools ... for above one thousand children."[3]

The National Society, a bastion of Anglicanism, responded with their own building campaign, generally emphasizing traditional Gothic structures. Under its auspices, the humanist educator Derwent Coleridge designed Gothic buildings for the teacher training school where he served as principal. For Coleridge, the Gothic style symbolized the liberal tradition in education, an education that was supposedly spacious and anti-utilitarian. Finally, legislators and the growing educational bureaucracy they created, aimed to shape both educational architecture and the architecture of education according to diverse purposes and agendas. In *Hard Times*, which Dickens dedicated to Carlyle, the utilitarian Gradgrind strives to shape a mass-producible, functional, and efficient education, repeatedly identified with a hyperrational, constrictive architectural space. Thus, architectural styles took on a symbolic resonance as embodiments of pedagogical styles; as suggested above, the century's contest between ornament and utility played out in the struggle between classical education, linked with traditional Gothic structures, and a new scientific pedagogy associated with a modern rectilinear architecture.

Set against this jumbled architectural skyline, Teufelsdröchk's jeremiad on contemporary educational practices and architecture issues not only an invitation but also a warning. Teufelsdröchk urgently demands a master architect to replace the bumbling hodmen who have attempted to educate him. Yet it is difficult to imagine how this new architect of the mind and spirit might foster Teufelsdröchk's own intellectual development. Although he suffers through three successive schools, Teufelsdröchk is triumphantly self-educated; his solitary reading and musings constitute a liminal self-education outside the walls, savored in an idyllic natural landscape. Teufelsdröchk soon surpasses his schoolmasters, who at best can only recognize his unique educational requirements and abilities. Thus, the work of the new educational architect is clearly far from simple; urgently needed, such an architect of education is also implicitly beside the point, at least in Teufelsdröchk's case. To the degree that it can be portrayed at all, the new architect's work is evoked as a negative quantity, as an escape from conventional social architecture that involves the demolition (or unbuilding) of the square enclosure.

Teufelsdröchk's eccentric *bildung*, it might be objected, can tell us little about the education of lesser mortals. A young prodigy, Teufelsdröchk remains, in Carlyle's depiction, a law unto himself. The translator of Goethe's seminal *bildungsroman, William Meister's Apprenticeship*, Carlyle clearly celebrates the individualized processes of *bildung* rather than the standards of an externally defined curriculum. At the same time, like that of other prophetic visionaries of individualism, Teufelsdröchk's rhetoric functions in part as a portal through which his readers supposedly glimpse their own recalcitrant individuality, a motive central to the subtly educative project of the *bildungsroman*. To the extent that we understand Teufelsdröchk, we allegedly become like him; we too are meant to resist the conventional architectural and educational structures that confine us. If, in one sense *bildung* and architecture (undefined and transcendent) are at one, in another sense *bildung* and building (historical and specific) are at odds. Carlyle's monitory parable typifies both a mid-century fascination with, and a concomitant ambivalence toward, an emerging architecture of education and its emblematic educational architecture.

Organizing the developing child's psychic space around the physical structures that contain and constrain his growing body, Carlyle traces a trajectory whereby the talented boy retains his "genius" only by escaping or repudiating the space of school, and positioning himself within a romanticized natural landscape. While his narrative appears to advocate a childhood outside the walls, Carlyle nevertheless finds himself in the position of calling for an educational architect to build new walls to define childhood experience. Carlyle's ambivalence helped to shape the contemporary commentary on literal and metaphorical educational architecture, and on the space of school and its pedagogy.

THE HISTORICAL BACKGROUND: PERSPECTIVES ON THE EMERGENCE OF SCHOOL SPACE

In 1850, in his first edition of *Social Statics*, Herbert Spencer attacks the proponents of state education for attempting to usurp the natural role of parents. Casting the development of a national school system as an institutional incursion into domestic territory, Spencer denounces the specter of a state educational bureaucracy as an appalling and unstoppable factory, whose product is a mechanized and standardized form of human consciousness. "[L]egislators," Spencer writes,

> exhibit to us the design and specification of a state machine, made up of masters, ushers, inspectors, and councils ... to be plentifully supplied with raw material, in the shape of little boys and girls, out of which it is to grind a population of well-trained men and women who shall be 'useful members of the community!' (299)

When Spencer denounced the prospect of state-run education, the great Education Act of 1870 was still two decades away, but extensive legislation had already attempted to standardize and regulate the voluntary schools. In 1833 the government had established grants for the building of schools, though such grants were available only to the National Society (founded 1811) and the British and Foreign School

Society (founded 1808). By 1846, other voluntary schools were eligible for *per capita* student grants as well as stipends for certified teachers and their pupil-teachers, advanced students who assisted teachers in the classroom.[4] In 1862 the new Revised Code attempted to guard against the relative subjectivity of inspectors' reports by correlating school grants to pupils' scores on standardized examinations.

At the same time, the government set standards indirectly by regulating teacher education. In 1846 it allocated grant money for normal schools to train teachers, dividing the funds equally between the National and the British and Foreign School Societies. Monies distributed to teacher training schools were dependent on pupils' examination scores, and after 1853 money was withheld unless prospective teachers stayed at the schools for more than one year. The Queen's Scholarships for future teachers, instituted in 1852, also encouraged attendance at the teacher training colleges.[5]

Although in hindsight the process of standardization may appear as an inevitable evolution, it naturally seemed far from inevitable at the time. Supporters of church-affiliated schools objected to government support of secular training schools for teachers. Bitter disputes between the British and Foreign School Society, established to protect the interests of dissenters, and the National Society, a fervently Anglican organization, also delayed the disbursement of monies to training schools. University-educated inspectors like Matthew Arnold were dismayed by what they perceived as schoolteachers' attempts to structure curricula solely to pass the necessary government inspections. Particularly after the institution of the Revised Code, schoolteachers were frequently accused of teaching for the examinations, repetitively training students, for instance, to offer rote readings of required passages. While the inspectors were often well intentioned and sometimes deeply concerned about students' progress, they also wielded the power to close or slowly destroy a school by withholding funds. From the schoolmasters' point of view, the inspectors could be guilty of bureaucratic tyranny and class arrogance. Thus, at every level, members of the burgeoning, increasingly regulated bureaucracy found grounds for objection to what they regarded as the bureaucratic interference and incompetence of others.

In part, what is at stake in the struggle toward (and against) school standardization is a new definition of school space. The mid-century saw the crucial transition from school space defined as a subset of a particular institutional or domestic realm to a new concept of professionalized school space. Exceptions to this general trend, the universities and public schools (which had not so much separated from, as wreathed themselves around, their church roots) occupied a unique and privileged position on the margins of the nineteenth-century education debates. Since medieval times their walls and towers had set apart their consecrated grounds, affirming a distinct school identity hardly found elsewhere. Thus, the educational storm that darkened the sky over Dickens's Coketown in *Hard Times* dissipated in the more serene weather of Winchester and Eton. To be sure, classical education at the elite schools could be regimented in the extreme. Nevertheless, it continued to pay lip service to individual differences in a way that the national schools rarely did. As parish schools and small private schools for poor and working-class children became increasingly absorbed into the state system, the elite schools thrived and expanded. Serving to institutionalize class differences, educating members of the aristocratic and governing classes, such institutions evoked images of a traditional society, just as the new national schools served as an emblem of unsettling social changes. At the same time, it is worth noting that new conceptions of teaching and learning in the national schools for poor and working-class children prefigured changes that would later spread to the teaching of middle-class and privileged children. The situation is analogous to changes in the profession of medicine described by Michel Foucault in *The Birth of the Clinic* (1963). As Foucault documents, the eighteenth- and nineteenth-century physicians tending the poor at charity hospitals eventually developed a rigorous, standardized medical practice that would ultimately revolutionize medicine for all classes. So too, the standardized pedagogy of the nineteenth-century national schools would set the tone for the widespread professionalization of pedagogy in the twentieth and twenty-first centuries.

In Victorian England the schools targeted for increasing government supervision included parish schools and dissenting academies, which placed education firmly within the moral and religious agenda of the church; the factory schools, relatively few in number but increasingly regulated, which attempted to educate a new generation of efficient, punctual, and orderly workers; and the numerous private schools, which continued to define themselves, strikingly, in domestic terms. Often such domestic schools occupied some part of the master's house, or if too large for such incorporation, integrated the master's residence into their own quasi-domestic spaces.[6] In fact, church space, work space, and home space had tended to incorporate an amorphously defined schoolroom, claiming to further an institutional or domestic agenda. Now, with government monies available to help build, staff, and supervise schools, school space was increasingly separated from previous institutional affiliations, and affirmed as an entity in its own right, with its own distinct spatial practices. In the language of inspectors' reports and school building codes, the new school emerges as an aggressively self-contained and independent space. Starting in 1839, applicants for government building grants had to submit to the Committee of Council exhaustive information about their proposed location and plans, including "the presence in the locality of tanneries, [and] slaughter-houses," as well as "structural details relating to walls, windows, roofs, floors, heating, and ventilation" (Ellis 67).

Gradually, schools ceased to be ancillary sites: a temporarily free workroom in a factory, a basement or a kitchen serving as a dame school, or like the Morton School in Brontë's *Jane Eyre*, a barn converted into a parish school. Similarly, the classroom itself underwent scrutiny and alteration. Increasingly, the single large schoolroom, which housed children of diverse ages, attainments, and abilities, was subdivided, sometimes by screens or curtains, into smaller areas separating students into ranked standards enforced by qualifying examinations. Eventually, following the German system, smaller classrooms become the norm, replacing the single schoolroom. Curriculum design was reflected in school architecture, as both became increasingly subdivided and hierarchical.

Useful as it is, however, the narrative just delineated (that of a sequential transition from marginal, subordinate, and nonstandard spaces toward a self-contained and standardized school locus) must be balanced by another story—one of contest and coexistence. A progressive narrative of standardization risks misrepresenting the shape of historical developments. In fact, the changes in school curricula and school spatial practices were incremental, multidirectional (retrograde as well as progressive), and far from consistent. One small instance serves as a metaphor for larger changes. Over the years, legislators debated the question: exactly how much space does a child need? As Ellis documents, from the 1830s onward, the Committee of Council's guidelines for school construction required a standard measure of square feet per individual pupil. Yet the spatial standards were both raised and lowered over the years, and the voluntary schools set their own standards:

> In the 1830's the National Society estimated that seven square feet per child was a reasonable allocation of space and regarded six square feet as a minimum provision. In the schools of the British and Foreign School Society the allocation of space per child was 7.7 square feet. Standards set by the Committee of Council fell from ten square feet in 1840 to six in 1845; after which they rose successively in 1856 to nine square feet.... After 1870 however the

> Committee's requirement for grant aided schools was reduced to
> eight square feet per pupil as compared with a recommended ten
> square feet for the more affluent board schools. (Ellis 68)

In sum, translating the schoolchild's needs into objective spatial standards was a difficult and contradictory process; whether the typical English child required 7 or 7.7 square feet, such government standards, as Ellis goes on to note, were not consistently enforced.[7] Once constructed, school buildings were recalcitrant entities of brick and stone, impervious to the latest batch of government standards. Even when legislative enactments suggest a progressive narrative, attempting to chart a schematic progress in practice from year to year or even decade to decade would be a quixotic enterprise. The more interesting story is one of "uneven developments," to borrow a phrase employed in another context by Mary Poovey in her study of nineteenth-century conceptions of gender.[8] Thus, as the century progressed, school inspectors and clergymen collaborated, despite their different agendas, to shape the Anglican parish schools. Similarly, private schools and dame schools coexisted with more standardized monitorial schools. The emergence of a self-contained school space led to fierce debates about how to construct the emerging schoolroom, and what agendas it might serve.

BUILDING SCHOOLHOUSES: GOTHIC AND MODERN

In his influential and comprehensive book, *School Architecture* (1874), E. R. Robson, the official architect of the London school board, questions the dominance of the Gothic style in school architecture. "Why," Robson demands, "should we take a great leap over the intervening centuries, and neglect the works therein produced, in order to reach an ideal thirteenth-century style belonging to a time of widely different popular habits?" (323).

Not only was the Gothic style inseparable from the tradition-steeped ethos of universities, public schools, and numerous private grammar schools; it also enjoyed a vogue during the mid-century's school-building expansion, and was the style of choice for many of the early Anglican National Society schools of the 1850s and 1860s. As John Ruskin tellingly observed in his essay "Traffic," "churches and schools are almost always Gothic, and the mansions and mills are never Gothic" (*Crown* 50). Having celebrated the Gothic impulse as a living embodiment of the universal striving for the ideal, Ruskin was disturbed by the reduction of Gothic architecture to a quaint museum style, suggesting a realm of sheltered morality suitable for schoolchildren and Sunday mornings. Thus, Victorian neo-Gothic architecture risked becoming a symbol, not of moral striving, but rather of a disengaged moral complacency.

Searching for a simpler and more modern style suited to easily available brick building materials (at times, Robson invokes "London brick" as enthusiastically as Ruskin celebrated the "stones of Venice") Robson asserts,

> The only really simple brick style available as a foundation is that of the time of the early Jameses, Queen Anne, and the early Georges.... The buildings then approach more nearly the spirit of our own time, and are unvariably true in point of construction and workmanlike feeling. Varying much in architectural merit, they [nevertheless] form the nucleus of a good modern style. (*School Architecture* 323)

While Robson did not invent the nineteenth-century version of the neo-Georgian or Queen Anne style, as it came to be called, he did help to popularize it, and to make it the hallmark of a new school architecture. For Robson, the neo-Georgian style appropriately embodies the spirit of the new, state-controlled board schools: "If a church should at once be recognized as a church by the character of its architecture, and a prison as a prison, so should a school-house be immediately known as a home of education" (321). In Robson's depiction, the neo-Georgian style marks the school's institutional agenda, its social mission of reconstructing human nature, like those complementary institutions, the penal system and the church. Beyond signifying institutionality, however, the new school architecture houses a realm of neutral secularism, free of the looming shadow of the church:

> a building in which the teaching of dogma is strictly forbidden, can have no pretense for using ... that symbolism which is so interwoven with every feature of church architecture as to be naturally regarded as its very life and soul. In its aim and object it should strive to express *civil* rather than ecclesiastical character. A continuation of the semi-ecclesiastical style which has hitherto been almost exclusively followed in England for National schools would appear to be inappropriate and lacking in anything to mark the great change which is coming over the education of the country. (321)

Though he searches for architectural precedents that will place his innovations within a solid English tradition, Robson's argument rings with a sense of new possibilities; an original and characteristic style is needed, he argues, to frame a new sort of school space, marking the "great change" occurring in education. Indeed, Robson goes on to affirm the imperative "to seek" an architectural style that is "wholly new or 'original'" (321). At the same time, endorsing a secularism that embodies civic values rather than sectarian doctrines, Robson speaks to a debate that had been vital since the early years of the century because dissenters had always resisted the high-church connotations of Gothic architecture, preferring instead variations on the Palladian, Elizabethan, or Italianate styles.[9]

By emphasizing the need for a modern civil style, then, Robson not only defines school space as a positive entity in its own right, self-contained and free of church influences; he also rhetorically places the new, state-defined school space beyond the reach of the enduring and often bitter debates between the Anglican National Society and the British and Foreign School Society, which included so many dissenters among its ranks.[10] Although the Education Act of 1870 made elementary education mandatory, the English educational "system" of Robson's day was still far from standardized, comprising a diverse network of educational institutions that included Anglican parish schools, Methodist and other dissenting academies, and numerous private schools from elite academies to poverty-stricken dame schools. Robson's definition of a new style of architecture, based in part on his extensive study of school buildings and school systems in Europe and America, signals the vision of a new more unitary educational system with a specific cultural agenda—an allegedly benevolent strengthening of state control over the education of the people.

If Robson's work emphasizes a secular and forward-looking functionalism, Derwent Coleridge, the principal of Saint Mark's Training College, emphasizes the importance of traditional architectural (and religious) forms. Coleridge wished to extend the provenance of ornament in both educational architecture and curricula, under the sheltering shadow of the Church of England. Thus, Coleridge (1862) deplores "the bald utilities and whitewashed parallelograms which have sometimes been set forth as a model" for the architecture of the state-sponsored teacher training schools (33). Commenting on Coleridge's assertion, Philip Collins emphasizes that the training colleges' "factory-like aridity" was often "symbolised by their buildings" (152). One London training college of the 1870s, as described by a student,

> "had no place for recreation worthy of the name, no library and reading-room; no pictures appeared on the walls of the dingy class-rooms.... The paved yard... [was] surrounded by forbidding

walls.... The men slept in cubicles... arranged in long rows.
(Birchenough 362–363)

The so-called "bald utilities" of training school architecture had their corollary in a baldly functional curriculum that strove to cram information into future teachers as quickly and efficiently as possible.

In contrast, Coleridge worked to bring Saint Mark's curriculum closer to the liberal education offered by universities. An architect, scholar, and the son of Samuel Taylor Coleridge, Derwent Coleridge designed the architectural plan for Saint Mark's new Practising School, where student teachers instructed their pupils. Constructed in the 1840s, the Practising School was an elegant octagonal building with arched windows and a Gothic exterior, blending appropriately with the Gothic chapel at Saint Mark's, which Coleridge also helped to design. Gothic school architecture affirmed the link between education and religion, as well as the importance of the classical and liberal arts tradition. The training college, Coleridge feelingly asserted, "must be an adapted copy, *mutatis mutandis*, of the elder educational institutions of the country, originally intended, even those of the higher class, with their noble courts, solemn chapels, and serious cloisters, for clerks full as humble as those whom I had to train" (33). In Coleridge's view, educating young teachers in the liberal tradition requires the "seriousness" and "solemnity" of Gothic architecture, evoking the tradition-hallowed campuses of the public schools and the universities.

For Coleridge, then, the training school's Gothic architecture provides a bridge between these schools and the universities; it affirms the need to extend the principles of a classical liberal education to its often working-class and upwardly mobile students within the beneficent shelter of the Church of England, as represented by the Anglican National Society. For Robson, in contrast, the medieval spires of neo-Gothic school architecture signal outdated educational practices and a narrow religious influence that impedes the modern professionalized pedagogical perspective. Robson is particularly dismayed by what he sees as the current preference for "ill-designed ornamentation within and without" (*School Architecture* 322). Thus, modern schools proclaim their scientific nature in their pared-down rectilinear lines, their moderate or restricted use of decorative architectural motifs, and their functional and inexpensive brick building materials.

Inside the schoolroom, Robson similarly emphasizes rectilinear, rationalized space, as we can see in his drawing of a "double classroom," showing "dual arrangement of desks" (Figure 1.1)—an efficient arrangement increasingly employed as schools moved from a single large schoolroom to the German system of separate classrooms. The room's minimal furniture and rigid lines of desks permit the two schoolmistresses to lecture and supervise their pupils with maximum efficiency and a minimum of distractions. At the same time, the rectilinear lines of an emerging professionalized classroom space (increasingly legislated and enforced by building codes and grants for school construction) serve as an apt embodiment of the disciplinary principles of the new scientific pedagogical method. As Robson asserts, "right angles and square corners are always preferable for the interior working of a school" (328).

As illustrated by Robson's sketches of the relationship between classroom furniture and classroom drills, (Figures 1.2 and 1.3), the lucid linearity of classroom space facilitates (and is mirrored by) the pupils' orchestrated, collective movements. As the teacher calls out appropriate commands, students collectively place their hands on their desks and lift their slates, or rise and step seamlessly to the side of their desks. Thus, architecture and pedagogy work together to ensure a specific type of classroom management, fostering a collective order that facilitates the efficient control of large numbers of working-class pupils. Beyond this, however, the classroom performance (of pupils as well as teachers) dramatizes both a rationalized classroom space and a professional pedagogical method that can, theoretically at least, be enforced in any properly constructed classroom throughout England.

THEORIZING SCHOOL SPACE: ROBSON, FARRAR, AND DICKENS

Such recent theorists of space as Michel de Certeau and Henri Lefebvre employ the term *spatial practices* to delineate everyday acts, often unacknowledged or taken for granted, that serve to define and characterize a space. Widely accepted but frequently unexamined spatial practices set apart self-contained or privileged spaces such as the schoolroom. In Robson's illustration, the linear and orderly arrangement of desks, ordained by both teacher and architect, reflects a contemporary spatial practice, reinforcing the schoolroom's orderly and regulated domain. For school architects and educational reformers, a linear arrangement of desks was considered a crucial component of the architectural space; thus, in Samuel F. Eveleth's *School-House Architecture* (1870), an interior plan includes the proper arrangement of school furniture (Figure 1.4). Just as importantly, spatial practices regulate not only the placement of furniture but also student behavior. The students' orchestrated, collective movements, rote recitations, and enforced silence embody the classroom's hierarchy of authority. Taken together, the dense network of spatial practices that characterize the schoolroom serve to distinguish it from other spatial realms, such as the territory of home and work. At the same time, the mass production of spatial practices required by the schoolroom—and the collective regulation of the schoolchildren's bodies—implicitly connect the space of school to the equally regulated and mechanized work space of the factory. In this sense, the spatial practices portrayed in Robson's drawing link working-class children to the factories that may already employ their parents—and might also constitute the children's future employment. Further, the mass production of learning in the schoolroom suggests that the children are themselves products, each to be shaped collectively by the same lessons and rules.

In his seminal work, *The Production of Space* (1974), Henri Lefebvre contrasts spatial practices with culturally mandated or validated *representations of space* in official documents, texts, and images. Robson's depiction of classroom space is such an official representation because it constructs a model schoolroom that would be in fact replicated in actual London schools, backed by the authority of an emerging government bureaucracy. As Lefebvre's distinction reminds us, Robson's representation of space is a complex construction built on a network of numerous spatial practices, some explicitly depicted and others merely implied. Such official representations of classroom space might be found in a variety of images and texts, including the language of school legislation, approved texts on classroom management, school inspectors' reports, and even some novels that present publicly sanctioned constructions of the culture of school. Although presented visually, Robson's drawing also exists as a discursive representation of space, one that mandates specific behaviors for teacher and students.

Both Certeau and Lefebvre recognize spatial practices as myriad, elusive, and difficult to quantify. Even while students affirm the teacher's authority by practicing mandated spatial behaviors, they may simultaneously enact contradictory spatial practices that covertly express their defiance. Farrar's *Eric* (1858) offers an evocative portrait of such mixed spatial practices when the young Eric enters his new classroom at the Roslyn School. On oblong benches, boys sit in neat rows, the picture of attention and discipline. As Eric advances between rows of benches to face the teacher at the front of the room, boys secretly extend their legs into the aisle to trip him. They go unpunished while Eric staggers forward, helpless and confused because the classroom overtly enforces the spatial practice of silence, which does not allow him to protest. As every schoolboy knows, what the teacher sees and hears limits what can be acknowledged in the classroom; the schoolmaster's field of vision determines the stage for the ritualized performance of learning. What occurs beyond that sphere is already murky, problematic, and unpredictable. Enjoying their double field of vision, the students in this case see more than the teacher. They develop both public and surreptitious spatial practices for classroom behavior.

Robson's official, idealized representation of the schoolroom excludes the students' covert spatial behaviors; Farrar's novel, in contrast, offers a tantalizing array of amusing, shocking, and defiant student practices. Although frequently didactic in tone and nominally written to enjoin schoolboys to morality and sexual purity, Farrar's fiction opens fascinating vistas into the surreptitious and clandestine side of school life. Like numerous other school fictions, Farrar's *Eric* invites us to consider how schoolboys use their bodies to protest adult restrictions even as they appear to conform to them. Unlike the intellectual productions of the mind, the body has no problem with logical contradictions. Enacting contradictory spatial practices, the child's body, so vividly portrayed in school fictions for all audiences, repeatedly undermines binary oppositions between obedience and rebellion. Regardless of their overt agendas, then, numerous school fictions for both adults and children perform the complex cultural work of both approving and undermining school authority. In the words of Greenblatt and Gallagher, the "art of the past" exemplifies a "double vision." Simultaneously "immersed in its time and place and yet somehow pulling out and away," literary works manifest "resistance as well as replication, friction as well as assimilation, subversion as well as orthodoxy."[11]

Lefebvre acknowledges this subtly subversive function of narrative and other forms of art by distinguishing officially sanctioned representations of space such as Robson's from imagistic, metaphorical, and emotionally saturated *spaces of representation* in the work of writers and artists.[12] Working largely through multilayered and complex images, such fictive spaces welcome us into the realm of subversive, or latently subversive, social practices. They convey a sense of how space is experienced by those *not* in official positions of power—by pupils, for instance, rather than by the educational establishment. For Lefebvre, then, such spaces of representation offer a subtext of symbolic associations and metaphoric elements that embody the "clandestine or underground side of social life" (33). They explore the lived experience of school space; in Farrar's depiction, the schoolroom reveals a covert spatial domain of disorder and confusion, contrary to its appearance of well-organized, well-regulated space. In this space, identical with the teacher's blind spots (what he cannot see), the human body resists the lucid architectural geometries that frame it.

Both official representations of space and subversive spaces of representation are discursive artifacts embodied in words or images. Further, there is nothing to prevent both from coexisting at different moments within the same text. Thus, a school narrative may combine widely endorsed codes of behavior appropriate to school space (representations of space) with metaphorical and allusive expressions of marginalized school experiences outside the official norms (spaces of representation). Lefebvre's goal is not to establish intrinsically pure and discrete realms of essentialized space, but rather to describe a dynamic interplay between spatial modalities.

While Farrar's *Eric* deploys a covert syntax of spatial practices to undermine some of its overt endorsements of school authority, Dickens's *Hard Times* mounts an overt attack on the emerging school system, formulating, through its subversive spaces of representation, a social critique that appears simultaneously forward-looking and nostalgic. Dickens's layered images, saturated with irony and anxiety, subversively undermine the foundations of Robson's rational and scientific schoolroom. In 1854, some twenty years before Robson's book appeared, the famous opening of *Hard Times* conflates images of rectilinear school architecture and a supposedly hyperrational pedagogical method in order to deconstruct both. Portraying Robson's aggressively defined school space as shorn of the softening influences of home or the moral agenda of the church, Dickens's *Hard Times* constructs a monstrously denuded space: Gradgrind's "bare... vault of a schoolroom" (1) subtly suggests a church stripped of its sacral trappings, reinforcing the separation of new professionalized schools from their earlier church affiliations. Tellingly, however, Gradgrind's schoolroom, so aggressively independent of both religious and domestic influences, is in fact indistinguishable from the rest of Coketown's warehouse and factory architecture. Indeed, like factory production, the model school founded by Gradgrind (a social reformer and member of Parliament) is designed for mass production, for implementation all across England. Existing in a world of other, similar attempts at standardization—exemplified, in the words of Gradgrind's ally Bounderby, by "your district schools and your model schools, and your training schools, and your whole kettle of fish of schools" (16)—Gradgrind's schoolroom prefigures the government standardization looming on the horizon.

As he lectures a group of pupils and their schoolmaster on the necessity of cramming facts into the "minds of reasoning animals" (1), Gradgrind not only dominates the classroom space of the unadorned model school he has founded, but also embodies its rectilinear architecture in his own person:

> The scene was a plain, bare monotonous vault of a school-room, and the speaker's square forefinger emphasized his observations by underscoring every sentence with a line on the schoolmaster's sleeve. The emphasis was helped by the speaker's square wall of a forehead, which had his eyebrows for its base, while his eyes found commodious cellarage in two dark caves, overshadowed by the wall. The emphasis was helped by the speaker's mouth,… wide, thin and hard-set… [and by his] square coat, square legs, square shoulders—nay, his very neckcloth, trained to take him by the throat with an unaccommodating grasp, like a stubborn fact. (1)

Just as facts must form and enclose the mind of the human reasoning animal, encasing the child's impulses in the hard sheath of principle, so too the schoolmasterly Gradgrind's human form is encased in a series of square enclosures. His body is reduced to linearity and angularity, from the square wall of his forehead to his square forefinger.

"Discipline," Foucault writes, "sometimes requires *enclosure*, the specification of a place heterogeneous to all others, closed in upon itself. It is the protective space of disciplinary monotony" (*Discipline* 141). In Carlyle's depiction of the "square enclosure," the school reflects a failed disciplinarity, which constrains but does not profoundly alter its "tumbling" students. In contrast, Gradgrind's physicality exemplifies Foucault's concept of the "docile body," "subjected" to practice and "discipline" (138). In Dickens's prescient, proto-Foucauldian image, the space of school inscribes its mark on the body, as school discipline is internalized. In fact, the passage's masterful tone of comic disjunction thrives on a series of mis-fittings as the human shape is impinged on and distorted by square enclosures, ending with the inhuman grip of the neckcloth.

Yet even here Dickens complicates the image of internalized disciplinarity. Crowning this series of squares that constrain Gradgrind's body, we find an image of defiant circularity, as Dickens offers a grotesque phrenological geography of a head bulging with facts: surrounded by sparse "hair" like "a plantation of firs to keep the wind from its shining surface," Gradgrind's scalp is "all covered with knobs, like the crust of a plum pie, as if the head had scarcely ware-house room for the hard facts stored inside" (1). As a counterpoint to the rectilinear architectural imagery ("ware-house room"), Dickens's metaphor evokes both external landscape (the "plantation of fir trees") and a humble domestic interior life (the "plum pie"). An explosion of undisciplined metaphoricity shatters Dickens's otherwise unified description of disciplinary control, undermining its "unaccommodating grasp" by introducing two realms outside the schoolroom: nature and domesticity. Exemplifying a similar resistance, Gradgrind's "knobby" head flaunts its recalcitrant curves, as rebelliously circular as the "tumbling" motion of Carlyle's ignorant "striplings" within the external limits of the Nameless University's "square enclosure." Gradgrind may attempt to square the circle, physically, intellectually, and morally, but circularity explodes out of its constraints nevertheless.

In Gradgrind's schoolroom, clearly, the human form is in jeopardy. Education is a species of deforming human architecture. Part of *Hard Times'* particular appeal—F. R. Leavis admired it as the sole work in which Dickens is "possessed by a comprehensive vision" (Leavis 228)—lies in the novel's startling ability to spatialize conflicting ideologies; it consistently contrasts the polarities of linearity and circularity throughout its narrative argument. Thus, the members of the "horse-riding," who embody, in Leavis's view, human charity and authentic emotion, have as their signature space the "ring" in which they perform; in opposition to the constrictions of Gradgrindery, they supposedly exhibit the unfettered human form, the emblem of unfettered hearts and minds. Throughout the novel, the rectilinear schoolroom and the circle of the horse-riding exist at opposite poles of experience, staging what Joseph Litvak (1992) denominates a "dialectical interplay" between "panoptic" and "ludic" forms of theatricality (118). As Gradgrind informs his new pupil Sissy Jupe, daughter of a performer in the "horse-riding," "We don't want to know anything about [the horse-riding], here.... You mustn't tell us about the ring, here" (4).

Like Carlyle, Dickens is adept at juxtaposing a circularity associated with the natural human form and free unimpeded human movement against a rectilinear order emblematic of school architecture and confining pedagogy. Like Derwent Coleridge attacking "bald parallelograms," Dickens satirizes oppressive rectilinearity. At the same time, of course, Dickens's fictive critique, far more than Coleridge's, is orchestrated through metaphor and image. As Victorian fictions participated in the education debates, their particular opportunity—and much of their power—derived from substituting for a burden of proof a weight and density of image. By extending the public debate into the realm of images, sense perceptions, and the layered emotions associated with them, fictional school scenes performed the cultural work of creating potentially subversive spaces of representation.

BUILDING THE MIND: TRAINS, LINEAR, AND ERRANT

As Penny Kane explains in *Victorian Families in Fact and Fiction* (1995), "The mid-nineteenth century saw the establishment of professional status for architects in 1834–35; mechanical engineers in 1847; solicitors in a series of Acts over the period; while the Medical Act of 1858 regulated surgeons, physicians, and apothecaries" (70). Architects, engineers, and physicians, of course, had a scientific basis for their professional practice, while solicitors interpreted established law; in contrast, teachers in elementary and secondary schools traditionally lacked a coherent theory to justify their professionalization. One German visitor, writing as late as 1876, asserted that "[t]eachers in England [in contrast to those in Germany] do not yet form a distinct *profession* .... and teachers, as a class, do not yet enjoy a full recognition, by the side of the other learned professions of clergymen, lawyers, and physicians" (Wiese 230).

In order for teachers to achieve a professional status, education would have to be considered, if not yet a science, at least a systematic undertaking regulated by scientific principles. And the groundwork for such a transformation of education existed in the emerging "science of mind," the study of "mental laws." In the words of Dugald Stewart, the nineteenth-century author of numerous treatises on mental development, "Would not Education be necessarily rendered more systematical and enlightened, if the powers and faculties on which it operates were more scientifically examined, and better understood?"[13] For Stewart, the potential science of education is to be a science of the human mind's powers and faculties. Systematical education becomes possible when we assume that such mental powers are subject to rational investigation and analysis, and that they conform to clearly articulated laws or principles, and thus can be predicted, modified, and tested.

Dugald Stewart's question serves as an epigraph for James Mill's *Analysis of the Phenomena of the Human Mind* (1829), a work later edited and expanded by his famous son, himself the product of Mill's own educational theories. Drawing heavily on Hume's theory of mental associations, as well as on the work of Locke and the more recent Scottish empiricists, Mill's cranky, compendious, and colossally ambitious work strives to formulate a new more rigorous psychology of association that would serve the needs of social theorists and educators. By Mill's time, theories of mental association had a long and venerable history, and association psychology had a widespread and growing following. (Its later adherents included Herbert Spencer.) Building on the work of the British empiricists, associationism portrayed a mind directly responding to and shaped by perceptual experience. Shunning

traditional Platonic conceptions of innate ideas that precede and structure our experience of physical reality, associationism tended to emphasize the mind's malleability, its capacity to be shaped and instructed by
direct experience. Denying preexistent ideas and absolute values, then,
association theory offered in their place a set of associative principles
that permit the mind to construct ideas as a result of direct sensations.

In Mill's view, however, contemporary association theory lacked a
unified scientific framework. His opus strives to systematize and clar-
ify the mysterious principles of mental association, filling in gaps and
fleshing out the provocative assertions of Locke, the subtleties of Hume,
and the speculations of the more recent Scottish theorists of mental
functioning.[14] At the heart of Mill's vision is his portrayal of the thinking process as a linear pattern of successive associations, or in Mill's
often repeated phrase, a "train of thought" that can be traced, analyzed
into its component parts, and directed to a specific destination. Though
it anticipates in some ways William James's influential formulation of
the "stream of consciousness," Mill's conception differs from James's
according to its metaphor. Unlike the stream, which flows unpredict-
ably, guided by mysterious currents, Mill's train of thought links particular ideas according to clear and describable laws or principles.

The metaphor of the train of thought is, of course, an old and
accepted one. As Locke emphasizes in his *Essay Concerning Human
Understanding* (1690), "it is not enough, that a Man has *Ideas* clear and
distinct… he must think in train."[15] Although Locke also develops the
concept of accidental mental associations, he views such links as irrational and dangerous impediments to logical thought.[16] In contrast,
Hume gives the concept of association a new coherence and centrality,
placing it at the very heart of the mental processes.[17] Hume had identified three dynamic principles of association—*contiguity*, *causation*, and
resemblance—which serve as forces possessed of a mysterious power
of gravitational attraction. Unsympathetic to his predecessor's subtle
and flexible empiricism, Mill aims to reduce the Humean principles
to a single category of relation.[18] Recasting Hume's *causation* as simple
contiguity in time, he impoverishes the complex Humean principle of
cause and effect, rendering it merely a sequential description. He then
proceeds to subordinate Hume's *resemblance* to his unitary vision:
Because we "are accustomed to see like things together" (*Analysis* 106),
Mill argues, *resemblance* is merely an example of contiguity of place,
another simple linear sequence, this time spatial rather than temporal.[19] According to Mill's tidy paradigm, then, two principles, *causation* and *resemblance*, are shown to be aspects of a third, contiguity in
time and place. Although *causation* is labeled *successive contiguity*, and

resemblance becomes *synchronous contiguity,* both forms of contiguity partake of the successive order, a linear movement from one thing to the next.[20]

The near equivalence of Mill's temporal and spatial trains of mental impressions emphasizes their relatively static quality. In Mill's map of the mind, space and time are symmetrically segmented and orderly. Similarly, objects, sensations, and words form themselves into symmetrical successions or trains. The engine of thought is linearity, embodied by positioning or contiguity. Ideas, carefully placed and secured, locked into a linear order by language, become building blocks. Flux hardens into architecture, as Mill implies in this illustration of how the mind associates ideas:

> Brick is one complex idea, mortar is another complex idea; these ideas, with ideas of position and quantity, compose my idea of a wall.... In the same manner my complex idea of glass, and wood, and others, compose my duplex idea of a window; and these duplex ideas, united together, compose my idea of a house. (*Analysis*, Vol. 1, Chap. 3, Sec. 12: 116)

It is easy enough to cast verbal stones at Mill's painstakingly explained "idea of a wall," and also at the solidity of the mental architecture he envisions. Yet his achievement—one acknowledged by the theorists of mental functioning who glossed the posthumous 1869 edition of his opus—was to develop an extensive, but simple and accessible blueprint of the mind and its mental constructions, one that imposed a reassuring order on the mysterious world within. Social thinkers in a variety of fields, including educators eager to develop a professional discipline based on the science of mind, would make use of the principles so firmly articulated by Mill, his colleagues, and his recent predecessors.

In particular, the increasingly literalized and unquestioned metaphor of the train of thought made its way into the popular imagination as into the scholarly and investigative writings of psychologists, medical men, and social philosophers. Given the railroad's status as an emblem of modernity and science, the train of thought gradually took on connotations of the railroad train's mechanistic drive. As William Carpenter wrote in *Principles of Mental Physiology* (1874), "our ideas are... linked in 'trains' or 'series' which further inosculate with each other like the branch lines of a railway" (429).[21] Hume minimized the directionality of the train of thought, casting it as an image of flux. For later thinkers, as for James Mill, the train of thought can be guided to a specific destination, almost as one might take a ticket for a certain station on the railway line.

In an 1815 article written for the *Encyclopedia Britannica*, some fourteen years before his *Analysis* was published, Mill enthusiastically anticipates an educational method that will implement the mental principles of association, directing thought processes into benign and useful channels:

> [T]he business of education is, to make certain feelings or thoughts take place instead of others. The business of education, then, is to work upon the mental successions. As the sequences among the letters or simple elements of speech, may be made to assume all the differences between nonsense and the most sublime philosophy, so the sequences, in the feelings which constitute human thought, may assume all the differences between the extreme of madness and of wickedness, and the greatest attainable heights of wisdom and virtue: And almost the whole of this is the effect of education. (*James Mill on Education* 52)

For Mill, the educator's ability to harness and direct the natural trains of thought may mean the difference between madness or wisdom, wickedness or virtue. Rigorous control of such mental trains is clearly necessary, but how are the trains to be harnessed? "It seems a law of human nature," Mill writes, "that the first sensations experienced produced the greatest effects; more especially, that the earliest repetitions of one sensation after another produce the deepest habit" (*Mill on Education* 92). Further, when children are "often made to conceive the trains [of thought] of other men, by the words, or other signs by which their feelings are betokened, those borrowed trains also become habitual" (99–100). Clearly, the gist of Mill's system reinforces an already prevalent emphasis on learning by drill and repetition. Yet the new pedagogy would expand the province of rote learning in innovative and far-reaching ways. It would encourage teachers to develop and construct extensive trains of thought that students could duplicate in order to practice *thinking in train*. The centerpiece of the scientific pedagogical method would be the child's performance of such borrowed trains of thought.

BUILDING PEDAGOGY: TRAINS AND CIRCLES, UTILITARIAN AND LIBERAL EDUCATION

Mill's *Analysis* sets the scene for the incorporation of association psychology into modern pedagogical methods, a move that would be fostered by the numerous teacher training colleges created to teach the new science of education. A striking instance is to be found in an educational manual by James Currie (1862), the principal of a teacher training school in Edinburgh.[22] Currie's text emphasizes the importance of "the well-known principles of association" (115) in developing "the power of connected thinking" (108). Carrying on his work in the great city where Hume had studied and where James Mill attended the lectures of Dugald Stewart, Currie, like Mill, cites the work of Reid, Stewart, and others who studied the mind's processes. In addition, Currie's text is pervaded by the language of association theory. For instance:

> The principle of *natural contiguity* may be illustrated in its application to the arrangement of the facts of geography and history. When we study the description of a country, we look for such associations as of its hills with its rivers, its rivers and its sea-coast with its towns, its groups of rivers with its slopes, its climate with its general aspect, and its vegetable productions. (115)

Clearly, the natural contiguity of place does yeoman's service in Currie's pedagogy. Geography, as a discipline, seems simply an extension of Mill's order of place or position. As we might expect, history symmetrically extends the order of time or succession:

> When we read a passage of descriptive history—the reign of a monarch, for instance—we endeavour to grasp the succession of events, by referring them to certain universal stages in the life of every monarch and of every man. Thus, his birth, education, early character, and accession; his predilections, as peaceable or warlike, and the directions and progress of their manifestation; the circumstances of his death: such a scheme may be applied everywhere, and serves as a net to apprehend and retain the complicated details which history records. (115)

Each discipline—whether geography or history—serves as a train of thought in two senses: First, it arises from a natural order or contiguity of sensations and objects: thus, hills naturally lead us to think of rivers, and rivers of towns (because they are often the sites of towns). Similarly, birth initiates a successive chain of biological events culminating in death. Such trains of thoughts can proceed and multiply *ad infinitum*.

What is more striking, however, from our contemporary perspective, is the virtuoso gusto with which Currie embraces these trains and many others, as he goes on to chart additional orders of succession, based on the Humean associative principles of resemblance and causality. Clearly, part of the educator's particular gift is a delight in coaxing out the most extensive and attenuated trains of thought. A train in this second sense is a willed accomplishment, a construction, albeit based on natural principles or laws of mind. The educator's vocation is thus training the train, analyzing and directing natural thought patterns to create disciplines, which are simply trains of trains. Currie's analysis of the "expression of thought," the "primary object in intellectual education" (116), insists on the link between mental training and developed trains of thought: "in training conception," Currie insists, "the issue to which the process should be carried is *words*; in training the judgment, it is *propositions*. In harmony with this exercise of the faculty of language, is the habit of expressing in our own language *trains of thought*" (116).

As in Mill's analysis, a precise correspondence exists between the mental landscape and the map of language: a single conception is accurately embodied in a word, and the faculty of judgment in a proposition. Such neat equations coexist, as in Mill, with what we might be tempted to call circular reasoning—were it not so aggressively linear and successive. Thus, thinking in train is natural. Knowing this, the skillful teacher trains his pupils to produce trains of thought.

The coherence of the new pedagogical method makes itself felt in the centrality that teacher training schools assigned to syntactical parsing, an occupation on which products of the liberal arts tradition, like the Oxford don Mr. Bell in Gaskell's *North and South* (1844-1855), looked askance. In a classical education, the parsing, or grammatical analysis, of Latin sentences facilitated the learning of a foreign language. Yet as Currie notes, the teacher training schools heavily emphasized the "scientific" parsing of English sentences (300). Currie defines parsing as the "ability to account, not only for the forms of individual words, but for the relations existing between words, by reference to the general practice of the language" (300). This study of relationships was regarded as an important "mental discipline" (302) that bridged the gap between phonetics (the study of associations between sounds and signs) and the "constructive power over language" (309) necessary for effective composition. Currie emphasizes the necessity of training students in a consistent and effective system of parsing; there were many systems to choose from. If the laborious recitations, elaborate tables, and often obscure terminology required by scientific parsing made it a cumbersome and time-consuming method of standardizing the pupils' use of grammar, parsing's real advantage was that it cast language as itself an orderly system of associations, reflecting, however indirectly, the principles of human mental functioning. Thus, parsing trained the young pupil's mind to produce logical associations; with its emphasis on language relations, it served as a basis for the development of relational trains of thought.

From the syntactical relations among single words, through the logical relations of complex thoughts, to the moral relations governing ethical behavior, the principles of association held good. Thus, like intellectual training, moral instruction also worked through the principles of linear association. As Currie emphasizes, from their earliest moments, children must be taught to form "a uniform bond of association, in virtue of which the child shall be led to desire to do what is right and to avoid what is wrong" (13). Thus, the parent's, and later the teacher's, effectiveness depends on "the steadiness with which a certain line of conduct is required from" the child (34); consistent ethical training impels the pupil to internalize a linear, progressive moral direction: "Thus it is that in the school life he feels every-where a power drawing him steadily in one direction; a power acting under one uniform purpose and in obedience to an understood law... [to which] the whole machinery of his nature [becomes] accustomed in its operations to give effect" (34-35). Once directed and guided along the proper track of associations—again the railroad metaphor suggests itself—the human machinery moves efficiently toward its goal.

Though more moderately expressed, Currie's elaborately documented trains of thought represent the same kind of thinking parodied in the famously tedious and oppressive lesson at Gradgrind's model school in *Hard Times*. Dickens's novel invokes the associative pedagogical methods so valued by both Currie and James Mill, insinuating a parodic rhetoric of association into its depiction of the intellectual formation of Gradgrind's own children, Tom and Louisa: "Almost as soon as [the children] could run alone, they had been made to run to the lecture-room. The first object with which they had an association ... was a large blackboard with a dry Ogre chalking ghastly white figures on it" (9). Gradgrind's rigorous control of childhood associations finds its crowning expression in the correct definition of a horse enunciated by the irritatingly proficient Bitzer, the model school's star pupil. Bitzer's definition embodies the principles of association at their most mechanical: "Quadruped. Graminivorous. Forty teeth, namely, twenty-four grinders, four eye-teeth, and twelve incisive. Sheds coat in the spring; in marshy countries, sheds hoofs, too. Hoofs hard, but requiring to be shod with iron. Age known by marks in mouth" (5).

Although it purports to follow a logical sequence, Bitzer's series of attributes lacks the subordination and relationality we expect from classical logical analysis. Instead, Bitzer's ludicrous definition gives equal weight to each aspect of the horse, just as Mill's description of temporal and spatial associations gives equal weight to each link in the train of perceptions. In Bitzer's anatomized "geography" of a horse, various aspects of the horse serve as identically functioning links forging a "train of thought." Thus, a statement as to the horse's eating habits leads to a description of its teeth, which in turn guides us to another aspect of the horse's appearance, its coat. The shedding of the coat then moves Bitzer to contemplate the shedding of the horse's hoofs, and so on. Or, in Dickens's words: "Thus (and much more) Bitzer" (5). Bitzer's mental stamina, his ability to continue the train of thought *ad nauseam* shows, not only that he is fully primed with facts, but also that he has mastered the pedagogical method of association.

Further, Bitzer's associative definition of a horse is surrounded by, and secured within, a net of professorial associations. Gradgrind demands the definition as a result of Sissy Jupe's statement that her father "belongs to the horse-riding" (4); similarly, the eminent "government officer" (a representative of the emerging national educational bureaucracy) follows up Bitzer's definition with the loaded question: "Would you paper a room with representations of horses?" (5). As the students soon learn, the correct answer is "no." Since horses don't normally walk on walls, wallpaper depicting horses is an error of "taste." "Taste is only another name for Fact," the official pronounces, adding, "This is a new principle, a discovery, a great discovery" (6).

In Dickens's parodic lesson, the horse serves as the pivot or nexus for various subordinated trains of thought; thanks to this nexus, the lesson moves, by means of leading questions, through a series of diverse topics to the enunciation of a great "principle." Outlandish as the lesson is, Dickens captures the form of the linguistic *object lesson* as it was envisioned in contemporary teacher training schools. After visiting a number of teacher training colleges in his capacity of school inspector, Matthew Arnold sadly records the unsatisfactory set-lessons that student teachers shaped around a single object or idea. Examples of such lessons included "a sketch of a lesson on the 'Hand,' a sketch of a lesson on the 'Isle of Wight,' on the 'Honey Bee,' on the 'Cause of Day and Night.'" As Arnold laments, "inevitably, the lesson becomes a means of showing the [student teacher's] own knowledge of his subject and power of arranging it, rather than his faculty of teaching" (Reports 281).[23]

In his manual, Currie describes several model object lessons, focusing rather on trains of thought than on the experimental examination of an object. One lesson, for example, entitled "The Eye" (*Principles and Practice* 385), embodies the same structure as the lesson in *Hard Times*. An introduction to the lesson relates the object to students' experience through questions easily answered: "What do we see with?" the instructor demands, and follows the pupils' predictable answer with yet another question: "How many eyes [have we]?" (Students are enjoined to point to each.) In the body of the lesson, the class is asked to name the position, shape, and parts of the eye, including such elements as "the dark little spot *in center*" and the "fine hair ... called *eye-lashes.*" The lesson's conclusion contains a principle supposedly derived from the train of thought, but in actuality a moralistic injunction: "[The] eye [is] given to *notice things*—use your eyes wherever you are" (385). Similarly, the Gradgrindian lesson begins with simple questions (about Sissy Jupe's father and his job as a "horse-breaker"), moves on to an anatomy of the horse, and ends with a great principle that also functions as a moral.

In Currie's teaching manual, the Pestalozzian object lesson, once the emblem of immediate and experiential learning, is attenuated to an abstraction, a merely formal exercise.[24] No longer experiencing a concrete object, touching, smelling, or tasting it, students learn to anatomize a described object or entity, tracing out various trains of thought for which it serves as the nexus. Clearly, the appeal of such abstract and formulaic object lessons was not their liveliness, nor even their ability, as Currie argues about the associative method in general, to cast a "net" that holds loose data in memory. In fact, the object lessons that Arnold records and that Dickens parodies are too tedious to be memorable. Rather, such linear tracings of trains of thought carried the imprimatur of the new "science of mind." They embodied mental laws easy to describe and transform into a simple pedagogical method. They appeal because they are relatively easy to justify and to duplicate; they fulfill the professional pedagogue's need for a balance between theory and practice.

British educators' adoption of the train of thought as the psychological and scientific basis of their pedagogical practice was a shrewd and effective move, yet it was undeniably complicated by the term's heritage of contradictory connotations. As noted above, Locke viewed mental associations as potentially dangerous and irrational, standing in opposition to authentic logical analysis (an objection that also pertains to Bitzer's associational definition above). Similarly, while Locke could employ the phrase "thinking in train" as a reference to coherent thought, he also used the term in an oppositional sense. Thus, he warns against "settle[d] habits of Thinking" that appear to be logical, but are mere "Trains of Motion in the Animal Spirits, which once set a going continue on in the same steps they have been used to."[25] Such deceptive "trains of motion" (mental prejudices or habits of thought randomly constructed) constitute the opposite of logical thinking.

Hume's complex depiction of the mental train exemplifies a rich texture of diverse moods and contradictory connotations, combining connotations of logic with images of irrationality and randomness. In one of his most eloquent metaphors for the mind, Hume depicts it as a commonwealth acting upon a set of coherent *laws*, the image of an albeit mysterious order:

> One thought chaces [*sic*] another, and draws after it a third, by which it is expell'd in its turn. In this respect, I cannot compare the soul more properly to anything than to a republic or commonwealth, in which the several members are united by the reciprocal ties of government and subordination, and give rise to other persons, who propagate the incessant changes of its members, but also its laws and constitutions; in like matter the same person may vary his character and disposition, as well as his impressions and ideas, without losing his identity. (*Treatise of Human Nature*, vol. 1:542)

Metaphorizing the mind as a commonwealth with a constitution, Hume here emphasizes its rationality, relative stability, and coherence. At the same time, however, Hume's vision is one of radical skepticism toward traditionally reified conceptions, questioning the very notions of mind and selfhood on which Mill and Currie based their pedagogical theories. As Hume emphasizes, "the thought alone finds personal identity, when reflecting on the train of past perceptions that compose a mind" (*Treatise*, vol. 1: Appendix 559). Or again: "Our notions of personal identity proceed entirely from the smooth and uninterrupted progress of the thought along a train of connected ideas" (vol. 1:541). Disputing the idea of a continuous self that can exist outside of or beyond its own perceptions, Hume emphasizes that "mankind" is only "a collection of different perceptions, which succeed each other with an inconceivable rapidity, and are in a perpetual flux and movement" (vol. 1:534).

Refining this image, Hume strikingly and famously depicts the mind as a theater enclosing, and offering a stage for, thought's successive pageants: "The mind is a kind of theatre, where several perceptions successively make their appearance; pass, re-pass, glide away, and mingle in an infinite variety of postures and situations" (vol. 1:534). On the other hand, Hume cautions us against taking even this highly fluid analogy too literally: "The comparison of the theatre must not mislead us. They are the successive perceptions only that constitute the mind: nor have we the most distant notion of the place, where these scenes are represented, or of the materials, of which it is compos'd" (vol. 1:534–535).

As Hume makes explicit, then, the individual mind or self as a fixed entity is an illusory concept, a reification of the process he wishes to foreground: "For my part, when I enter most intimately into what I call *myself*, I always stumble on some particular perception or other.... I never can catch *myself* at any time without a perception, and never can observe any thing but perception" (vol. 1:534). The theater, the enclosure "where these scenes are represented," is thus illusory, or at least indescribable given our current state of knowledge. On this insubstantial stage, the vivid pageant of perceptions advances. As Hume describes it here, the "train" of human perceptions exhibits no particular order. The successive pageant's forward movement is an embodiment not of progress but of flux, of endless changes whose significance eludes us.

The irrational aspects of mental trains of association (so richly depicted in the work of Locke and Hume) would be exploited in John Henry Newman's eloquent attack on the new scientific utilitarian education and its reliance on associative training. In 1809, *The Edinburgh Review* mounted an attack on the traditional classical education offered at Oxford and Cambridge, prompting a flurry of defensive writing, of which Newman's influential *The Idea of a University* (1852) is an aftershock or an echo. Thus, Newman's wide-ranging essay is in part a counterattack on what he sees as the utilitarian model of learning, in which students accumulate unrelated facts, amassing information without fully integrating and synthesizing it.

Newman links such mechanical instruction by association with a deadening linearity, the sign of feeble or vitiated thought that can lead to extremes of irrationality. Thus, those who have overstimulated their memories in the course of a mechanical education endure a flattening of the intellect that is akin to madness: "they have no power of self-control; they passively endure the succession of impulses which are evolved out of the original exciting cause; they are passed on from one idea to another and go steadily forward, plodding along one line of thought" (*Idea, Discourse VI*, vol. vii:102). Displaying a truly Lockean suspicion of "associations," Newman equates the associative train with mental "Derangement": "The mind, once set in motion, is henceforth deprived of the power of initiation, and becomes the victim of a train of associations, one thought suggesting another... as if by a mechanical process" (*Idea, Discourse VI*, vol. vii:102).

In contrast, the dynamic processes of imagination and reason are evoked by nonlinear images, emphasizing circularity and three-dimensionality: "We know," Newman writes, "not by a direct and simple vision, not at a glance, but, as it were, by piecemeal and accumulation, by a mental process, by going round an object" (*Idea, Discourse VII*, vol. i:109). Similarly, connected or systematic thought manifests itself, not in a linear succession, but rather in a three-dimensional system of planetary relations: "It is not the mere addition to our knowledge that is the illumination [provided by education]; but the locomotion, the movement onwards, of that mental centre, to which... the accumulating mass of our acquirements, gravitates" (*Idea, Discourse VI*, vol. v:98). Evoking a Humean gravitational attraction at the heart of mental functioning, Newman's solar system model of "the enlargement of mind" (*Idea, Discourse VI*, vol. iii:95) is the antithesis of James Mill's linear paradigm.

MENTAL GOVERNMENT IN THE THEATER OF PHANTOMS: SCHOOLROOM INTERIORS AND STYLES OF INTERIORITY

As we might expect, Newman has no more use than Carlyle for square enclosures. For him, the university serves as the ground on which young men form a rich, intellectual community. Such a meeting of minds is more important than meeting "three times a week... in chill lecture rooms" (*Idea, Discourse VI*, vol. ix:107). Of course, as it is hardly necessary to underline, the great Gothic edifices of university architecture stand behind Newman's elegant and sonorous sentences. Attending carefully to the metaphors that govern the text, we find that Newman's argument (like that of *Hard Times*) is substantially about space. Above all, the university is spacious—it permits the individual mind to develop and expand, in contrast to the cramping and narrowing influences of the world of business and the professions. Newman's spacious sentences, with room for pleasing images and surprising metaphors, evoke both an intellectual and architectural spaciousness. The "chill lecture rooms" can be gently dismissed in part because the university as an institution is such a great and towering presence.

In contrast, for Currie and the new breed of professional teachers, the rectilinear and regulated schoolroom has a crucial significance as the site of a regulated and professional activity, perhaps analogous to the barrister's courtroom or the physician's surgery. As Peter Sandiford writes in *The Training of Teachers in England and Wales* (1910), the "customary method of extending educational facilities at that time [the 1830s] was to build a school, appoint a master, and then send him to be trained" (38). Sandiford is writing specifically about the highly standardized monitorial system of teaching as implemented by the Kildare Place Society in Ireland. Still, the chronology he records is typical not only of the monitorial movement, but also of the new emphasis placed on the school's physical plant in the British national system. A prime object of the Kildare Society was the "fitting up of schoolhouses upon a suitable plan" (37). Once money was raised to build a proper school, a teacher could be supplied relatively easily. Teacher training by the Kildare Society typically took only six weeks.

As we have seen, James Mill affirms a seamless congruence between the orders of the mental and the physical realm, as well as between time and space. It is hardly surprising, then, that educators like Currie believed they could shape the physical terrain of the schoolroom in a manner conducive to the cultivation of the mental landscape. "The best shape for the school-room," Currie affirms, "is the oblong, about twice as long as it is broad; being that in which a larger proportion of the entire space is available for teaching than in the square or any other form" (*Principles and Practice* 181). While the efficient Currie prefers the utilitarian oblong to the square enclosure satirized by Carlyle, he clearly endorses the linearity that Carlyle questions.

In Currie's manual, the schoolroom's oblong space contains a proliferation of other oblong enclosures that stand for a methodical and systematic pedagogy. Throughout Currie's text, exquisitely ruled tables flaunt their elegant oblong columns and boxes, illustrating everything from a "register of merit" for recording student grades to a tripartite Bible lesson plan, and an analysis of parts of a sentence. The oblong is not only the shape of the classroom; it also most accurately shapes and encloses the categories of thought that are the classroom's reason for existence. In one sense, the classroom is a series of boxes within boxes; it is that emblem of methodical analysis, the uniformly ruled "table" of information. School life offers a dazzling array of tables: tables to record grades, tables of attendance and absences, tables of class materials, of expenses, multiplication tables, tables of verbs, and tables enshrining the anatomized parts of a sentence—just as glass cases showcase geological specimens in the Gradgrinds' aggressively rectilinear house. As in Foucault's analysis, space is not only enclosed and partitioned, but is ranked in a hierarchy of classification, a "permanent grid" (145): "Thus, the classroom would form a single great table, with many different entries, under the scrupulously 'classificatory' eye of the master" (147).

Within the mandatory oblong schoolroom, Currie's manual allows for various arrangements of school furniture, depending on the nature and number of the pupils and teachers; all arrangements, notably, include a series of benches or writing desks in parallel rows, often arranged along an inclined plane, as in Gradgrind's model school. One interesting example offered by Currie is the "tripartite system of arrangement," based on the assumption that students' activities fall into a tripartite order: (1) those requiring "thoughtful exposition," such as Bible and grammar lessons with the teacher, (2) reading aloud and spelling, implicitly more mechanical activities to be performed with a pupil-teacher or assistant, and (3) quiet "desk-lessons" such as "writing" and "slate arithmetic" (135–136), which can be carried on alone.

The division of studies and activities is then reflected in the physical arrangement of the schoolroom:

> An ordinary school-room of oblong shape might be... divided into three equal compartments, separated by curtains from each other; let the middle compartment be fitted with parallel benches and desks for the silent lessons in writing, drawing, and slate arithmetic: of the remaining two, let one have a gallery for oral instruction, subdivided if necessary, and the other be furnished with seats for small [groups] engaged in reading. From a raised desk or platform at the end of the room the teacher can superintend the hourly changes. (139)

In some respects, the tripartite arrangement, like Robson's double schoolroom, is a sensible way station on the road from the traditional large schoolroom to a system of divided classrooms. Endorsed by the Committee of Council, it was in effect by the 1850s, and came to be "specially favoured by British schools" (Birchenough 273). At the same time, the tripartite system is also particularly in line with the spirit of Currie's manual. Students are placed in boxlike divisions, each characteristic of a subject and an activity. Thus, there is reading space, exposition space, and quiet lesson space. Students move between these spaces at regular intervals, exemplifying the order of succession.

Not only spatially but also temporally, the tripartite schoolroom exemplifies the successive order of the mental train. The compartmentalized space—its three contiguous areas filled with their parallel benches, writing desks, and seats for reading—exemplifies a rationalized contiguity of place; the hourly changes by which students move from one contiguous area to the next exemplify contiguity in time. Time is thus symmetrical with space, giving us exposition time, reading time, and quiet lesson time. If the pupils watch and listen to the teacher on his raised platform, at least during exposition time, the teacher also watches the shifting pageant of pupils moving through their intervals of time and space.

Enacting the clarity of the order of succession in its time schedule, its physical arrangement, and its activities, Currie's schoolroom exists as a theater of linearity. In contrast to the fleeting pageants embodied in Hume's eloquent image of the mind as theater, Currie's teacher and pupils enact a pageant of self-contained presence in a controlled structure that subordinates space and time to its own ends. Also in contrast to Hume's qualified metaphor, Currie's schoolroom might be regarded as a literalized metaphor embodied in brick and wood, imaging the terrain of mind as mapped by association psychology. Arguably, the tripartite schoolroom fuses the two meanings of *train* exemplified in Hume's contrasting images of the theater and the commonwealth. Under the teacher's supervision, the schoolroom partakes of both the specular quality of the pageant as well as the purposeful and orderly change of the commonwealth's government, in Hume's depiction.

Certainly, Currie's ideal school instructs pupils in the art of self-government, controlling, training, and governing the faculties of the mind. Subdued and purposeful, the classroom offers us an emblem of the mind at its most rational, apparently divorced from play and pageantry. In what sense, then, can we also register our contradictory feeling that activity in the tripartite schoolroom is also a performance? Where are we to locate its performative and decorative aspects?

For all their earnest rationality, the elaborate and elaborated trains of thought offered by both Currie and Gradgrind—typical in different ways of contemporary educators—exhibit a baroque and decorative quality. Dickens's portrait of Gradgrind's schoolroom uncovers its dramatic and performative aspect; although they fit within the formal principles of association theory, the connections that link the discrete parts of the novel's model object lesson seem outrageous and absurd, enacting a mad flamboyance.

Similarly, Matthew Arnold was disturbed by what he took to be the purely performative aspects of the object lessons taught by student teachers. He pities the audience of pupils "wearied" by "a number of these performances, one after another," and asserts that the bewildered students learn little from such exercises. A school inspector, he adds, could more effectively gauge the apprentice teacher's capacities by seeing a five-minute reading lesson than by "witnessing this much more pretentious performance" (*Reports* 281). While spinning the attenuated and virtuoso trains of thought that constitute the linguistic object lesson, the trained teacher performs a pageant of professionalism, dramatically enacting the link between practice and theory. In this context, instruction of individual students is less important than the virtuoso display of the pageant. Both pupils and teachers, in other words, engage in a pageant that serves to manifest mental government—the rationality of the mental processes.

As Dickens effectively dramatizes, the model object lesson in Gradgrind's schoolroom may proclaim the new reign of facts, but it is less about substance than about style. Despite its assertion of a new utility that displaces decoration, the lesson is simply decorative in a new sense: it replaces images of quadrupeds on wallpaper with ornamental nets of words woven around objects, or gaudy trains of language, like banners stamped with images of the associative, mechanical mind. In

Dickens's narrative, utility and ornament, apparently in opposition, are unmasked as permeable categories because styles of architecture, of language, and of interiority are ornamental in complementary ways.

As the linear mental trains cultivated by Gradgrindery proliferate and become decoratively baroque, as utilitarianism is recast as a style, a species of ornamentation, Dickens's work exults in a new fusion that might be described as utilitarian Gothic. Gradgrindery, according to Dickens, produces not existence lived in a dreary monotone, but horrific excess, nightmares of rationality. Although it attacks a form of pedagogy initially designed for working-class children, *Hard Times* prophetically predicts that the new scientific pedagogical method cannot ultimately be contained by class boundaries. Thus, Gradgrind's socially privileged children are maimed by the new pedagogy even though they don't attend the model school. Trapped in a marriage with the grotesque husband chosen by her father on supposedly rational principles, Louisa Gradgrind undergoes a species of mental torture; similarly, her morally enfeebled brother sinks into criminality and frames the innocent workman Stephen Blackpool, who must make a nighttime journey through a dangerous region of old mines in order to clear himself. Through its vitiation of Tom's character, then, Gradgrindery is implicated in the exiled Blackpool's horrific death in the coal pits, transformed into a "poor, crushed human creature" (*Hard Times* 271). If Gradgrind's school of hyperrationality metaphorically deforms the human, it is now implicated in a literal, physical maiming and death. For Dickens, Gradgrindery is a pedagogical discourse that can kill.

To a striking degree, *Hard Times* generates narrative by literalizing its metaphors. The mechanisms of plot and the complexities of character rigorously enact the emotional connotations of its language. Bitzer's skill in forging mechanical trains of language associations generates an equally mechanical calculus of action (an admittedly distorting parody of Bentham's utilitarian "moral calculus") that leads him to betray both Gradgrind and Tom. Gradgrind's designation of the horse-riding ring as a forbidden realm that cannot even be mentioned in school does indeed seem to generate an alternate world run on principles diametrically opposed to his own.

In fact, *Hard Times* offers only one cure for Gradgrindery's lethal emphasis on mechanical mental training, its tendency to recast the child's mind as a classificatory grid. That cure resides in the errant and wayward paths of narrative. As Dickens laments,

> No Gradgrind had ever associated a cow in a field with that famous cow with the crumpled horn who swallowed Tom Thumb; it had

never heard of those celebrities, and had only been introduced to a cow as a gramnivorous ruminating quadruped with several stomachs. (8)

As Gradgrind rigorously trains his children's mental associations, he outlaws stories and storytelling; Gradgrind repeatedly stands in opposition to fiction's peculiar methods of knowing and learning, associated here with improvisatory linguistic play, vicarious identification, metaphor, and symbol. Tom Thumb's story, it need hardly be emphasized, invokes a classic fairy tale metaphor for childhood: the tiny boy in an outsize world, who can outwit the looming adults and giant animals who threaten him. Earlier in the novel, the government officer who visits Gradgrind's model school denounces the practice of adorning carpets with flowers since human beings don't normally walk on flowers. For Dickens, the new pedagogy's supposed disdain for imaginative play involves a misapprehension of the utility of metaphor. Unlike the iron links of the pedagogue's associative chain leading in one inexorable direction, metaphor is a vehicle for jumping off the tracks of the train, for forging illicit and circuitous connections not dreamed of in Gradgrind's philosophy. Opposing the metaphorical aspects of fiction and fairy tale, Gradgrind's institutionalization of childhood is seen as a threat to fiction's unique educative project.

2

FROM FELIX'S COTTAGE TO MISS TEMPLE'S PARLOR

Domestic Instruction and the Paradox of the Teacher's Room

[I]t is reasonable to expect that in a large school there should be set apart a small room for the use of the teacher, both for business and for his retirement during intervals.

—**James Currie,** ***The Principles and Practice of Common School Education***

The cottage of my protectors had been the only school in which I had studied human nature.

—**Mary Shelley,** *Frankenstein*

In *The Practice of Everyday Life* (1980), Michel de Certeau argues that stories "traverse and organize places; they select and link them together; they make sentences and itineraries out of them." Thus, stories "are spatial trajectories" (115). Numerous nineteenth-century fictions map trajectories between coercive and idealized school spaces, associated with the realms of institutionality and domesticity. Depending on how the school scenes are staged, sequenced, and linked, such narrative pathways implicitly reassure readers that school abuses can be corrected, or warn them of disturbing trends on the educational horizon. Charlotte Brontë's *Jane Eyre* (1847) charts a path from Lowood under Brocklehurst's cruel reign to its more benign management by Miss Temple after Brocklehurst's role has been curtailed. Brontë's novels *The Professor* (1857) and *Villette* (1853) also map a corrective itinerary, replacing the unsatisfactory schools where their protagonists teach with the benignant and domesticated academies they later found and operate. Similarly, Dickens's *David Copperfield* (1849–1850) frees its protagonist from Mr. Creakle's abusive school (run like a factory as a purely commercial venture) by seeing him safely through the gates of the idealized academy headed by the fatherly Dr. Strong. Through such juxtapositions and implicit comparisons, numerous mid-century novels both critique and "correct" current educational abuses. Conversely, other novels map an ominous transition from nurturing educational spaces to a coercive and mind-numbing institutionality. Gaskell's *North and South*, for instance, depicts one parish school's transition from a familial and nurturing site (conducted by the gentle Margaret Hale) to an increasingly regimented space under the purview of the state inspectorate. George Eliot's *Middlemarch* (1871–1872), in so many ways a novel of education, juxtaposes the practical moral education received by Mary Garth and her siblings in the informal dame school of their mother's kitchen against Fred Vincey's superficial institutional schooling, associated with upward mobility and the quest for social status.

Such contrasting pairs of schools reflect a similar dualism in nonfictional educational discourse.[1] As explored in the previous chapter, James Currie (1862) situates his scientific, professional pedagogical method, with its rigid subject divisions and rote lessons, within the efficient, rectilinear spaces of the new standardized classroom; yet he also maps a site for more informal, domestic interactions between teacher and pupils. Thus, he affirms the need for a "teacher's room" for "retirement" and "business" when the schoolmaster's "dwelling-house" is not "contiguous to the school building." Primarily a domestic retreat for teachers, substituting for their too-distant home, the room also serves as a haven for "pupil-teachers" and as a "library" (182), which the teacher "must encourage" the schoolchildren to use "by interesting himself in what they read." Welcoming students into this semidomesticated space, the wise teacher "draw[s] out thereby their general intelligence" (180–181). A nurturing annex to the classroom, the teacher's room fosters a different set of spatial practices. Rather than listening silently or collectively reciting rote lessons aloud, students can speak individually, sharing ideas and knowledge derived from freely chosen reading rather than preordained lessons.

The subject of this chapter is the *teacher's room*, in its dialectical interplay with institutionality, as evoked in school narratives. As the plan of the typical national school became standardized, the teacher's room, used for both retirement and business, became a fixture. In *School Architecture* (1874), Robson includes the teacher's "private rooms" (220) in the typical school plan as a matter of course,[2] as did many other architects (Figure 2.1). The teacher's room aptly embodies the dynamic of domestic education when detached from the private household and confined within the precincts of school space. A schoolroom that defies the conventions of institutionalized schooling, the teacher's room evokes the less regimented space of home. On the other hand, the teacher's room is a home that is temporary and provisional, and admission to it must be earned by the diligent pupil; thus the space reveals the provisionality of domestic attachments, the germs of institutionality located at the very heart of home, an insight emphasized by numerous critics from Jürgen Habermas to Michel Foucault and their successors. In the words of Nancy Armstrong (1987), "the power of domestic surveillance," helped to establish "the need for the kind of surveillance upon which modern institutions are based" (19). Habermas's (1962) spatial metaphor of a familial "intimate sphere" situated at the core of the "sphere of the market" (55) offers an illuminating analogy. Serving as "an agent of society," the bourgeois family also proclaims itself "the anticipated emancipation from society" (55). Replicating the patriarchal ownership structures of the market, the family produces intimacy and comfort as products; yet this production can only occur, of course, when male authority is obscured by the fiction that all members of the family circle are free and equal. Often cast by Victorian novelists as oppositional to institutional space, the teacher's room more accurately illustrates the link between home space and institutionality.

As I argue in this chapter, the constellation of images and assumptions that constitutes the rhetoric of domestic education permeates the nineteenth-century literature of education at a time when schooling increasingly takes place outside the home. This rhetoric serves two apparently contradictory functions. Representatives of institutionalized education employ it as rhetorical window dressing to temper a standardizing agenda that might otherwise seem threatening. Alternatively, their opponents often deploy the rhetoric of domesticity as part of an influential but admittedly ambivalent critique of the trend toward an institutionalized, standardized pedagogy. While Victorian novelists generally fall into the latter category, their work requires yet another level of analysis. Drawing on the *bildungsroman*'s valorization of individualism and individualized education, Victorian fictions respond to the education debates with a variety of narrative and formal strategies. In particular, they dramatize in narrative form, the philosophic oppositions staked out in educational discourse, clothing ideas and agendas in human form. The "parental" instruction of teachers like Dickens's Dr. Strong and Brontë's Miss Temple—rhetorically staged as "domestic" despite its school setting—suggests both a corrective for institutional education and a standard against which it must be judged.[3] Yet the demands of fictive narrative also expose latent contradictions in both the theoretical discourse and popular assumptions about domestic education.

The protean, domesticated space of the teacher's room can take many forms; in this respect it is analogous to Lefebvre's conception of the clandestine spaces of representation that so often emerge in the varied metaphors and fertile, vivid images created by storytellers. "Dwelling-space" or "the indoor space of family life," Lefebvre (1974) contends, "exemplifies a spatial practice which... is close, in concrete terms, to the work of art" (166). The realm of home allows for a measure of artistic improvisation and the experience (or illusion) of creating one's own space. Similarly, the teacher's room facilitates an experience of improvisatory intellectual play, linked with images of self-education or even self-creation. Like the teacher's room, the present chapter is also somewhat protean, crossing generic boundaries and historical divides, as it draws on Mary Shelley's pre-Victorian fantasy *Frankenstein*, (1816), the educational theories of Rousseau and Spencer, and the fictive schoolrooms of Hughes, Brontë, and Dickens. Only such an eclectic and synthetic approach can evoke the mixed associations and assumptions behind the image of the teacher's room.

THE CIRCLE OF INTIMACY: MARY SHELLEY'S CHILD-MONSTER

[Felix's] reading had puzzled me extremely at first; but, by degrees, I discovered that he uttered many of the same sounds when he read as when he talked. I conjectured, therefore, that he found on the paper signs for speech which he understood, and I ardently longed to comprehend these also.... I applied... my whole mind to the endeavour: for I easily perceived that, although I eagerly longed to discover myself to the cottagers, I ought not to make the attempt until I had first become master of their language; which knowledge might ... make them overlook the deformity of my figure. (*Frankenstein* 90)

These earnest words, spoken by Victor Frankenstein's unnamed and hapless creation, record a memorable scene of domestic instruction. Hiding out in a hovel adjoining a poor but well-kept cottage, the monster

spies on the cottagers through a crack in the wall, lea
its, family relationships, and ultimately their languag
unwitting lessons briefly tame the monster's tumult
by resentment and longing. Yet the childlike monster .
to a devastating degree, believing that if he can only learn his ~
well enough, he will be admitted into the glowing and serene domestic
space that has been for so long the fixed object of his gaze. Mastering
language, he believes, will win him this privilege:

> I formed in my imagination a thousand pictures of presenting
> myself to them.... I imagined that they would be disgusted, until,
> by my gentle demeanour and conciliating words, I should first
> win their favour, and afterwards their love.
>
> These thoughts exhilarated me, and led me to apply with fresh
> ardour to the acquiring the art of language. (91)

The key to domestic instruction, according to numerous thinkers
from Rousseau to Spencer, is simple: by learning his lessons well, the
child, like Victor's lonely monster, hopes to gain the love and approval
of admired adults. Shelley's monster has been seen as an emblem of
various oppressed groups, including women and the colonial subjects
of empire.[4] Yet the analogue most clearly suggested by Shelley's text is
that of an undisciplined and uneducated child rejected by his maker or
father. The goal of the monster's quest is most importantly to reunite
with his lost father, an aim he realizes only when they die together in
an Arctic wasteland.

If the dominant spatial metaphor for the work of the standardized,
regulated schoolroom is the straight line—emblem of directed thought,
individual intellectual progress, and collective social amelioration—a
major metaphor for domestic education is the entrance into the *family circle*, also cast as the penetration of previously closed spaces, or
the movement from the marginal to the privileged center. Within the
home, the child works his way from the nursery to the domestic hearth,
attaining only gradually the inmost sanctuary of family life. Similarly,
Frankenstein's monster envisions entering his mentors' closed cottage,
and leaving his own monstrousness behind.

By delineating the limits of education and its ultimate inability to
civilize its nonhuman protagonist, the novel serves as a failed *bildungsroman*. Shelley's narrative postulates the ability to profit from a human-
istic education as a defining characteristic separating the human and
the monstrous; although the monster grasps his mentors' lessons intellectually, he fails to internalize them, choosing not the code of civilized

society, but an aberrant program of revenge. At the same time, however, by portraying the childlike monster as a talented and motivated student, albeit an ultimately unsuccessful one, Shelley also problematizes the boundaries between the human and the monstrous, between the child-pupil and the horrendous and unassimilable Other.

Ultimately, the plight of Frankenstein's hapless creation calls into question the agendas and purposes of domestic education itself. The cottagers, of course, have two pupils: the monster and the Turkish visitor Safie, an exoticized Other, female and foreign. As part of the human family, Safie can be educated and incorporated into the cottagers' familial circle through marriage to the young Felix, who serves as the virtual head of the family, supporting his sister and blind father. Tellingly, Safie's condemnation of her own culture serves as a prerequisite for her full admission into Felix's European family, presented as both normative and idealized. Domestic education, we are reminded, thrives on polarities; it is all about otherness. Promising the ultimate dream of inclusion, the ideal of domestic education also draws boundaries and excludes those beyond its magic circle. Utopian in its aims, it implicitly condemns—and often shuns—the world beyond its walls.

As embodied in Shelley's novel, the monster's domestic education includes three defining elements: first, he finds mentors whom he perceives as surrogate parents or prospective family members, and who can therefore inspire his love and admiration, establishing an implicit if admittedly illusory "familial" relationship. Second, the monster's vicarious lessons in literacy foreground a defining characteristic of domestic instruction: its mysterious methodology and refusal to be confined within disciplinary boundaries. Implicitly shaping his character as they explicitly instruct him in language and letters, the monster's lessons civilize the "savage" pupil through a process so subtle as to appear invisible. While mastering intellectual challenges, the monster grows adept in affective subtleties and distinctions. Striving to connect sounds with signs, he also absorbs lessons about family relations. As he joyfully discovers, and later narrates to his creator:

> the youth and his companion had each of them several names, but the old man had only one, which was *father*. The girl was called *sister*, or *Agatha*; and the youth *Felix*, *brother*, or *son*. I cannot describe the delight I felt when I learned the ideas appropriate to each of these sounds, and was able to pronounce them. (89)

As the monster's lesson in literacy becomes simultaneously a lesson in familial love, he learns that language cannot describe its own delights. Images of domestic education frequently bring together the lessons of the spoken word and a nonverbal or indescribable experience of comity and delight.

Third, as the monster unhappily learns, domestic education is confined to designated members of the familial circle of intimacy, and carries with it an implicit threat of exile that can lead to a rigorous internalization of knowledge and codes of behavior. By his nature, Mary Shelley's exiled monster can never penetrate the domestic sanctuary; unlike a human child, he cannot shed his "monstrousness," except perhaps in the sightless eyes of Felix's blind father, who briefly welcomes him into the cottage. The monster's incomparable solitude foregrounds domestic education's exclusionary nature, its linkage to a site that is moral rather than visible, eternally shifting yet eternally stable. While it can take place on the elegant estate of Rousseau's *Émile* or in Felix's humble cottage, domestic education is dependent on the magic circle of an assumed intimacy.

The monster's fruitless lesson suggests that domestic education, in contrast to Gradgrind's educational mill, defies standardization and imitation. It achieves its aim with Safie, the woman Felix loves and marries, even though Shelley portrays her as less studious—and less adept—than the monster. In contrast, the hopeful monster's acquisition of a "gentle" demeanor, a moral vision, and the capacity for reason are swept away when he is rejected by the family he aspires to join. At our own peril do we nourish the illusion that domestic education can extend beyond the familial circle of intimacy. Thus, domestic education thrives on a rhetoric of dualism; its circle of intimacy is evoked *in relation to* a flawed counter-space, an alien or uncomprehending world. For Shelley's monster, that counter-space involves the terror of isolation and the dangers of unmediated nature; for Safie, it comprises the supposed flaws of non-Western culture. In later novels of education, such as those by Dickens and Charlotte Brontë, the dominant threat is more likely to involve the encroachments of institutionality and commercial exchange. Just as home is a protective shelter that reminds us of the vast spaces outside its walls, so domestic education tends to be staged against allegedly more coercive forms of instruction and human relations.

Shelley's portrayal of domestic education offers a rich field for spatial analysis. In his depictions of human habitations, the monster seems especially drawn to the hearth fires where the occupants gather for meals. Similarly, he marvels at the "tapers" used by his neighbors as a "means of prolonging light" (86) as they while away their evenings reading and playing musical instruments. In *School Architecture*, E. R. Robson notes approvingly the homely and domestic connotations of the school hearth,[5] and brightly burning hearth fires figure prominently in numerous scenes of domestic education, from Lizzie Hexam's inspirational stories by the fireside in Dickens's *Our Mutual Friend*[6] to Jane Eyre's ambrosial feast in Miss Temple's parlor, discussed later in this chapter. In Shelley's novel, as in these other works, the light and warmth of the domestic hearth typify a commonality of the intellect and affections, inextricably intertwined. Unlike the regimented schoolroom, which arranges its occupants in geometrical rows, the glowing domestic hearth fosters a different spatial practice, as family members gather in a circle around it.

At the same time, the monster experiences only reflected light and warmth, the anticipation of domestic comity rather than its presence. In fact, both novels and works of nonfictional educational discourse frequently orchestrate their domestic critique of institutionalized education through variations on the theme of absence and presence. Like the glowing interior of Felix's cottage, the redemptive vision of domestic education seems most compelling when it is least available within the actualities of a character's present experience. As with any normative and prescriptive ideal, idealized domesticity thrives by detaching its mesmerizing "truth" from the literal. To a true believer, a hundred dysfunctional families only serve to confirm, rather than undermine, the primacy of the domestic ideal, once it has been internalized and naturalized. In the nineteenth-century literature of education, the dream of "domestic education" is continually invoked as a normative ideal enshrined in an individual's earliest memories of family life, as well as in the collective vision of a utopian, familial society yet to be achieved. Shelley's fantastic parable prefigures narrative patterns in Victorian school fictions, while also embodying images of domestic instruction from a rich repository dating back to Rousseau's *Émile* (1762) and *Julie, or the New Heloise* (1761). To fully contextualize portrayals of domestic education in later works, we must turn briefly to the Rousseauian heritage that helped to forge the dilemma of Shelley's child-monster.

DOMESTIC INSTRUCTION AND EDUCATIONAL DISCOURSE

Rousseau's *Émile* famously defines the project of domestic education as one polarity within a contrasting pair: "From… necessarily opposed objects come two contrary forms of education—the one, public and common [*publique et commune*]; the other, individual and domestic [*particulière et domestique*]" (40).[7] Although education in the home is as old as the family itself, Rousseau glamorizes domestic instruction as a new and sophisticated enterprise, dominated not by mothers and nurses but rather by philosophers of education engaged in reenvisioning the limits of the human. In contrast to public education, which produces a "citizen," who serves the state, "domestic education or the education of nature" supposedly unveils the "natural man" (41). As Rousseau ringingly proclaims of his pupil in *Émile*, "Living is the job I want to teach him" (40). Allegedly defined less by social roles than by an understanding of the human condition, the product of domestic education "best knows how to bear the goods and ills of this life" (42).

A fascinating hybrid of fictive and educational discourse, *Émile* anticipates the idyllic educational vision of Shelley's outcast monster. The idealized tutor Jean-Jacques is, of course, a fictionalized version of the author, the tutor that Rousseau imagines he might have become had he devoted himself to the occupation of teaching. Throughout Émile's childhood, Jean-Jacques devotes himself solely to his chosen pupil; a man of exceptional talents and character, he immerses himself in every detail of his pupil's life, asserting, "the same man can give only one education" (51). Jean-Jacques practices a mysterious experiential instruction that elides disciplinary boundaries. Equally suspicious of textbooks and rote learning, he educates his pupil invisibly as they converse together while walking or gardening. Unlike the Victorian school architect E. R. Robson (1874), who would worry that teachers might "forget the difference between work and leisure" (221), Jean-Jacques makes schoolwork as pleasant as leisure, and leisure as productive as work; in fact, his most profound lessons are taught through playful, apparently casual and impromptu activities.

Considered as a novel, *Émile* depicts in excruciating detail the daily process of character formation in a domestic setting. This cultivation of an individual sensibility came to characterize the German *bildungsroman,* and later left its stamp on the English novel of development. According to Fritz Martini, Karl Morgenstern was the first to coin the term *bildungsroman*, later popularized by, and often attributed to, Wilhelm Dilthey. In an 1820 essay sketching out the genre's history, Morgenstern identified *Émile* as an important early example of the genre.[8] Later, the influential Dilthey would affirm that "*Bildungsromane*... reflect the interest in inner culture that Rousseau had inspired in Germany."[9] A classic novel of maturation, *Émile* tracks the time and space between two births. Beginning with the preceptor's introduction to Émile as an infant, it chronicles the young pupil's development through childhood, adolescence, and young manhood, ending with his marriage and impending fatherhood.

Yet while it includes the major markers of a life as envisioned by numerous novels of development, *Émile*'s reach extends well beyond them. Judged by novelistic norms, its principles of selectivity are daring indeed. In Book I, the conscientious tutor devotes considerable time to choosing Émile's nurse and considering how her diet will affect the quality of the breast milk she produces. By the end of the work, in Book V, he is monitoring the frequency of sexual relations between Émile and his new wife, and advising them, in avuncular fashion, on the proper methods of managing their sexual commerce to promote health, love, and enjoyment. Concerning himself with all aspects of Émile's charac- ter and development, the devoted (or intrusive) tutor is easily as eccen- tric a preceptor as Sterne's Walter Shandy. At odd hours he fires off pistols, rifles, grapeshot, and even canons in the young child's hearing to forestall a fear of loud noises. He requires members of the household to come before Émile adorned in masks ranging from the "pleasant" to the "hideous" in order to school him in courage. He exposes his charge to "ugly, disgusting, peculiar animals," including "snakes, toads, cray- fish" to prevent timidity in the face of new objects (*Émile* 63). In a some- what similar vein, when Émile has reached maturity, the tutor falsely leads him to believe that Sophie (the woman he loves) is dead, in order to further refine his understanding of love.

While skeptical readers might expect interesting, though perhaps not the desired, results from Jean-Jacques's pedagogical methods, Rous- seau adroitly forestalls any negative consequences. Tellingly, he begins his long mentorship of Émile with a refusal; as he disarmingly recounts, he has adamantly refused to mentor an actual child whose father has sought him out because he doubts both his powers and his methods. Instead, his narrative of Émile will serve as a test case, an experiment, which others may draw on if they will. Dispensing, then, with the prob- lematic literal child, Rousseau proceeds to invent Émile, assigning him such traits and circumstances as please the tutor: "Émile is an orphan. It makes no difference whether he has his father and mother. Charged with their duties, I inherit all their rights. He ought to honor his par- ents, but he ought to obey only me. This is my first, or rather, my sole condition" (53). In the capacity of fiction writer, Rousseau eases his pro- jected role of teacher. As he makes Émile an orphan, he ensures that his first condition can be met without difficulty; at the same time, he holds those who follow in his footsteps to a condition nearly impossible to enforce in the emotionally fraught circumstances of actual family life.

As Rousseau acknowledges in another context, "The real world has its limits; the imaginary world is infinite" (81). As a "real" teacher blessed with an "imaginary" student, Rousseau, or his idealized alter ego Jean-Jacques, is freed from the limitations of the actual. The fascination of Rousseau's hybrid work derives less from its status as fiction or educational treatise than from its ability to be both, or perhaps neither. The dynamic slide from "real" to "imaginary," and "imaginary" to "real" repeatedly energizes the work at key points in the narrative. Thus, at a moment of intensely wrought, highly charged language, when he is engaged in protecting his pupil from the "dangerous supplement" of masturbation (a rhetorical moment given additional force for contemporary readers by Derrida's virtuoso reading of it), Rousseau enjoins us, "Remember that I am no longer speaking of my pupil here, but of yours" (334).

As Rousseau's imaginary pupil merges with the real pupils of real tutors, the separate genres of novel and educational treatise turn inside out, revealing themselves to be twin sides of one fabric. Just as Rousseauian domestic education elides disciplinary boundaries, so too Rousseau's *Émile* breaks down generic boundaries, as we see in the often cited game of "Robinson Crusoe" that Émile plays in Book III, midway through the chronicle of his education. Asserting that he "hate[s] books," Rousseau nevertheless celebrates one "marvelous book" that will "for a long time compose" Émile's "whole library" (184). For Rousseau, *Robinson Crusoe* also merges two genres; it is not only a novel but "the most felicitous treatise on natural education" (184): "This novel, disencumbered of all its rigmarole, beginning with Robinson's shipwreck near his island and ending with the arrival of the ship which comes to take him from it, will be both Émile's entertainment and instruction throughout the period which is dealt with here" (185).

Robinson Crusoe, then, is to be Émile's portable schoolroom. Its narrative structure—its beginning in one place and ending in another, its fusion of spatial and temporal orders—is clearly a significant aspect of its educative function, as is Émile's ability to interpret it through an essentializing critical reading that "disencumber[s]" it of its inessential "rigmarole." As Richard Barney affirms in *Plots of Enlightenment* (1999), *Robinson Crusoe* "supplies a crucial link between English pedagogical theory and discourse during the 1700s and Rousseau's work, which has been called 'the first *bildungsroman*'" (308). According to Barney, "the value of this novel" for Rousseau lies in its ability to teach Émile the "lessons of self-sufficiency and moral detachment" (307). While Barney's analysis is no doubt correct, "moral detachment" seems a weak phrase to characterize the profound and disorienting engagement with the novel that Émile experiences as he reenacts Crusoe's feverish and desperate activity: "I want it," Rousseau says of the novel, "to make him dizzy. I want him to be busy with his mansion, his goats, his plantation"

(*Émile* 185). Émile's "moral detachment" from the conventions of the social world is to be earned by a passionate and dogged moral engagement with the world of the novel. This fierce readerly identification with the text leads to his ability to literalize and translate it into the realm of the actual world. Thus, Émile is required to construct an actual "island," complete with goats, a plantation, and Crusoe's crudely built "mansion." As Rousseau emphasizes:

> I want [Émile]… to think he is Robinson himself, to see himself dressed in skins, wearing a large cap, carrying a large saber and all the rest of the character's grotesque equipment…. I want him to worry about the hero's conduct; to investigate whether he omitted anything, whether there was nothing to do better; to note Robinson's failings attentively; and to profit from them so as not to fall into them himself in such a situation. (*Émile* 185)

Thus, Émile must act out the novel while performing a rigorous critical reading that moves through processes of identification, analysis, and evaluation, ending in a final revised and more objectified identification. And, of course, this is what Rousseau also wishes readers to do with *Émile*, as they read, analyze, and literalize his great work of fiction, transforming his imaginary Émile into a host of real pupils who will be educated according to the master's pedagogical principles.

The Rousseauian model of active, potentially subversive reading recurs in Certeau's "politics of reading," in which "there *already* exists, though it is surreptitious or even repressed, an experience other than passivity." Invoking the novel Rousseau admired, Certeau lyrically asserts, "the reader produces gardens that miniaturize and collate a world, like a Robinson Crusoe discovering an island." Furthermore, the reader's improvisatory play or "jesting" introduces "plurality and difference into the written system of a society and a text. He is thus a novelist" (*Practice* 173). Like the Rousseauian dynamic, this model of reading (associated most saliently with narrative) allows readers to discard or recreate aspects of the text. It acknowledges that novels may attempt to set up an authoritarian lecture room in the mind, forcing readers into passivity; yet it also allows for an experience of reading analogous to Rousseau's dream of domestic education, which takes place in an imaginary schoolroom defined by an experience of intimacy. In this specific and limited sense, fiction is Crusoe's "island," that imaginary and shifting space that the reader both "discovers" and "produces" (*Practice* 173). In Rousseau's vision, then, the fictive processes that call readers to acts of identification, analysis, and recreation are themselves profoundly educative.

Like *Émile*, Rousseau's equally influential *New Heloise* also celebrates domestic education, as its protagonist Julie wisely instructs her children without seeming to, subtly shaping character by means of inspiring conversation, gentle manners, and a protective maternal instinct. Julie perfects a method of teaching so natural that it is virtually invisible: "one never sees her urge" her children "to speak or to keep quiet, nor prescribe or forbid them this or that... one would think she was content to see them and love them" (*Heloise* 459). So subtle is Julie's domestic instruction that one is apt to mistake her behavior for "indolence" (459). Yet "under this semblance of negligence," we are assured, lies "the most vigilant attention that a mother's tenderness ever paid" (460).

Pressed to explain her method, Julie reveals that its guiding "principle" is "to see my children happy" (464). Shunning specific elucidations, she conjures vague, idealized pictures of free children "running bare-headed in the sun" (466). Affirming its own naturalness, the rhetoric of domestic education is invested in mystifying or obscuring its own pedagogical methods. Allegedly working through subtle personal affinities rather than through a clearly defined pedagogical method, the mechanisms of domestic instruction remain tantalizingly unseen. Following Rousseau's paradigm, later portrayals of domestic education are similarly rich in lessons whose transformative effects are felt while their content cannot be fully expressed by the pupil. In the same pedagogical and rhetorical vein, Jane Eyre proves herself a skillful governess when she wins the affection of the willful child Adèle, correcting her charge's wayward impulses in a process gestured at but never fully dramatized.

Although Rousseau's dramatic portrait of domestic education carried a powerful appeal, it also embodied contradictory assumptions that rendered it nearly impossible to implement. In its attempt to salvage a realm of nature undefiled by culture, Rousseau's apparently lucid distinction between the two is always in danger of breaking down. Thus, the project of domestic instruction often ignores or elides crucial differences in gender and class; in its project of liberating the child's full potential, it can also obscure the cultural locations of authority and power. In an effort to elevate the role of the male tutor, Rousseau strives to masculinize domestic spaces and agendas, sometimes leading to confusions of rhetoric. Serving as a surrogate father, the tutor in fact supersedes parents of both genders. *Émile* clearly peripheralizes the role of mothers and female nurses, even to the degree that the tutor rigorously controls all aspects of the wet nurse's diet. Furthermore, the nearly omniscient tutor Jean-Jacques can anticipate every beat of his pupil's emotional pulse. Explaining Émile's docile acceptance of his stewardship, Jean-Jacques emphasizes his moral mastery over his pupil's character:

> It has taken fifteen years of care to contrive this hold [over Émile] for myself.... It is true that I leave him *the appearance of independence* [italics mine], but he was never better subjected to me; for now he is subjected because he wants to be. As long as I was unable to make myself master of his will, I remained master of his person; I was never a step away from him. Now I sometimes leave him to himself, because I govern him always. In leaving him, I embrace him, and I say to him in a confident manner, "*Émile*, I entrust you to my friend; I deliver you to his decent heart. It will answer to me for you!" (332–333)

Émile can be safely "entrusted to" a friend only because Jean-Jacques now "govern[s] him always" through the pupil's internalization of the master's authority.

Émile's supposed progress from youth to maturity ends on an oddly discordant note. In the work's final scene, the former pupil, now a man and soon to be a father, begs his preceptor to continue supervising him and his new wife: "Advise us and govern us," he urges the tutor. "We shall be docile. As long as I live, I shall need you" (480). Rousseau's narrative inspires us to question whether Émile's vaunted maturity is as illusory as his earlier appearance of independence. Is the tutor's goal, indeed, the formation of a self-possessed free agent, or rather the creation of a docile being eternally dependent on the tutor's superior wisdom? In other words, is Émile a successful product of domestic education because he remains, in crucial ways, a child? Does domestic education, as defined by Rousseau, risk keeping a child forever locked in a supposedly idyllic childhood? Does it ultimately unsuit him for the world outside childhood's carefully constructed Eden?

ROUSSEAU IN ENGLAND: SPENCER'S DOCILE CHILD

In recent decades, scholars have tended to downplay Rousseau's influence on English educational thought,[10] assuming that Locke's educational ideas carried far more weight with an English audience, and emphasizing an English suspicion of the radical French thinker. This view fails to acknowledge the tremendous influence that Rousseau exercised, even on his detractors, as both an early novelist and a seminal educational and political thinker. Beyond this, however, such scholars fail to recognize that the Rousseauian legacy reentered England in a more acceptable and less radical form in the late eighteenth and early nineteenth centuries, carried by ardent Continental disciples of Rousseau like Johann Pestalozzi and Freidrich Froebel, the founder of the *kindergarten* movement.

In 1781, Johann Heinrich Pestalozzi published the first installment of the great, hybrid work that he never completed in a lifetime of writing. Part novel, part educational discourse in the tradition of *Émile*, Pestalozzi's *Leonard and Gertrude* eventually grew to many hundreds of pages as its author continued to revise it throughout his life. Like Rousseau's idealized portrait of education in *Émile* (an avid reader of Rousseau's works, Pestalozzi not only named his son Jean-Jacques but also modeled his early training on that of Émile) Pestalozzi's writings mingle a talent for fictive narrative with luminous evocations of an educational ideal. *Leonard and Gertrude*, which made its author famous, offers a utopian vision of education as a fusion of a scientific method derived from nature and an idealized domestic comity that integrates its members into a familial relation. In the novel's highly romanticized portrait of rural life, the expert male teacher, who has been hired to start a local country school, is so impressed with Gertrude's mysterious ability to motivate the students in her informal dame school that he models his pedagogy on hers.[11]

The novel's unfinished state seems emblematic of the famous Pestalozzian method, which continued to inspire and fascinate educators and educational theorists in part because, in its ultimate incompleteness, it remained open to interpretation. Primarily, Pestalozzi advocates a form of Rousseauian experiential learning, conducted through a series of *object lessons* involving direct contact with objects in nature. Combining diverse impulses, the Pestalozzian vision provided a critique of institutional education even as it offered a supposedly scientific method for the aspiring pedagogue of the teacher training schools. For its English proponents (including such diverse figures as Maria Edgeworth, Robert Owen, and Herbert Spencer), Pestalozzian education bridged gaps between institutionality and domesticity, as well as between standardization and inspired improvisation. For Herbert Spencer, the Pestalozzian vision was a "great truth" (*Education* 118), offering the promise of revolutionizing education, even though "the due realization of the Pestalozzian idea remains to be achieved" (119). Above all, the famed Pestalozzian method celebrated the Rousseauian ideal of domestic education, and strove to implement a loving, parental approach even in schools outside the home. According to Pestalozzi, "the only genuine basis for popular education… is parental sympathy, which… awakens the confidence of love in the hearts of children…. It is in the sanctity of the home... that we must seek the starting point of our science of education" (*Pestalozzi's Educational Writings* 204-205).

Despite Rousseau and Pestalozzi's eloquent rhetorical evocations of parental, particularly maternal, affection, their portraits of domestic education in practice emphasize a familial love that appears far from unconditional. In the same tradition, a century later, their ambivalent intellectual descendant Herbert Spencer encourages parents and teachers to withhold the expression of affection at key moments when the pupil fails to learn appropriately. Notably, Spencer's depiction of an individual family draws on the rhetorical tradition established by Rousseau's great parable of domestic education. As in Shelley's novel, both Rousseau and Spencer metaphorically locate the "monster" within the child. Both at times liken children to "savages" bursting with impulses that must be refined and civilized.[12] For both writers, parental affection is a tool to be wielded with a knife-edge precision in order to fully tame the supposedly "savage" child.

Describing a father who manipulates the methods of domestic education as skillfully as Jean-Jacques, Spencer conjures an idyllic picture of family life:

> He makes himself thoroughly his children's friend. The evening is longed for by them because he will be at home.... Thus possessing their perfect confidence and affection, he finds that the simple display of his approbation or disapprobation gives him abundant power of control. (*Education* 193)

Spencer's enchanting scene darkens, however, when we learn that the father's deft emotional manipulations can be more painful than physical violence: "The mere withholding of the usual caresses, is a source of the keenest distress—produces a much more prolonged fit of crying than a beating would do" (194).

Spencer's father deftly employs his daily absence to make his nightly presence more valued. Yet even at home he can render himself figuratively absent, withdrawing his love and affection by withholding the usual caresses, so that his pupil-children will be forced to petition for his metaphorical return. Like Shelley's eighteenth-century monster, Spencer's nineteenth-century child lives in fear of an impending absence. While domestic education welcomes its chosen subjects into the familial circle, offering the ultimate myth of inclusion, it does so, as Spencer emphasizes, at the cost of an abiding fear of exile:

> the dread of this purely moral penalty [of parental rejection] is, [the father] says, ever present during his absence; so much so, that

frequently during the day his children inquire of their mama how they have behaved, and whether the report will be good. Recently, the eldest, an active urchin of five in one of those bursts of animal spirits common in healthy children, committed sundry extravagances during his mama's absence—cut off part of his brother's hair and wounded himself with a razor taken from his father's dressing-case. Hearing of these occurrences on his return, the father did not speak to the boy either that night or next morning. Not only was the tribulation great, but the subsequent effect was, that when, a few days after, the mamma was about to go out, she was earnestly entreated by the boy not to do so; and on inquiry, it appeared his fear was that he might again transgress in her absence. (*Education* 194)

As we are informed three times, childish transgressions and excesses are liable to occur during the father's or mother's absence. Yet rather than looking forward to such temporary escapes from parental control, the children dread them; the father's trick of performing his return as a punishing absence results in the boy's internalization of the father's values, in a process analogous to the formation of the Freudian superego. The father's moral dimension renders him, as Spencer emphasizes, "ever present during his absence." Just as Émile can be left alone with a friend only because his master Jean-Jacques "govern[s] him always," so too the mother in Spencer's family portrait can serve as a surrogate for the father only because his authority has been rigorously internalized. Thus, Spencer's story embodies the internal logic of Rousseau's successful paradigm.

Spencer's analysis offers insights into the apparent invisibility of domestic education's processes, in contrast to the externalized, highly performative methods of the school lesson. If the "animal spirits" of Spencer's child link him to the brute strength and brutish impulses of Shelley's monster, both child and monster strive to master their impulses internally, invisibly, as a condition of their inclusion in the family circle. As the child emphatically learns in Spencer's narrative, transgression, once so delightful, has come to mean exile.

While even the most standardized school might strive to incorporate elements of domestic education, schools in a schoolmaster or schoolmistress's house were uniquely positioned to offer the attractions of a familial atmosphere. In 1817, a year after the publication of *Frankenstein*, the following newspaper advertisement promised to deliver the fully domestic education that Mary Shelley's outcast monster dreamed of:

> TO PARENTS AND GUARDIANS: A LADY who has been accustomed to the Education of Children, and who now keeps a Day School in an airy Situation in town, is desirous of receiving under her care three or four YOUNG LADIES as Boarders... They will be treated with the tenderest attention, be constantly under her immediate inspection, and form in every respect part of her family. (Jordan 151)

Here, the quasi-domestic space that Currie and others attempted to institutionalize has not yet shrunk to the restricted and peripheral teacher's room. Instead, the teacher offers the whole of her house as the site of familial instruction. Constantly under the schoolmistress's immediate gaze, and "in every respect" part of her domestic circle, the students enjoy an inclusive relation with their mentor that may be more intense than that afforded by the majority of contemporary parents. The schoolmistress's constant preoccupation with her pupils evokes the almost preternatural presence of Rousseau's Jean-Jacques and Spencer's canny father in the lives of the children they "govern." At the same time, the dynamic whereby domesticity and institutionality reinforce each other is already, of course, in place. The schoolmistress will treat her students with the tenderest affection, but they will also be objects of "inspection." Half a century later, school inspection in the hands of the government would be a double-edged sword, as inspectors' reports were both praised for correcting the abuses of previously unregulated schools and condemned for eroding individual freedom and parental prerogatives.

Because of the high currency of domestic education during the Victorian era, writers of fiction and nonfiction alike frequently invoke it to describe schools that might seem to us anything but domestic. Even the proponents of the century's various forms of institutionalized or standardized education employ the rhetoric of domestic instruction as a justification for their diverse agendas. Joseph Lancaster, founder of the notorious Lancastrian monitorial system, whereby a single schoolmaster could instruct five hundred pupils in one schoolroom, was supposedly known for "his love of, and devotion to the lads under his charge," regarding many of them "as his 'family,' a term which he used for many years in this enlarged sense" (Binns 8). Similarly, in 1865, Lord Shaftesbury, president of the Ragged School Union, emphasized that teachers within the movement must have "more than [the] ordinary sense of duty" that suffices for other teachers. Instead, "there must be affection; there must be love" (Montague 291). In a series of lectures, Frederick Dennison Maurice utilized the rhetoric of domestic education to valorize church schools over a falsely familial state education:

we (Churchmen) have an Education which assumes men to be members of one family ... universal, limited by no conditions of time or country... This principle underlies all our education, and is the very meaning of it... The State rushes in and says,... "We will make you members of one family, whether you like it or no. You shall love by Act of Parliament, and embrace by an Order in Council." (quoted in Birchenough 78–79)

Although they varied greatly as a result of the presiding clergymen's interests and agendas, the parish schools defended by Maurice as familial tended, in practice, to be socially stratified institutions that endeavored, often harshly, to reconcile working-class pupils to their current economic and political status. School conditions were often atrocious, fostering epidemic disease, and schoolmasters and clergymen were not above beating their pupils for infractions that might seem minor today. Pupils were charged school fees that their parents frequently could ill afford; many students were reprimanded and sent home for failure to pay.[13] Flawed as they were, the emerging national schools sought to rectify such abuses by establishing building codes, monitoring schoolmasters' conduct, and eventually providing free education. Yet Maurice confidently portrays the church schools as authentically familial, no more deterred by such troubling discrepancies than numerous other advocates of a supposedly parental and domestic education. The project of distinguishing one's own genuinely domestic education from the false claims of other groups or institutions is, as we shall see, central to the rhetoric of domestic instruction, which thrives on such dualistic paradigms.

Finally, middle-class reformers and writers, who appreciated the value of individualized domestic education for relatively privileged children, too often failed to extend their insights to working-class children. In his essay, "The Domestic and the Official Curriculum in Nineteenth-Century England,"[14] David Vincent suggests that the working-class "domestic curriculum was a rich and complex... programme of learning" that has been misunderstood because of the modern equation of literacy with education (Hilton 171). According to Vincent, official schooling was only part of a "broader programme of discovery" fostered by the working-class home (172). As Vincent demonstrates, working-class domestic education embodied a dynamic similar to that endorsed by Rousseau. Often including an apprenticeship to a relative or familiar member of the community, it crossed disciplinary boundaries to provide a wide array of diverse skills. Just as importantly, parents and relatives served as domestic mentors who instructed as much by example as by words, a form of experiential learning that institutional schools could hardly match.[15] Vincent's analysis serves as a corrective to generalized middle-class suspicions of working-class home education. "To very poor children, the school is a substitute for a home," asserted the Report of the Newcastle Commission on the State of Popular Education. "[T]hey frequently have no other experience of domestic comfort and decency."[16] A writer in the *The Poor Man's Guardian*, however, responded irately to such sweeping and superior claims: "You have starved the father and the mother, and then take the babe [to school] to rescue it from want, crime, ignorance, and nakedness, consequent on living at home."[17] From this perspective, the institutionalization of education for working-class children is both a result of, and an exacerbating factor in, a widespread attack on working-class domesticity.

DOMESTIC SPACE AND THE NOVEL'S
PORTABLE SCHOOLROOM

Just as Rousseau's experiential pedagogy filtered, sometimes by indirect routes, into English educational thought, so too the Rousseauian novel of education shaped the English novel of development, in part through the rich tradition of the German *bildungsroman*. In lectures given in 1819 and 1820, Karl Morgenstern, the professor and scholar who first employed the word, struggled with many of the inherent contradictions that still plague contemporary scholars' use of the term today.[18] Morgenstern establishes an enduring keynote of the genre, the central relation between a fictive hero's growth and an actual reader's emotional and intellectual development: the genre "could well be called the *Bildungsroman*," Morgenstern affirms, "first and foremost because of its content, because it presents the hero's *Bildung* from its inception and continuation until a certain stage of completion; secondly, however, because precisely through this presentation it encourages the cultivation of the reader more fully than any other type of novel."[19]

For Fritz Martini, Morgenstern's definition unwisely sacrifices precision in the interests of breadth: "Morgenstern's initial thesis that every good novel is, in the end, a Bildungsroman" allows the term to be used imprecisely and "leaves only the banal conclusion that one can learn something about the individuality and nationality of the author from every novel 'which wishes to have a claim to something more than mere fleeting entertainment'" (Hardin 21). As Martini notes, beyond Morgenstern's "naïve" critical methods, the persistent difficulty of defining the genre lies in the fact that it has less to do with "formal structural laws" than with such elements as "content, theme, and ideology and with [the genre's] intended effect and function." Thus, the *bildungsroman* "appears not as a categorical aesthetic form, but as a historical form deriving from specific and limited historical conditions" (Hardin 24). With due respect to Martini's wise lucidity, Morgenstern's creative confusion is useful precisely *because* it illuminates correspondences in works acknowledged as formally divergent. His dynamic approach to defining the genre can help us understand the creative cross-fertilizations that breed in the murky areas between distinct generic traditions.

Morgenstern's implicit suggestion that the *bildungsroman* represents not only an aesthetic genre or a historical category but also an enduring and dynamic impulse within the novel informs the history that I trace in this and remaining chapters. Thus, I locate elements of the genre in such larger multiplot novels as Dickens's *Dombey and Son* (1846–1848), and find a reduced and formulaic version of it in the popular school novel. My use of the term is largely adjectival in purpose, not meant to extend a categorical entity but rather to locate impulses and gestures derived from that entity. As I identify *bildungsromanic* elements, however, I respect Morgenstern's dynamic relation whereby novels claim to cultivate their readers' sensibilities by portraying their fictive protagonists' growth and development. Thus, I invoke by the term Émile's readerly relation to *Robinson Crusoe*, summoning up an experiential self-cultivation on the part of readers, which stands in opposition to the didactic impulse in educational novels. In this sense, *Tom Brown's Schooldays* (1857) merges overtly didactic impulses expressed in the narrator's sermonizing exhortations to his readers, and *bildungsromanic* impulses embodied in attempts to lead younger readers through a process of vicarious identification with the stages of Tom's character formation.

My aim here is not to endorse the work of the *bildungsroman* over the didactic project; instead, I wish to explore how Victorian novels exploit elements of the traditional *bildungsroman* to stake out a territory within the English education debates. Given that the *bildungsromanic* tradition is suspicious of any standardized model of education mandated or imposed from without, the English novel of education and development is far from a neutral site in the conflict between domestic and institutional education. Rather, in their implicit aim of cultivating the reader's sensibility through a process of experiential learning, novels of education repeatedly stack the deck against the forces of institutional education; thus, nineteenth-century English *bildungsromane* cast standardized schooling as an attack on novelistic ways of knowing and learning. As we have seen, domestic instruction resists multiplication and standardization. Rousseau's contention that "the same man can give only one education" (51) calls into question the compromises of classroom education and stands as an implicit critique of the centu-ry's trend toward larger and more regulated schools. Despite its internal flaws and contradictions, the rhetoric of domestic education effectively militates against the search for a professional and standardized peda-gogical method.

Crucial to my argument, then, is the contention that Victorian nov-els implicitly ally themselves with a Rousseauian experiential domes-tic education (in contrast to institutional education), and characterize themselves as inhabiting a species of domestic space, analogous in my argument to the teacher's room. As we have seen, Rousseau links domestic education to fiction, and in fact makes reading *Robinson Crusoe*, in the private spaces of home, the centerpiece of his experi-ential instruction. Similarly, in *Hard Times*, Dickens casts the errant narrative structures of fairy tale and fable as crucial counters to the hierarchical grids and categorical linearities of Gradgrindian educa-tion. Brontë's *Jane Eyre* allows its schoolgirl heroines to escape from schoolwork through the tangled narratives of storytelling, daydream-ing, and memory, constructing a jeopardized domesticity at the heart of an oppressively institutional charity school.

In their attempts to idealize domestic education, fictive portrayals—even more than Spencer and Rousseau—minimize the inspective aspect of the teacher's parental role, casting the process of internalization as invisible or mysterious. This crucial erasure of the inspective aspects of domestic education certainly enables Victorian novels to benefit from a false dichotomy, to carve out sanctuaries of familial inclusion, staged as utterly uncoercive alternatives to the harsh and coercive lessons of institutional schools. Novels are then free to offer their narratives as unproblematic instruments of an individualized domestic instruction, promising a wholehearted and pure identification with the child against adult disciplinary institutions. In the remainder of this chapter, how-ever, my goal is not merely to expose this particular novelistic brand of bad faith. Rather, I will contend that such selective erasures also per-mitted novels of education to make relative judgments about various educational institutions and institutional possibilities.

In a similar way, Herbert Spencer frequently denominates a domestic and familial approach to education as "uncoercive."[20] The Spencerian parental interactions that we have examined are clearly both coercive and manipulative. Although they may be equally humiliating, however, they are still less overtly brutal than the common alternative invoked by Spencer (i.e., physical beatings). Thus, I aim to tread lightly, neither endorsing nor merely attacking the nineteenth-century novel of educa-tion's claim to be singing on the side of the angels. Rather, I examine the complex ways in which the novel's self-consciously naive picture of domestic innocence enables a limited critique of social institutions, while simultaneously tempering widespread social anxieties with its consoling fictions of a supposedly liberating domestic instruction.

Finally, I should add that I am not arguing that all nineteenth-century novelists supported, endorsed, or even approved of the works and ideas of Rousseau. I do contend, however, that the *bildungsromanic* tradition within the novel emphasizes individual development to such a degree that any form of standardized and institutionalized education was questioned and qualified by the novel as a genre. Further, in more specific terms, the novelists I investigate frequently make their stand in favor of a private, domestic, and individual education. Dickens, as I have argued above, deeply distrusted the institutional nature of the national schools. Even Thomas Hughes, who celebrates an institutional education at Rugby, nevertheless implicitly limits the role of institutionality by equating Rugby's most successful achievements with the idiosyncratic character of its famous headmaster, Thomas Arnold. Rugby is successful less because of an institutional agenda than because of one man's individual energies and pursuits. Similarly, Charlotte Brontë expressed admiration for some of Rousseau's pedagogical techniques and principles; in fact, according to Gaskell's biography of her, Patrick Brontë drew on Rousseauian methods and theories while raising Charlotte and her siblings. Brontë's novels allude to Rousseau's works, and the title character of her novel *Shirley* (1849) ardently praises Rousseau and his writing.[21]

MISS TEMPLE'S ROOM

Perhaps the most famous type in Victorian fiction of the failed charity school, Brontë's Lowood was read as a record of outrageous actualities, stimulating Mrs. Gaskell's somewhat skittish defense of the novel's alleged depiction of the Cowan Bridge School.[22] At Lowood, domestic space shrinks to isolated pockets of resistance, overshadowed by an oppressive institutionality associated with the church and a charitable foundation. A numinous and mutable extensivity, domestic space fills up dark corners and empty fireplaces, as transient and shifting as sunlight on a wintry afternoon.

Even in the bleakest novels of school life, domestic space is rarely completely eliminated. Thus, in Gradgrind's dreary school, a debate over home decoration opens vistas of a corrective domestic norm when a visiting school official denounces flowers on rugs and horses on wallpaper. His injunctions against ornament exemplify educational reformers' attempts to extend the hegemonic regime of school principles into domestic territory;[23] in Dickens's narrative, however, the hegemonic impulse is stymied when the recalcitrant schoolgirl Sissy Jupe defends ornamental carpets. Conjuring up a still unregulated home space as a subversive presence in the sterile schoolroom, Sissy is one of those supremely domestic fictional children who import a breath of home life into the harsh world of school—and occasionally succeed in humanizing and civilizing their classmates. Another example is George Arthur in *Tom Brown's Schooldays*, who repeatedly exhorts his cohorts to act on the morality of love that his pious parents have taught him. (Arthur's mother is the only parent who ever appears at Rugby, and her transformative domestic aura instantly enchants the rough and ready Tom.) Such domestic and domesticating schoolchildren may not shine in the competitive spaces of the schoolroom or the playing field, but their generous actions subtly ameliorate the impersonal school atmosphere.[24]

Like Arthur, the home-loving Helen Burns in *Jane Eyre* also transforms and educates the protagonist of the novel in which she makes a cameo appearance. Like Sissy Jupe, she conjures up a magic circle of home space around her, even in the oppressive gloom of Lowood Institution. When her nemesis, the rule-bound Miss Scatcherd, punishes her for inattention by forcing her to stand in the center of the schoolroom, Helen surprises Jane with her calm demeanor: "She looks," Jane speculates, "as if she were thinking of something beyond her punishment—beyond her situation: of something not round nor before her... her sight seems turned in, gone down into her heart: she is looking at what she can remember" (58). Helen later confesses to Jane that her thoughts "continually rove away" from the schoolroom: "I fall into a sort of dream. Sometimes I think I am in Northumberland, and that... I hear... the bubbling of a little brook which runs through Deepden, near our house" (64). If Helen escapes coercive school discipline by forging narratives that merge memory and dream, her surreptitious daydreams of home also enlarge the psychic space of the schoolroom. As noted earlier, in the late 1840s, when *Jane Eyre* was written, the government insisted that nationally funded schools allocate six square feet of space per individual child. Helen multiplies this space exponentially through the power of her daydreams, although physically she pays the price of standing for hours in a confined position as punishment. Like Farrar in *Eric* (1858), Brontë illuminates children's clandestine spatial practices, opening secret vistas that official representations of space fail to include.

As Helen explains to Jane, she holds a "creed" that "no one ever taught me," the belief that Heaven is open to all. Helen's heresy—an implicit critique of Brocklehurst's hellfire religion—makes "Eternity" not "a terror and an abyss" but "a mighty home" (67). On a humbler note, Helen also transforms the schoolroom's marginal spaces into a place of domestic comfort. After a day of harsh lessons, she "kneels" in the "dim glare of the embers" of the dying schoolroom fire (62); here she reveals to Jane both her dreams of Deepden and her vision of a domesticated Heaven. Brontë's evocative image—the crouching girl, the nearly exhausted fire—sums up the schoolgirls' necessary conversion of marginal school spaces into a domestic realm of before and after; thus, Helen's ameliorative narrative charts a path from memories of a lost home to dreams of a future home—to be realized, in Helen's case, only in death.

In schoolboy narratives such as Farrar's *Eric,* Martineau's *Crofton Boys,* Hughes's *Tom Brown's Schooldays,* and Dickens's *David Copperfield,* the dormitory serves as a transgressive counterpoint to the teacher's room, an antidomestic space where exile from parental presence opens a realm of violent and frequently sadistic pleasures. *Tom Brown's Schooldays,* for instance, inverts the serene comforts of the domestic fireside when Flashman and his fellow bullies gather around the great dormitory hearth to torture Tom by roasting him over the fire (183). In contrast to such scenes in schoolboy fiction, *Jane Eyre's* dormitory fosters no girlish transgressions; rather, dormitory space is fully under the regime of institutionality. Lowood's bleak living quarters mortify flesh and spirit, converting nourishment and rest into instruments of death. A dormitory so cold that water freezes in the ewers and a refectory that serves up a "nauseous mess" of porridge "as bad as rotten potatoes" (51) leave no room for stolen pleasures, much less for the harmonies of domesticity, which must be conjured instead by domestic mentors like Helen.

Brontë drives home the point by allowing Helen to instruct the naive Jane in the pervasive nature of institutionality. Disturbed by the word "institution" on Lowood's sign, Jane reads the name "over and over again": "I felt that an explanation belonged to [the words], and was unable fully to penetrate their import. I was still pondering the signification of 'Institution,'... when the sound of a cough close behind me made me turn my head. I saw a girl sitting on a stone bench near" (55). Introduced by the cough that signifies her martyrdom to Lowood's oppressive institutionality, Jane's domestic child-mentor enters the narrative. Twice Jane asks Helen to explain Lowood's strange name:

"What is Lowood Institution?"

"This house where you are come to live."

"And why do they call it Institution? Is it in any way different from other schools?" (55–56)

Jane instinctively rejects Helen's first palliative answer—that Lowood is simply a house where she can live. She continues to question Lowood's name until Helen reveals that it is "partly a charity-school" for orphans. Twice banished from a domestic relation, first by the loss of a parent and second by their exile from home itself, the schoolgirls now derive their identity from the institution in which they reside. As Helen explains, they are not just schoolchildren but "charity children" (56).

In this aggressively institutional school, domestic space reemerges provisionally within the sanctum of Miss Temple's room, where a clandestine feast by the fireside redirects Jane's faltering school career. Helen's mentorship prepares Jane for an intimate friendship with the benevolent head teacher. After Mr. Brocklehurst, the school's hypocritical founder, publicly accuses Jane of lying, both Helen and Miss Temple arrive to comfort Jane.[25] Miss Temple's mentorship of Jane reveals the three aspects of domestic instruction that Rousseau delineated and for which Shelley's outcast monster longed. First, the supremely domestic Miss Temple fulfills the role of surrogate parent, admitting the unkempt and isolated girls into her bright parlor, as idealized as Shelley's description of Felix's rural cottage. Summoning the schoolgirls to her side, Miss Temple rewards them with kisses. As the school bell banishes them from her domestic sanctuary, she draws them "to her heart," calling them "my children!" (86).

Second, Miss Temple's assumption of the parental role fosters an instruction that elides disciplinary boundaries and educates Jane's intellect and affections simultaneously. Miss Temple's conversation with Helen fills Jane "with wonder" (85). In a similar way, Shelley's monster records, "Every conversation of the cottagers now opened new wonders to me" (*Frankenstein* 96). As Helen and Miss Temple introduce Jane to new themes and ideas, they also inspire her to emulate their knowledge: "They conversed of things I had never heard of! of nations and times past: of countries far away: of secrets of nature discovered or guessed at: they spoke of books: how many they had read! What stores of knowledge they possessed!" (*Jane Eyre* 85). Brontë's punctuation infuses an emotional drama into these lines, which might otherwise seem flat in their generality. Brief fragmentary sentences war with the conjunctive force of the four successive colons. Serial revelations and illuminations, initially dazzlingly distinct in Jane's eyes, merge into a synthetic conversation, flowing from history to geography, from nature to books.

Unlike the regulated classroom's "borrowed trains of thought," so carefully orchestrated in their associations, Miss Temple's domestic instruction engages in playful improvisations. Schoolgirl and schoolmistress participate equally; lessons are replaced by conversation; for Jane, the rapt listener, the classroom's drill gives way to the wondering absorption characteristic of domestic education; here, genuine learning is signaled by Jane's passive silence, the antithesis of the school regimen of question-and-answer. In *Hard Times*, both Gradgrind and the schoolteacher McChoakumchild do their best to outlaw the child's sense of "wonder" (*Hard Times* 49), which clearly flourishes in Miss Temple's room and Felix's cottage. When the precocious Helen caps her intellectual performance—which we are asked to read as a nonperformance, the natural expression of Helen's "unique mind" (*Jane Eyre* 85)—by reading a page of Virgil, Jane finds "my organ of Veneration expanding at every sounding line" (85–86).

True to the dynamic of domestic education, then, Miss Temple's parental care sparks an intellectual and emotional fire in Helen, her chosen pupil. As in *Frankenstein*, the vivid domestic imagery reinforces emotional content. Weaving together images of light, warmth, and radiance, the scene in Miss Temple's room analogizes the comforting fire on the hearth with the ardent fire in the heart. Miss Temple's "brilliant fire" illuminates and animates Helen's internal landscape, "kindling" her extraordinary powers: "They woke, they kindled; first, they glowed in the bright tint of her cheek... then they shone in the liquid lustre of her eyes." Jane identifies Helen's unusual beauty as an inward fire, a quality of "radiance" (85).

Finally, as Jane recognizes, she and Helen have been chosen from Lowood's many students for privileged inclusion in the circle of intimacy. This serendipitous inclusion, however, only emphasizes the imminence of exile. The delights of Miss Temple's room are stolen from, and constrained by, the looming realm of institutionality. When the bedtime bell interrupts Helen's reading, "no delay" can "be admitted" (86). Like Helen's comforting lessons in the corners of the schoolroom, Miss Temple's fleeting feast is a species of truancy, partaking of the marginal and the subversive, followed by absence and exile. For Jane, then, domesticity and institutionality form an oppositional, but oddly reciprocal, relation. Just as the monster's isolation makes the cottagers' hearth appear to burn more brightly, Jane's status as a charity child heightens the radiance of Miss Temple's room.

If home is figured forth—or more accurately, conjured into existence by—the hearth, love is repeatedly equated with the food that nourishes the "famished" girls: "We feasted that evening," Jane records, "as on nectar and ambrosia; and not the least delight of the entertainment was the smile of gratification with which our hostess regarded us, as we satisfied our famished appetites on the delicate fare she liberally supplied" (84). When the housekeeper, "a woman after Mr. Brocklehurst's own heart, made up of equal parts of whalebone and iron" (84), denies more toast to the feasters, Miss Temple offers her own seedcake, previously hidden in a drawer. Supplementing the refectory's fare with its own secret but generous stores, Miss Temple's room corrects Brocklehurstian institutionality.

According to Rita Felski, "home" serves as "the privileged symbol" of everyday life. Enmeshed in the quotidian, it constitutes "a base, a taken-for-granted grounding" (Felski 85). At Lowood, this common assumption is reversed: institutionality forms the ground of daily experience, dominating the quotidian, while the domestic realm partakes of the visionary and the phantasmagorical. Brilliantly luminous and miraculously satisfying, the scene of ambrosial feasts and intimacy, Miss Temple's room embodies the radiance of a dream, heightened by the bleak school architecture and time schedules that surround it. Miss Temple's idealized wisdom disentangles moral complexities with ease, immediately recognizing Mrs. Reed's culpability and Jane's innocence in the old power struggle that continues to haunt Jane's existence at Lowood. Miss Temple's room, then, can be usefully read as a novelistic capitulation to wish fulfillment, a visionary moment that compensates for the horrors of Brocklehurstian institutionality. Jane perhaps tacitly acknowledges this when her new relationship with Miss Temple (along with the public exoneration that it brings her) enables her to abandon the nightly fantasy of sumptuous banquets with which she once wooed her hungry body to sleep: "That night on going to bed, I forgot to prepare in imagination the Barmecide supper of hot roast potatoes, or white bread and new milk, with which I was wont to amuse my inward cravings."[26] As Jane notes, she "feast[s] instead on the spectacle of ideal drawings" and French translations that she now hopes to produce (87). Miss Temple's feast effectively realizes her pupil's self-consoling dream, leaving Jane free to fantasize about artistic and intellectual accomplishments. Thanks to Miss Temple, Jane makes the transition from famished child to dedicated student, having turned her hunger for parental approval into an appetite for independent accomplishment.

If Miss Temple's parlor stands in opposition to Brocklehurst's austere refectory, Miss Temple's bedchamber offers a similar contrast with the pernicious dormitory. Searching for Helen during the school's deadly typhus epidemic, Jane finds her ensconced in a "crib" in Miss Temple's room, where the hearth-fire's once brilliant illumination has dwindled to a single "unsnuffed candle" burning "dimly." Though dying of tuberculosis, Helen still offers warmth and comfort; she shares her quilt with Jane, inquiring solicitously, "Are you warm, darling?" (97). Sheathed in white curtains, Helen's crib evokes an ominous shroud, foregrounding the failure of Lowood's institutional provisions; even the parental Miss Temple can no longer compensate for the institution's lethal failure to nourish its charges.

Yet as Lowood's institutional education sinks to its nadir, domestic education ascends to new heights of transformative eloquence. Even on her deathbed, Helen teaches and comforts Jane with her portrait of a domesticated Heaven. Looking forward to "my long home—my last home" (95), Helen paints the perfect domestic relation, complete union with the "mighty, universal Parent" (96). To be sure, Helen takes her place in a long tradition of pious child-invalids, and her elevating rhetoric is not uncommon. Still, its contextualization within the rhetoric and tropes of domestic education serves as one more argument in Brontë's case against institutionality. Lowood, as Jane's probing questions about its name and Helen's unsatisfactory answers make clear, is a failure insofar as it is institutional. The only solution to its evils is to domesticate it by placing it under the management of the surrogate parent Miss Temple. Indeed, when Miss Temple leaves the school to marry and manage her own household, Lowood once again becomes untenable for Jane.

Jane's progress typifies the course of a successful domestic education, in which the parental relation with a teacher fortifies one to face a world characterized as institutional; in contrast, Helen's decline embodies the alternate narrative of a characteristically domestic sensibility destroyed by an institutionality that fails to nourish. Helen's dream of a vast domesticated Heaven evokes the Bachelardian conception of "intimate immensity." For Bachelard (1958), "immensity is within ourselves... as soon as we become motionless, we are elsewhere; we are dreaming in a world that is immense" (184). In Bachelardian terms, such experiences of outward immensities can be seen as subjective soundings of a mysterious "self."

If Bachelard's celebration of a transcendent subjective plentitude raises issues beyond the scope of this chapter, his analysis nevertheless shines a light on Helen's creative domestication of what might seem an unfriendly and unhomely world. For Bachelard, daydreaming and domesticity are profoundly linked. The "chief benefit of the house" is that it "shelters daydreaming" (6). Dreaming of "the house we were born in, in the utmost depth of reverie, we participate" in an "original warmth" (7) that is fictively embodied in the warmth and radiance of Miss Temple's room. In daydreams of home, we encounter what Bachelard regards as a staple of the domestic archetype: "always in our daydreams," he writes, "the house is a large cradle" (7). Helen's domestic meditations are implicitly identified as daydreams. Mystified by Helen's detached serenity, Jane asks herself: "I have heard of day-dreams—is she in a day-dream now?" (58). Bachelard's romantic evo-cation of the house's maternal and nourishing aspects is congruent, to a degree, with Helen's perpetual work of domestication. Emphasizing the "nostalgic aura" surrounding Bachelard's depiction of home, Henri Lefebvre (1974) nevertheless acknowledges the influence of this tradi-tional view of domesticity: "Bachelard's writings—the importance of which are beyond question—deal with this idea [of home] in a most emotional and indeed moving way. The dwelling passes… for a special, still sacred, quasi-religious… space…. The House is as much cosmic as it is human" (121). Taking a similar approach to the spaces of domestic-ity, Michel de Certeau (1980) states the matter in a lucid, epigrammatic form: "There is no place that is not haunted by many different spirits… [and memories]. Haunted places are the only ones people can live in" (108). Whether dreaming of Deepden or of death, Helen draws on the nourishing and transformative paradigms of domesticity and domestic instruction. Like a visionary magic lantern, her dreams project Miss Temple's radiant room onto the dark and vast spaces of her world.

Brontë's text, however, allows neither Jane nor her readers to inhabit Helen's serene plenitudes. The frightening voids, so conveniently exor-cised by Helen's domesticating vision, assert their presence even in Miss Temple's room. On her first visit, in order to win the schoolmistress's love, Jane is forced to recount her ghostly visitation in the Red Room at the home of her guardian, Mrs. Reed. In Miss Temple's domestic sanc-tuary, then, she must reexperience her old fears and self-doubts. An image of the blank terrors, gaps, and abysses within the home and the self, the Red Room is arguably the shadow that haunts the luminous spaces of domesticity. In Jane's second foray into Miss Temple's room, Helen's shrouded "crib" fuses Bachelard's domestic cradle with associa-tions of the grave. Obsessively questioning Helen's comforting asser-tions, Jane produces a litany of doubt: "Where is God? What is God?" (*Jane Eyre* 96) "You are sure, then, Helen, that there is such a place as Heaven; and that our souls can get to it when we die?" (96) "Where is that region? Does it exist?" (96). Jane's questions, spoken and unspo-ken, answered and unanswered, serve as a skeptical counterpoint to Helen's domesticated cosmos. The positive images of domestic instruc-tion within Lowood's oppressive institutional realm are both attacked from without and jeopardized from within; even Miss Temple's room opens up spaces for doubts and uncertainties, for unexpected abysses that resist the domesticating urge.

DOMESTIC EDUCATION REALIZED:
THE PERILS OF PRESENCE

As we have seen, domestic education defies institutional boundaries, whether disciplinary divisions or the literal bounds of the schoolroom's oblong enclosure. Deprived of both home and parents, Frankenstein's disinherited "progeny" is reduced to learning by a literal defiance of boundaries. Exploiting the permeable border between his lonely hovel and the adjoining cottage, he gazes and listens through cracks in the moldering walls. Numerous Victorian fictions reinscribe this connection between domestic education and the transgression of boundaries.[27] For Jane and Helen, the feast in Miss Temple's room merges love and discipline, affection and instruction, the two realms that institutionality strives, according to the novel's logic, to sunder. Further, Helen's last act of domestic instruction, conducted on her deathbed, combines a moral sermon and a mortal embrace, as Miss Temple's room both shrinks to a tomb and opens on a visionary eternity that erases all divisions.

Schools that embody the domestic model, like Dr. Strong's academy in *David Copperfield*, conform to a similar spatial patterning. David absorbs the benefits of the Doctor's moral atmosphere in the teacher's private rooms. In fact, the Doctor himself is never even portrayed in the schoolroom, unlike the infamous Creakle, the antidomestic headmaster of David's previous school. Adept at juxtaposing the idealizing rhetoric of domestic education against de-idealized depictions of schools that grotesquely violate the norms of the domestic code,[28] Dickens celebrates and defends the domestic realm. Yet in his only fully realized depiction of a domesticated school, he also raises questions that go to the heart of domestic education, even when it functions as a model of harmonious presence.

David Copperfield has emerged as an increasingly problematic *bildungsroman* in recent literary criticism, as critics read David's development as morally skewed. Thus, recent readers are apt to find, not the intellectual and moral growth celebrated by earlier scholars, but rather occlusion and self-deception in the service of a willful self-patterning complicit with bourgeois standards of success.[29] The process that once was denominated "moral growth" is now more frequently read as "psychic repression." Yet for all the probing of David's socialization and development, little attention has been paid to the role of school in fostering, or interacting, with David's highly reactive and adaptive sensibility. If David's self-deceptions and compromises are intriguingly congruent with those of the society he describes and strives to master, aspects of his aspirations and fears are reflected and magnified by the educational institutions he attends. While many readers persuasively emphasize David's desire to adapt himself to the standards of commercial success, they risk impoverishing the work's complexity by ignoring David's concomitant suspicion of the commercial project. David's divided impulses and actions must also be read as attempts to guard and fortify a protected home space against the commercial assault, to construct a self that can repel, as well as make use of, the incursions of commercialism.

Within its many plots and subplots, the novel returns repetitively to scenes that embody an overriding, almost archetypal threat: the incursion of the commercial impulse and commercial values into the vulnerable and threatened realm of domesticity. To cite only two major examples: just as David's childhood idyll is disrupted by his mother's marriage to the ruthless businessman Murdstone, later in the novel the commercially minded Uriah Heep serves as the secret enemy in the house of David's friends, the Wickfields. In the first instance, home is ruthlessly destroyed by Murdstone and his sister, and the death of David's mother coincides with David's expulsion into the commercial world. In the second instance near the novel's close, however, home is triumphantly protected, as the grasping Uriah Heep is expelled from the sacrosanct home space. Eventually Heep reemerges in the realm of benighted institutionality, as an inmate in a mismanaged jail where Heep's hypocrisy earns him the status of a model prisoner. The novel's generalized tension between the realms of commerce and home is further illustrated by Micawber's financial irresponsibility and Dora's inability to manage a household budget, traits that make both characters unwitting enemies within the house, undermining domestic security in a threateningly commercial world. Finally, the enduring commercial threat to a vulnerable domesticity also emerges tellingly in Dickens's portrait of domestic education, as Dr. Strong's benign academy falls prey to those money-grubbing enemies within the house, his wife's mother and her cousin Jack Maldon.

In presenting a contrasting pair of schools, one idealized and one debased, *David Copperfield* follows a trope common to many novels of education. Exemplifying an oppositional relationship between institutionality and domesticity, the novel charts David's journey from Mr. Creakle's school, dominated by its cruel master, to Dr. Strong's academy, shaped by the Doctor's kindness and innocence. In *Dickens and Education* (1963), Philip Collins emphasizes the linkage between the two academies, affirming that Dickens portrays them "in terms of simple moral antithesis" (116). In Collins's view, Dr. Strong's school serves partly as a "wish-fulfillment," a somewhat abstract fantasy for Dickens, who has just relived, through his evocation of Creakle's pernicious academy, his sufferings as a student at Wellington House. Focusing on the autobiographical elements of the novel, and indirectly linking the portrait of Strong's academy with Dickens's somewhat misleading claim that he had "distinguished himself at school" (Collins 13), Collins argues that, in *David Copperfield,* "Dickens departs from fact, to indulge his dream-self in an idyllic period at a happy school where he flourishes and becomes head boy" (Collins 118). Collins's argument that the invention of Strong's academy served as a willed corrective of Dickens's own personal history smacks of the *ad hominem* authorial analysis that is neither verifiable nor particularly profitable; yet his assertion is nevertheless insightful when directed to the novel rather than its author. For Doctor Strong's "idyllic" academy clearly does serve a corrective and reassuring function within the fictive world of the novel, just as Miss Temple's room corrects, or at least mitigates, Lowood's corrosive realm of institutionality.

In David's words, as different as "good" and "evil," the schools diverge most profoundly not in their curricula, which remain largely undescribed, but in their relations to domestic space and the ideal of domestic instruction. Because he keeps school at home, Creakle can expect to be judged by domestic standards. Strikingly, however, he flamboyantly violates every norm of the domestic model of education.[30] First, Creakle is unfit to serve as a teacher or surrogate parent because his own domestic affairs are in disorder. He tyrannizes over his wife and daughter, and has banished his son from the house for criticizing him. "My flesh and blood," Creakle announces, "when it rises against me, is not my flesh and blood. I discard it" (*David Copperfield* 82). Second, Creakle's lessons are ineffective not only because of his ignorance and cruelty, but also because they rigidly commodify and compartmentalize learning, divorcing it from the transformative human agenda of domestic education. Creakle regards his academy simply as a money-making business: he takes up "the schooling business after being bankrupt in hops" (86). Like a harsh factory master, Creakle begins each day by ordering, "now get to work, every boy!" (89). Reinforcing the factory or workhouse atmosphere, Creakle makes "the round of the schoolroom," beating the boys with his cane so that "half the establishment was writhing and crying before the day's work began" (89). Third, Creakle betrays domestic education's promise of entrance into the circle of intimacy by maintaining rigid divisions between home and school space, between the schoolroom and the teacher's rooms. Creakle's apartments are distinctly separate from the space inhabited by his pupils: "Mr. Creakle's part of the house was a good deal more comfortable than ours," David narrates, "and he had a snug bit of garden that looked pleasant after the [schoolboys'] dusty playground" (81). Entering into Mr. Creakle's private rooms is a rare and perilous enterprise, fraught with anxiety. As David emphasizes, "It seemed to me a bold thing even to take notice that the passage looked comfortable, as I went on my way trembling to Mr Creakle's presence" (81). The difficulty of penetrating into Creakle's domestic spaces recalls the foiled attempt of Frankenstein's creation to enter Felix's cottage. In fact, Creakle permits only one pupil into his private rooms, the wealthy "parlour-boarder" Steerforth (87), an exception designed to emphasize the school's commercial basis; similarly, "a coal-merchant's son" who attends the school as "a set-off against the coal-bill" is "called on that account 'Exchange or Barter'" (87). As the commercial impulse pervades the school, admission into the teacher's room must be bought and paid for. Rich pupils are converted into customers, poor pupils into commodities.

While he strives to keep the teacher's rooms utterly separate from the schoolroom, never permitting his pupils to enjoy his own private and familial comforts, Creakle betrays the code even within the domestic realm, neglecting or willfully breaking family ties. He is equally tyrannical, selfish, and sadistic in his capacities as a teacher and as a father. Ironically, then, Creakle's attempt to separate the pedagogical from the domestic is subverted by his identical behavior in each realm, which perversely conflates pedagogical and parental roles. Tellingly, his son objects to Creakle's sadistic treatment of both his students *and* his wife. Thus, in a profound sense, the text undermines Creakle's attempt to delineate a fixed boundary between the spaces of school and home, and his flagrant violation of the standards of domestic education serves ultimately to reinforce its norms.

Dr. Strong's academy, in contrast, attempts to render fully present the ideals and assumptions of domestic education. In virtually every respect, Doctor Strong's utopian school corrects the clear abuses of Creakle's. First, David repeatedly portrays the Doctor as a surrogate parent for both his young wife and the boys, emphasizing an implicit relation between the Doctor's domestic and school life: "It was very pleasant to see the Doctor with his pretty young wife. He had a fatherly, benignant way of showing his fondness for her, which seemed to express a good man" (238). The Doctor's fatherly relation to his young wife, which typifies his "goodness," is echoed by his fatherly affection for his schoolboys, who are "warmly attached" to the school and are known proudly in the neighborhood as "Doctor Strong's boys" (237).

Second, unlike Creakle, who commodifies and compartmentalizes learning, the Doctor bridges the disciplinary divisions of institutional schooling; he instructs David not only intellectually but also morally, and he educates as much through his gentle and redemptive presence as through his schoolroom lessons. In his analysis of Strong's school as an authorial daydream, a wishful re-creation of Dickens's own past, Philip Collins emphasizes the vague generalities that permeate Dickens's descriptions, blurring the school's outlines in a haze of abstraction. "The first scene establishes certain moral and social qualities," Collins writes, "but neither then nor later is Dickens explicit about the school's organization or curriculum" (*Dickens and Education* 117). Further, Collins argues, "It is not clear even what sort of school Dickens is representing here" (117). As Collins documents, even Dickens's contemporaries seemed confused. While its venerable buildings evoke a long-established grammar school, Strong's ability to appoint his own successor suggests a private school fully under his own control. Thomas Hughes, Collins records, suggested a third alternative, seeing in the Doctor's academy an implementation of the "new education"— the "'progressive' ideas of Froebel and the other continental reformers, which had affected only a few private schools" (117).

While Collins faults the portrait for its "vagueness" (117), in contrast to Dickens's more vivid depiction of Creakle's academy, the dynamic I am tracing suggests a different reading. A narrative focus on spirit rather than method, on "moral and social qualities" rather than "organisation and curriculum," typically characterizes portraits of domestic education, from the indescribable delight of Mary Shelley's monster to Jane Eyre's wonder in Miss Temple's room. According to the paradigm of domestic education, Doctor Strong's classroom methods are less significant than his character and his ability to inspire his students: "My school-days! The silent gliding on of my existence—the unseen, unfelt progress of my life—from childhood up to youth!" (*David Copperfield* 265). These exclamatory fragments introducing a chapter of David's school recollections dreamily evoke the invisible but transformative lessons of domestic instruction. Reminding us of Certeau's contention that domestic spaces are always in some sense "haunted" (*Practice* 108), if only by our own "unseen" and "unfelt" past, the passage summons up the Rousseauian contention that feeling at home is the prerequisite for educating the child's sensibility and emotions.

In contrast to the vague depictions of the schoolroom, the Doctor is rendered vividly present in his private rooms—his parlor and his library, not to mention his garden. His presence becomes a trifle ghostly only in the schoolroom, which is described, tellingly, in the absence of school lessons; indeed, the schoolroom itself is perhaps best characterized as an "absence"; after remarking merely that it is a "pretty large hall, on the quietest side of the house," Dickens omits further description, painting instead a lengthy portrait of the enlivening vistas of natural growth visible through its windows—the "secluded garden" and the potted aloe plants, "symbolical" to David "of silence and retirement" (*David Copperfield* 228). Rather than an enclosure, oblong or otherwise, the Doctor's schoolroom appears most saliently as an opening, a window onto varied vistas. While the standardized classroom is a locus of divisions, Dr. Strong's schoolroom dissolves even its own boundaries. In Dr. Strong's domestic academy, space is amorphous, flexible, and open.

Thus, Collins's claim that Creakle's school is more effectively described than Strong's appears misleading. Nevertheless, Collins is certainly correct in focusing on differences in language between the Creakle and Strong sections of the novel; the portraits of the novel's contrasting pair of schools counterpoise dystopian irony with the idealizing abstractions of domestic education to such a degree that the same word can have opposite meanings when applied to Creakle or to Strong. "Miserable little propitiators of a remorseless Idol," David bitterly writes of the schoolboys' submission to Creakle, "how abject we were to him!" (90). In contrast, he affirms approvingly of Doctor Strong: "the doctor himself was the idol of the whole school; and it must have been a badly composed school if he had been anything else" (238). Institutional and domestic education exist in the different worlds of satire and idyll, of irony and ideal; words are necessarily transformed as they enter the oppositional worlds of Creakle and Strong. Thus, the novel emphasizes the unstated and numinous component of domestic education; understanding this idealizing aspect allows readers to scan the emotional registers that differentiate "Idol" from "idol."

Finally, exemplifying a third aspect of domestic education, the benign Doctor immediately welcomes David into the circle of intimacy from which Creakle has excluded him; unlike the authoritarian Creakle, Strong fosters permeability between the realms of home and school. Meeting the Doctor in his private library for the first time, David finds his nervousness instantly defused by Strong's beautiful young wife Annie, who is "sitting at work, not far off" (226). As David nervously shakes hands with the absent-minded and preoccupied Doctor, Annie "kneel[s] down to put Dr Strong's shoes on, and button[s] his gaiters" with "great cheerfulness and quickness" (226). Annie's domestic ministrations to the disheveled Doctor transform him from an intimidating and eccentric master into a gentle husband, converting his absent-minded preoccupation into a charming oddity. In contrast to Creakle's rigid division between school space and his domestic quarters, Dr. Strong invites David into his private rooms, including him in a family party in the parlor where the Doctor appears as a benign domestic mentor, fostering the comfort of all.

At the same time, however, David's entrance into Strong's domestic circle allows him glimpses of a troubled home life, raising a flood of doubts and questions that will eventually impact on David's experience of school life. In novels of school experience, portraits of the schoolmaster's domestic relations can come to seem almost obligatory. Thus, *Tom Brown's Schooldays* depicts the awe-inspiring Thomas Arnold frolicking with his children in his study, and *Jane Eyre* emphasizes the Reverend Brocklehurst's hypocrisy by portraying his pride in his haughty and gaudily dressed wife and daughters. Yet Dickens foregrounds Dr. Strong's domestic life in a particularly telling way, showing the good-hearted man at the mercy of his wife's mercenary relatives, who seem likely to "swarm the Doctor out of house and home" (237). In contrast to the stingy Creakle, who has already exiled his son from home, the Doctor is so recklessly generous to every member of his family that he may no longer be master in his own house. His innocent trust in his wife and her family appear to lead to domestic disorder when Annie is suspected of a love affair with her charming cousin, Jack Maldon.

The Doctor's very commitment to domesticity, then, seems to call into question his wisdom, his fitness to serve as a preceptor to the young. The specter of Annie's domestic betrayal jeopardizes not only the Doctor's family but also his school. As David records,

> The impending shadow of... a great disgrace... fell like a stain upon the quiet place where I had worked and played as a boy, and did it a cruel wrong. I had no pleasure in thinking, any more, of the grave old broad-leaved aloe-trees which remained shut up in themselves a hundred years together... and the congenial sound of the Cathedral bell hovering above them all. It was as if the tranquil sanctuary of my boyhood had been sacked before my face, and its peace and honour given to the winds. (282)

David's insistence that Annie's error could taint the whole of his school experience, retroactively demolishing the domestic sanctuary, may ring oddly in the ears of modern readers; yet here we are at the heart of domestic education's assumptions and motives. In *Dr Wortle's School* (1880), Trollope exploits a similar dilemma; the suspicion that a teacher at Wortle's private academy may be living in a bigamous relation with his wife threatens to destroy an institution that strives to merge home and school by ensconcing a schoolmaster's wife as a surrogate mother to his pupils. Thus, Annie's sexual betrayal of Strong would also constitute a betrayal of David, a second maternal failure, echoing that of the weak mother who betrayed his father's memory for Murdstone.

Because of his domestic shame, Dr. Strong's cloistered school risks becoming a defiled Eden, casting David retroactively out of the paradise of memory. Yet the ultimate vindication of Annie's honor, love and fidelity, eventually redeems what at first seems the schoolmaster's blind and reckless faith in the power of domestic ties, restoring his school to its proper place in David's narrative. In a novel that, as we have noted, deals repeatedly with incursions of commercial self-interest into the domestic realm, the ultimate triumph of Dr. Strong's domestic school reverberates throughout the work. At the same time, Dickens's portrait also hints at hidden anxieties about the vulnerability of both the domestic realm itself and a school so grounded in its ethos. For if domesticity cultivates the selflessness and generosity that provide an escape from society's rampant commercialism, these very treasured qualities may render the household unable to protect itself from commercial incursions. The innocent disciples of domesticity can hardly be prepared to mount a defense against the onslaught of commercial self-interest. And within the model of domestic education, these paradoxes are multiplied. If the family model of instruction educates children for domesticity, will it render them unfit, as adults, for the world of strife and business? Is Dr. Strong's radical innocence, finally, a weakness or a strength? Does he, indeed, live up to his name, or is he like so many characters in this novel, the dupe of his own good intentions and his willfully innocent misreading of others' motives?

The question is especially pertinent because Annie is not only Dr. Strong's wife but his former "pupil." Dickens's portrait of the Strongs literalizes the idyllic metaphor of domestic education, as the teacher and pupil join to become a family in fact. As Annie ardently asserts,

> my first associations with knowledge of any kind were inseparable from a patient friend and teacher....[The Doctor] stored my mind with its first treasures, and stamped his character upon them all. They never could have been, I think, as good as they have been to me, if I had taken them from any other hands. (659)

Though Annie never quite grasps the issues at stake in the Doctor's great work, his Greek dictionary, she passively absorbs, by a mysterious process of osmosis, the moral lessons of his character. Or to vary the metaphor, bringing it more into line with Dickens's own language,

Annie's mind has been stamped with the Doctor's imprint. Annie's fervent words aptly sum up the mysterious domestic lessons that transcend their nominal content in the service of a numinous realm of presence. Thus Annie's body (corrupt or innocent?) figures forth the dilemma of domestic education.

To put the problem another way—to place it clearly within the context of the traditional language of domestic education—the central question is whether the transforming goodness of the parental impulse can tame (or train) the child's wayward impulses. Annie confirms the Doctor's successful teaching when she admits her former predisposition in favor of her cousin Jack Maldon, and thanks her husband and teacher "for having saved me from the first mistaken impulse of my undisciplined heart" (661). Thus, while domestic education valorizes the natural maternal or parental impulse, and is confirmed by the child's voluntary emulation, it paradoxically requires the child's willingness to curb the natural "impulses" of the "undisciplined heart" in order to vindicate the natural goodness of humanity. Dickens resoundingly resolves the matter in a single highly charged scene in which Annie delivers a monologue explaining her motives. As we learn, her appearance of guilt stems only from an innocence so rigorous that it agonizes over the possibility that guilt might wrongly be imputed to her. According to this paradoxical principle, an appearance of extreme guilt is actually the sign of extreme innocence.

Yet the issue remains troubling. Rousseau's Julie, the peerless mother of *The New Heloise*, educates her children with exquisite domestic tact and grace. Julie's refined sensibilities are in part the creation of her admirable and charming tutor, whom she continues to love even after her marriage to a man of her own class. Succumbing gladly to a fever that saves her from the adulterous resumption of that illicit love, Julie attains a beautiful and self-annihilating virtue. Perhaps it is no accident that Rousseau's immensely popular tale of Julie's suicidal virtue is also a narrative of idealized domestic education. For domestic education, as it educates the individual for a higher standard than the world endorses or understands, raises the fear that it may ultimately unfit the individual for the world. In the words of Herbert Spencer:

> Is it not that education of whatever kind has for its proximate end to prepare a child for the business of life—to produce a citizen who, at the same time that he is well conducted, is also able to make his way in the world?... And if by any system of culture an ideal human being could be produced, is it not doubtful whether he would be fit for the world as it now is? May we not, on the

contrary, suspect that his too keen sense of rectitude, and too ele-
vated standard of conduct, would make life alike intolerable and
impossible? (*Education* 169)

Pushed to its limits, idealized domestic education, following the example of Julie, risks annihilating itself. An admittedly powerful critique
of educational institutions, capable of closing schools and discrediting
pedagogical reputations, the rhetoric of domestic education serves as
a magic mirror, reflecting a visionary realm—the world as it could be.
When invoked as an image that could replace current practice, however,
the "mirror crack[s] from side to side" as surely as the Lady of Shalott's
enchanted glass in Tennyson's poem; because it can never transform
the world into its own paradisal image, the idealized vision of domestic
instruction must be consigned to the realm of impossibility.

As we have seen, the cluster of assumptions and tropes that constitute
the rhetoric of domestic education can be conjured to discredit current
educational practice, as in Brontë's exposé of Brocklehurstian institutionality or Dickens's portrait of Creakle's profit-driven school (which
Matthew Arnold identified as typical of English private school education). At the same time, the consoling vision of an idealized domestic
education can "correct" current abuses by portraying parental teachers
like Miss Temple or familial academies like Dr. Strong's. By its very
nature, however, the home space represented by the domesticated anti-
schoolroom—the teacher's room—is, of course, limited, provisional,
and subject to constant attack. While this sanctified space resonates
eloquently as a dramatic and sometimes dreamlike vision, it remains
an ideal that is most vivid when least realized, most compelling when it
dwells in the realm of absence and dream. Attempts to realize it within
the territory of actual experience draw us once again into a terrain
of absences and empty spaces. The narrative vista opens onto Helen's
consoling but ultimately self-annihilating daydream, like a spiderweb
straddling an abyss; or in the case of Doctor Strong's Edenic academy,
the radical innocence of domesticity becomes a space of extreme vulnerability: a sanctuary redeemed only by its barricading walls, a woman's body that figures, by turns, its guilt and innocence, a latent wound
that invites commercial and institutional incursions.

Of course, the mid-century novel of education's tendency to portray
domestic instruction, less as a fully present reality than as a species
of dream or wish fulfillment, underlines a widespread idealization of
the mysterious transformations of domestic education even as schools
were being increasingly standardized within a burgeoning educational
"system." In a sense, the dualistic vision that juxtaposes a threatened

home space against the looming presence of an institutionalized world has its corollary in the novel's tendency to cast itself as a space of dissent within an increasingly regulated society. Thus, the glowing dream of Miss Temple's room demands to be read not only against the backdrop of Lowood, but also against the background of an increasingly institutionalized English educational landscape. Drawing implicitly on the traditional *bildungsroman's* promise of transforming the reader's character as it depicts the character formation of a fictive hero or heroine, mid-century novels of education, whether *bildungsromane* or not, ally themselves by implication with the anti-institutional spaces they celebrate as sanctuaries within a hostile world; such works of fiction position themselves as sheltering sanctuaries of the imagination, set against the looming presence of institutionality, affirming the dualistic dynamic of domestic education both within and without the novel's generic borders. As they delineate domestic and institutionalized schoolrooms, Victorian writers are also mapping out the territory of Victorian childhood. To an extent, the Victorians desired to enshrine childhood in an idealized domestic space, arguing that the lessons of home were all that children needed. Yet the urgency of social reform and industrial progress moved Victorians to push children into the institutionalized space of standardized schools and standardized pedagogy. In this sense, domestic education could symbolize a lost or vanishing past, while institutionalized instruction points toward an uneasy future in which the amorphous state of childhood will be curtailed, dissected, and standardized.

3

LEVEL PLAYING FIELDS AND LOCKED GARDENS
Nature at School

A proper school garden may, must, and is destined to be the place
where children are happiest.

> —Erasmus Schwab, *The School Garden*

Deception is a primary object of the landscape gardener.

> —Reginald Blomfield, *The Formal Garden in England*

During the Victorian era, proponents of the school garden movement
dreamed of a garden attached to every schoolroom—a space for coop-
erative work and communal games, fostering both body and spirit. Just
as the teacher's room signified the need for nurturing surrogate parents
to temper the rigors of institutionality, so the garden aimed to reintegrate the lessons of nature into the institutional domain. Sometimes
viewed as a liberating anti-classroom with its own distinct spatial practices, the garden minimizes or obscures the role of adult authority figures, allowing children to interact in allegedly "natural" ways—to run,
shout, fight, work, and play. In the vivid scenes of Victorian school narratives, the garden builds a bridge between cultivated and wild nature;
it aims to domesticate nature and childhood simultaneously. In this
sense, the garden becomes a quasi-domestic space that embodies elements of Rousseauian education. Yet paradoxically, the link between
childhood and nature reveals inhibiting as well as liberating aspects. In
works as diverse as *David Copperfield*, *Jane Eyre*, and *Alice's Adventures
in Wonderland*, assumptions about child-nature reveal and reinforce

self-perpetuating gender stereotypes. At the same time, in *The Crofton Boys* and *Tom Brown's Schooldays*, exuberant games in the boys' school garden also open vistas into adult fears about children's "natural depravity." The image of the *wild child*, an emblem of untrammeled nature, draws on both traditional Christian morality and pseudoscientific fears about the devolution of the human species. In sum, the school garden becomes yet another site for staging a fictive critique of institutionalized education; at the same time this critique is also blunted by conflicting assumptions about how nature, culture, and gender shape human character.

SCHOOLING NATURE: ROUSSEAU AND THE ORIGINS OF PROPERTY

In Book II of *Émile* (1762), Jean-Jacques, the sagacious tutor, teaches Émile his first lesson on the origins of property in the natural and nurturing spaces of the garden. In this crafty and many-layered lesson, the natural and the social, which Rousseau so often portrays as oppositional foils, appear to share a deeper correspondence, a unity that makes the process of education possible. For Rousseau, the circumscribed space of the garden is analogous to the ideal schoolroom, in which the pupil's sensibility grows according to natural laws, but cultivated by human hands. Thus, the domestic garden becomes an apt schoolroom for one of Émile's seminal lessons.

Rousseau initiates his lesson in the garden by emphasizing that the proper sequence of education corrects the common mistake of "speaking at first to children of their duties, and never of their rights" (97). Correcting this pedagogical error, he contends that the "first idea which must be given to [the child] is... less that of liberty than that of property" (98). Property and liberty are, implicitly, symmetrical rights; as Rousseau argues, the right of property must be learned first because a "child does not attack persons but things" (97). By extension, then, a property violation is an attack on *things*, while a violation of liberty consists in an attack on *persons*. An understanding of property, for Rousseau, is thus a foundation for liberty, and finally, for the whole process of education.

So often in Rousseau's theory of education, ontogeny recapitulates phylogeny, as the individual education follows the steps and markers of historical social evolution. In this instance, too, Émile must experience the right of property in its original form: "The thing to do therefore is to go back to the origin of property, for it is there that the first idea of it ought to be born" (98). Inspired by watching a gardener at work, Émile, with the help of his tutor, plants beans. As a result of his cultivation of nature, he experiences an intoxicating sense of ownership, which the tutor encourages, even though he may already suspect it to be false. Telling Émile, "This [garden] belongs to you," Jean-Jacques "make[s] him feel that he has put his time, his labor, his effort, finally his person there; that there is in this earth something of himself that he can claim against anyone whomsoever" (98).[1] But disillusionment is just around the corner: "One fine day he arrives eagerly with the watering can in his hand. O what a sight! O pain! All the beans are rooted out, the plot is torn up. O what has become of my labor.... Who has stolen my goods?" (98).

Émile's first lesson about property is the joy of possession; his second is the pain of its loss. His third lesson will reconcile thesis and antithesis in a synthesis that balances pleasure and pain. Learning that Robert, the estate gardener has rooted up his beans, Émile confronts him only to find himself attacked. He, and not Robert, is the criminal, the thief, because he planted his beans in Robert's melon garden, and in the process has destroyed some rare and valuable seeds. Finally, instruction in the sanctity of property comes not from Jean-Jacques, the wily bystander, but rather from the indignant gardener. "Each respects the labor of others," Robert informs Émile, formulating the principle with Rousseauian clarity, "so that his own will be secure" (99).

Émile's protest—"But I don't have a garden" (99)—rings with the ontological helplessness of the child, seeking, implicitly, for adult resolution. This is exactly the state to which Jean-Jacques wishes to bring him, an acknowledgment of "true need, natural need" (86), as opposed to the false needs inspired by caprice or the desire for dominance. Robert answers in the spirit of *amour de soi*, the innate self-love that has the force of a natural law: "What do I care [if you don't have a garden]? If you ruin mine, I won't let you go around in it" (99). But now the tutor interposes with the insight of reason, just as historically the laws of property intervened to resolve warring self-interests in favor of mutual good:

Jean-Jacques: Couldn't we propose an arrangement with the good Robert? Let him grant us, my little friend and me, a corner of his garden to cultivate on condition that he will have half the produce.
Robert: I grant it to you without condition. But remember that I will go and plow up your beans if you touch my melons. (99)

The episode is rich in the distinctive layering that permeates Émile's encounters with his tutor. Apparently a casual dispute about the humblest of activities, the lesson both recapitulates a posited seminal moment in human history and enables Émile to experience the violation and reaffirmation of what Rousseau casts as a basic and "primary" right. In Rousseau's words, "In this model of the way of inculcating primary notions in children one sees how the idea of property naturally goes back to the right of the first occupant by labor. This is clear, distinct, simple, and within the child's reach. From there to the right of property and to exchange there is only a step" (99).

Clear and simple admittedly, and yet the lesson is also a masterwork of indirection and withholding. Émile learns without realizing he is learning, because Jean-Jacques knows when *not* to speak, permitting the child his crucial illusion of ownership, allowing nature and the gardener to teach their inevitable lessons. Clearly, as the child cultivates the garden, the garden, with the help of the tutor, is cultivating him. The principles of government, of political and social relations, Rousseau suggests, need not be encountered for the first time in books. Eternally at work in the rich and unfolding natural world, they are always to be discovered there. Throughout *Émile*, the rhetoric of education intertwines seamlessly with the language of gardening, cultivation, and growth. Rousseau states the connection explicitly: "Plants are shaped by cultivation, and men by education" (38). Thus, "innate principle[s]" "bloom";[2] skillful masters must allow childhood to "ripen" (94), and nurturing mothers must "cultivate and water the young plant" because "its fruits will one day be [their] delights" (38). In Rousseau's parable of learning, the garden, apparently the casual annex of the schoolroom, the site of recreation from its more regulated demands, is transformed into the schoolroom's truest emblem and most central space.

As Derrida has illuminated in the context of "writing," Rousseau's myth of origins can become as luminously reflective as a hall of mirrors because the point of "origin," lost in its inception, leads us always to another signifier in the chain.[3] In the lesson in the garden, Émile gains his first idea of property by returning to a point of origin—"the origin of property"—which is ever present in nature's immanence, yet always receding. Émile's discovery of property, its pleasures, losses, and limitations, enacts a fall placed at the indecipherable origin of human social relations, a source that remains privileged and veiled.

In this sense, Rousseau offers the reader, and Jean-Jacques offers Émile, a luminous myth of an authentic reading of nature's principles, one that can never be verified, but may nevertheless be useful in forming Émile's character. But the situation is even more complex, for the property rights in dispute are, of course, more staged than authentic. Robert's sturdy defense of "his" garden masks the fact that the garden in question belongs to Émile's father, and eventually, by inheritance, to

Émile. Robert's melons — which he claims with such assurance—will ripen in order to be eaten by Émile and his tutor, as Robert himself points out. Similarly, Jean-Jacques's humble request that "the good Robert... grant us... a corner of his garden" is not, as it first appears, the plea of a suppliant, but rather the triumphant and corrective intervention of reason. As Émile's "governor," Jean-Jacques casts himself as Robert's social superior; according to Rousseau's educational theories, the tutor ought to exercise dominion over the whole of his charge's estate, insofar as it impinges on his pupil's intellectual and moral development.

Thus, although Jean-Jacques claims to teach Émile an authentic principle of social relations, as revealed in a simple, natural encounter, its social relations are carefully orchestrated for a desired effect. Ardently defending his property, Robert is no more the owner of the garden than Émile was when he unwittingly invaded it and Jean-Jacques, equally ardently, asserted: "This belongs to you." Both claims of ownership are inauthentic, yet each is staged as authentic and natural by the clever tutor. The privileged naturalness and authenticity of the garden, then, is constructed as rigorously, in its way, as the schoolhouse walls. Equally important to note here is the purpose of Rousseau's construction, the seamless transformation of nature into property. In Rousseau's parable, nature, through its innate laws, sanctions its fair division into tracts of workable land. Nature endorses its own taming.

As Richard Barney (1999) has documented, the rhetorical conflation of gardening and teaching, of natural cultivation and the pedagogical project, has a long history in the literature of education:

> [T]he metaphor of gardening was not only ubiquitous in the pages of the educational works by Locke, Mary Astell, Francois Fénelon, Thomas Sheridan, Damaris Masham, William King, and many others, but it also became the most frequently invoked figure in even the most casual remarks on education or personality during the eighteenth century. (95)

While he draws on and modifies the rhetoric of his predecessors, particularly that of Locke, Rousseau also strikes a new note by transforming a rhetorical analogy into both an educational site and a pedagogical method. In *Émile*, the garden is not only a metaphor for the schoolroom, but serves as a literal schoolroom. In the words of Dorothy Gardiner (1929):

> Following on the counsels of Locke and Fénelon, and... the example of Queen Mary II, the occupation of gardening was coming into favour [in England in the late eighteenth century], and

> is constantly recommended as a subject to be taught even in the
> boarding-school.... The taste thus implanted was greatly encour-
> aged by the appearance of Rousseau's *Émile*. (357–358)

Rousseau's dynamic transformation of the garden into a site of instruction resonates throughout the burgeoning literature of education, from
Pestalozzi to Spencer. For poor urban children, innovative nineteenth-
century educators would strive to incorporate gardening into the curriculum, finding a redemptive lesson in the processes of nature. By
the end of the century, "nature study rambles," roof gardens, and the
reclamation of urban land for workable school gardens were becoming popular pedagogical devices in London schools. In 1892 in Surrey,
evening school gardens were founded for working boys, who were given
marks for "good workmanship, orderly arrangement and condition of
crops, and for neatness of plats, edgings, and paths" (Sipe 24). Similarly,
for the privileged descendants of Émile, the garden continued to exercise its appeal as a pedagogical site. John Stuart Mill's father famously
instructed his son on long walks. In Harriet Martineau's *Deerbrook*
(1839), a summerhouse in the garden serves as a pleasant schoolroom
for children of the wealthy merchant class. Locke had long ago endorsed
the teaching of gardening to children of the upper classes, and student
gardeners helped to maintain part of the grounds at Rugby.

The international school garden movement, exemplified by Erasmus
Schwab's influential treatise of 1870, viewed the act of gardening as
morally elevating for students of all classes. A German school inspector, Schwab received favorable responses to his book from enthusiasts
all over Europe, including England. As Schwab writes, "A proper school
garden may, must, and is destined to be the place where children are
happiest" (*The School Garden* 22). Serving as the cheerful heart of the
school, the school garden not only inspires students to work contentedly at their more regimented tasks, but also lays the groundwork for a
moral and intellectual education: "The school garden will be peculiarly
a school of correct and specific judgment, of circumspect reflection, a
fountain of the purest and most innocent joys of children and youth—a
communion with nature" (23).

For Schwab, this communion is not only moral and aesthetic but
also physical. He praises the Austrian law of 1869 that required every
public school to maintain a "gymnastic ground" for pupils as well
as a teacher's garden, and an area for "agricultural experiment" (53).
For urban children, the gymnastic ground is even more important.
As he cautions, "the gymnastic [field] and playground must be in or
near the garden. The garden work and movement in the fresh air are,

in a sanitary point of view, inestimable to city children" (61). As in Rousseau's parable, Schwab's school garden has a dual and contradictory function. While it redeems children in a fallen world by exposing them to authentic nature, it also serves the social function of converting nature into property, a workable resource to be divided and shared. In Schwab's utopian view, this collective conversion can redeem and refashion not only individuals but a society. The sense of community is fostered by shared work and common property in the garden: "The clear perception that the community is a great family with an inseparable bond of union, does not proceed so much from the school room as it will from the school garden" (24–25).

As Schwab himself asserts in closing, he has stated "nothing new" but rather has given voice to "a thought which is floating as it were in the air" (75). Pestalozzi's emphasis on natural Rousseauian education and Froebel's creation of *kindergartens* (or child gardens) had already heavily influenced English educational thought. In fact, the rich literature of English school novels records the evolution of Schwab's "floating" idea. In many school narratives, a natural space, circumscribed for safety and cultivation—whether the pupils' garden, the school close, or the playing field—takes on crucial symbolic significance, as it mediates between raw nature and the structured realm of social relations. Paradoxically, this privileged "natural" site exists both inside and outside the school walls. Separated from the school proper, it is nevertheless also a walled enclosure. An escape from school regimentation, the garden can also become the place where the school's most important lessons are learned. Yet as Rousseau's lesson in the garden reminds us, even there nature must be staged and constructed. The form of that construction offers insights into the educational assumptions and expectations at work in the nineteenth century's vigorous and complex literature of education.

As the English school garden movement addressed itself increasingly to instructing and inspiring rural and urban children of the working classes, novels of education—especially the popular genre of schoolboy literature—focused primarily on children of the middle and upper classes. While the school garden movement aimed to create a Rousseauian moment by assigning garden plots to poor urban children for whom the possession of property was a new and perhaps utopian idea, the privileged boys of school novels learned to anticipate the acquisition of property and the taming of nature as their birthright. In the remainder of this chapter, as I examine the school garden in novels of education, I necessarily concentrate on privileged children of the middle and upper classes, educated as prospective property holders or their associates. Diverse as they are, Hugh Proctor's small rural boarding school in Martineau's *The Crofton Boys* (1841), Tom Brown's prestigious public school, Jane Eyre's Lowood, and Alice's day school in *Alice's Adventures in Wonderland* assume for their students a degree of future leisure and liberty rarely envisioned for their working-class compatriots.

Given the centrality of the concept of *nature* in novelistic depictions of education, the school garden, a supposedly natural site adjacent to the classroom, tends to transform itself from a marginal to a dominant space. While nature in school novels may appear as a moral norm or guide in the Rousseauian sense (as it does at times in Hughes's *Tom Brown*), it is just as apt to appear as a monster that cries out to be tamed. Equated with raw nature, the unschooled human nature of the child must be pruned and developed; just as in Rousseau's garden, nature is converted into property, so the raw material of the child is transformed, at school, into a self-governing individual. The school garden partly typifies the attempt to enact this conversion of child into individual by natural means, implying, as in the Rousseauian parable, Nature's endorsement of such taming. Yet the garden's status as nature and property leads to unsettling contradictions. Paradoxically, nature emerges as both an innate quality to be modified and a lesson to be learned, both raw material and ideal. An analogy frequently drawn between education and natural evolution can require the child to appear by turns as an unspoiled innocent and a "primitive" savage. Similarly, the collective free play of boys' brutality may be justified as the only effective way of refining away the brutality of the individual boy. Finally, an examination of boys' gardens and girls' gardens foregrounds the construction of a gendered nature. While the boys' garden shapes a public identity, linking the development of individuality with work in the external world, the girls' garden emphasizes a veiled and private identity, linking individuality with interior and domestic spaces. As boys are schooled to tame nature, in order to become the proud possessors of property, girls are trained to see themselves as property under cultivation, taming their own wild spaces through self-regulation and self-control.

GENDERED GARDENS: GROWING BOYS AND GIRLS

In *Education: Intellectual, Moral, and Physical* (1861), published nearly a century after *Émile*, Herbert Spencer compares two school gardens, the first belonging to a boys' school and the second to a school for girls.[4] The passage is long, but best quoted in its entirety because it self-consciously epitomizes a tradition of gendered descriptions of school gardens, present in many school narratives. Spencer's emblematic images and striking contrasts dramatize how nineteenth-century schools constructed nature differently for boys and girls:

> It chances, somewhat strangely, that we have daily opportunity of drawing a comparison. We have both a boy's and a girl's school within view; and the contrast between them is remarkable. In the one case, nearly the whole of a large garden is turned into an open, gravelled space, affording ample scope for games, and supplied with poles and horizontal bars for gymnastic exercises. Every day before breakfast, again towards eleven o'clock, again at mid-day, again in the afternoon, and once more after school is over, the neighborhood is awakened by a chorus of shouts and laughter as the boys rush out to play; and for as long as they remain, both eyes and ears give proof that they are absorbed in that enjoyable activity which makes the pulse bound and ensures the healthful activity of every organ. How unlike is the picture offered by the "Establishment for Young Ladies"! Until the fact was pointed out, we actually did not know that we had a girls' school as close to us as the school for boys. The garden, equally large with the other, affords no sign whatever of any provision for juvenile recreation; but is entirely laid out with prim grassplots, gravel-walks, shrubs, and flowers, after the usual suburban style. During five months we have not once had our attention drawn to the premises by a shout or a laugh. Occasionally girls may be observed sauntering along the paths with their lesson-books in their hands, or else walking arm-in-arm. Once, indeed, we saw one chase another round the garden; but, with this exception, nothing like vigorous exertion has been visible.

Why this astonishing difference? (253–254)[5]

Spencer's description stands as an illustration of how schools define and shape nature, as manifested in the garden, to mirror a gendered inner nature, nowhere visible, yet accepted nevertheless as an unchanging norm. As clear and pointed as the illustrations for a moral fable, the passage forges an iron link between environment and behavior. Spencer's primary concern here, of course, is with socialization, not with an innate child-nature, which is present if at all as a blank slate. At the same time, Spencer's depiction subtly valorizes the boys' garden as natural, promoting the "healthful activity of every organ," in stark contrast to the artificial girls' garden. Thus, the boys' garden is an "open" and level space, unbeautiful and stripped for action. This "gravelled" field implies not only the lack of artificial constraints and restrictions, but also a sort of rough democracy of the spirit. Regardless of their inherited social privileges, all the schoolboys can compete on an equal footing in their vigorous games and exercises. Constructed, or rather cleared for free play, this site of unconstrained energies is analogous to nature as a leveled field, permitting maximum freedom.

In contrast, the girls' garden is ornamental and restrictive. "Gravel-walks" direct the girls' footsteps into circumscribed paths; "prim grassplots" and shrubs inspire prim and restrained behavior. Except for one dramatic exception that proves the rule, the girls in the garden are silent and barely visible. For five months, the girls' school has kept its mere existence a secret from the essayist. At first nearly opaque, the garden gradually offers a few images of female behavior. It shows us girls in solitary study with their lesson books, girls arm in arm in acts of friendship, and even an isolated instance of transgressive, unwomanly behavior. We need not be surprised when an observer as different as Paul Emanuel in Brontë's *Villette* (1853) spies on the garden of a girls' school and finds secret love letters and hints of illicit assignations. Strikingly, the girls' gardens in school novels foster both cloistered obedience and clandestine acts.

While the boys' school playgrounds are rough-and-tumble affairs where the group rules, girls' gardens emerge as oases of solitude, suitable for prayers and *billets-doux*, devotions, deceptions, and indiscretions. The boys' playground generally exhibits the open transparency evident in Spencer's description. In contrast, the girls' garden thrives on the opacity that Spencer locates there; its spatial practices become visible only gradually. Time in the boys' garden is a disciplined and repetitive round of hours, signaled by phrases invoking the stages of the day—"before breakfast," "toward eleven," "midday," "afternoon," "after school"—each filled with activity. In the girls' garden, months go by before anything happens, and then we have solitary instances rather than general hubbub. Time has the shape, not of a repetitive cycle, but of a slow revelation.

LEVEL PLAYING FIELDS: TAMING
NATURE, CLAIMING PROPERTY

If Spencer's graveled playground seems a long way from Rousseau's lesson in the garden, how much more distant are the playing fields that pervade the genre of popular nineteenth-century schoolboy fiction. Experiencing solitary "transports of joy" as he watches his beans sprout in the garden, Émile seems light years away from the rough-and-tumble games of Tom Brown and his unruly cohorts (*Émile* 98). Despite the numerous and obvious distinctions to be drawn, however, striking parallels emerge. In both *Émile* and many of the popular schoolboy novels, the garden—or the playground—first appears as an annex, a natural space peripheral to the educational project, and then emerges gradually as the site where real education begins. Whether linked with Rousseauian natural laws and rights or with a debased human nature that must be pruned and guided, the garden perennially offers itself as a metaphor for the "natural" maturation that occurs outside, adjacent to, or even in opposition to the classroom.

For Émile, the first lesson about social relations derives from gardening, and feeling "that there is in this earth something of himself" (98). For Thomas Arnold, the brilliant Rugby headmaster who helped to inspire *Tom Brown's Schooldays*, gardening—and the pedagogical cultivation it stands for—would seem to be a less pleasant activity. "I am inclined to think that the trials of a school are useful to a boy's after character," he writes, in a letter of 1831, "and thus I dread not to expose my boys to it; while on the other hand, the immediate effect of it is so ugly, that, like washing one's hands with earth, one shrinks from dirt[y]ing them so grievously in the first stage of the process" (Stanley 243-244). In Rousseau's image of Émile at work in the garden, contact with the earth is a transporting and revelatory experience; for Arnold, such contact constitutes an antibaptism, a washing that soils. Arnold's recoil from the inevitable taint of earth is in keeping with the emphasis he places on the trials of school life. Clearly, both Rousseau and Arnold, and indeed, the whole tradition of educational literature that shaped their thought, grapple with the tension between nature and discipline, between individual liberty and institutional authority. Rousseau, in *Émile,* generally casts nature as benevolent or neutral. Ineluctably unfolding its laws to the mind of the pupil, nature—whether portrayed as an unchanging norm, or an inspirational guide—can be invoked as a transcendent and pristine concept. At the same time, nature can be figured forth as innate animal impulse, as raw human nature. In this sense, it is a neutral concept because *amour de soi*, the hallmark of raw human nature, can be turned toward good or evil. Raw human nature, though not a tabula rasa in the Lockean sense, nevertheless exists to be shaped and guided by the laws of overarching Nature, made manifest through experience and reason.

To Arnold, however, raw human nature appears far from neutral. Corrupted by original sin, the "evil of boy-nature" (Stanley *Life of Arnold* 137) calls for strict mechanisms of correction, in order to transform un-Christian boys into Christian men. For Arnold, as for many other contemporary educators, such a correction is not to be accomplished only through the example and guidance of a Christian master. Paradoxically, the correction of wayward "boy-nature" occurs by means of what Joseph Conrad's imperial representative *Tuan* Jim experiences as immersion in "the destructive element" (*Lord Jim* 20).[6] According to Arnold's public school model, boys hone and refine their flawed characters in part by striving with other flawed boys like themselves. "Washing [their] hands with earth," they submit themselves to an antibaptism in raw human nature within the boys' culture that thrives inside the semiprotective confines of the school walls.

As exemplified in a letter of 1828, Arnold's concept of boy-nature associates "the natural imperfect state of boyhood" with "the low standard of morals" that prevailed in "the boyhood of the human race," a principle that, according to his biographer Stanley, guided his pedagogy (Stanley 68). Boys are savages, or at least primitives. Fearing that "where the intellect is low, the animal part will predominate" (Stanley 346), Arnold strove to raise his students' characters through a process of intellectual and moral evolution. Decades before the publication of Darwin's *Origin of Species*, we can observe the specific cultural vision that colored the reception of Darwin's theories, inspiring Herbert Spencer's celebrated vision of the "survival of the fittest." It is unfair to link Arnold too closely to the often simplistic and sometimes even brutal ethos at work in the tradition of popular schoolboy novels. His troubled and qualified endorsement of boys' schools already distances him from that tradition. His legendary reforms at Rugby strove to place religion at the center of school life, and to recast school traditions in a more humane form. Nevertheless, Arnold's ambivalence toward unleashing the "natural" forces at work in character education can serve as an apt starting point for our investigations.

For many readers, *Tom Brown's Schooldays* famously epitomizes the boys' school novel. As critics like Beverly Lyon Clark (1996) and Claudia Nelson (1991) have documented, however, it draws on a rich and conflicted tradition of schoolboy tales, often written by women, and designed for moral and religious edification. E. J. May's *Dashwood Priory, or Mortimer's College Life* (1856), for instance, depicts a pair of ethereal and spiritualized boys who exercise a missionary influence on their often worldly classmates. In Clark's words, "there was an older tradition of school story, beginning with the first book-length story for children, Sarah Fielding's *The Governess* (1749), and continuing with such books as Mary Wollstonecraft's *Original Stories from Real Life*

(1788), Charles and Mary Lamb's *Mrs. Leicester's School* (1809), and Harriet Martineau's *The Crofton Boys* (1841)."[7]

A particularly interesting example of the genre, published a decade and a half before *Tom Brown* (1857), *The Crofton Boys* is modeled after an incident of a boy injured at school, recorded in a biography of Walter Scott. As Martineau emphasizes in her preface, children can expect the double pleasure of reading her fictionalized version now and the true record of the historical incident when they are older. Promising a safely diluted introduction to real-life drama, the preface implicitly claims for the novel an agenda analogous to that of the preparatory school itself: Martineau's fiction will both rehearse and distance the crises and resolutions of impending adult life.

Martineau's tale, narrated in a limpidly graceful, conversational style, records the grim history of an initially unruly boy who finally learns self-restraint when his foot is amputated after a severe injury. Sent to school at an unusually young age because of his failure to respond to home lessons, Hugh Proctor defiantly resists the bullying of his older classmates, and in consequence is injured in the rough-and-tumble games on the playground. Like many schoolboy novels, *The Crofton Boys* depicts adults as oddly passive, relatively helpless to educate a boy until he has been softened up by the harsh schooling administered by his peers. Typically, then, the well-intentioned but recklessly impetuous Hugh learns his most important lessons in discipline and self-control on the playground, through contact with rough, unvarnished boy-nature.

Even before he arrives at Crofton, Hugh sees the playground as the true center of the school. When his older brother Phil comes home from school on holidays, Hugh "ask[s] every question that could be imagined about the playground at the Crofton school" (*The Crofton Boys* 9). On the verge of leaving his sheltered domestic world for Crofton, Hugh's thoughts revert once again to the playground and games with the other boys: "Then it quickly passed through his mind that instead of... the little yard [at home], there would be the playground" (44). Similarly, the playground looms large as Hugh approaches the school. His initial contact with his fellow classmates occurs even before he enters the school building. As his coach passes the playground for the first time, "some of the boys" lean "over the pales which separated the playground from the road" (69) and call out the taunting nickname "Prater," earned when a school usher overheard Hugh talking too much on the journey to Crofton. In the playground, pupils are "named," identified, and ranked by the boys themselves in a hierarchy that affects a student's daily life more profoundly than the masters' academic rankings.

Hugh's initial entry into the playground pits his exuberant physicality against spatial limits. His exultation in his new freedom is punctured by the taunts and jibes of his schoolmates and by his own disappointment at discovering the fixed boundaries of his provisional liberty. Released into the "open air," reveling in the presence of trees and "green fields," Hugh "scream[s] with pleasure" (92). Yet his joy turns to misery as disappointments rain on him in quick succession. He is scolded for running "out of bounds" (93), mocked for attempting to feast on inedible raw chestnuts, and finally driven out of a ball game after his inept efforts to play with the older boys. At his lowest ebb, skulking on the edges of the garden, Hugh encounters Firth, the noble older boy who serves as a role model and mentor for much of the novel. Firth instructs Hugh in the unwritten code of the schoolboys. As he makes clear, the playground exacts its own characteristic spatial practices, defining it as a realm controlled by the boys themselves: Hugh must "push" his "own way" (98) and "prove" that he "can shift for" himself (99). Firth also explains that in the boys' garden, gender is not a given but must be earned. As a new pupil, Hugh will be stigmatized as a "Betty" until the older boys "see what you are made of" (100). Through his manly, self-controlled behavior, Hugh must overcome the shame of being "brought up with girls," a defect signified by his overly long, girlish locks, which Firth obligingly offers to cut for him (99).

If Firth offers a warning benignly couched in an offer of sympathy and friendship, the playground itself sends Hugh a more violent and urgent message. Moments after Hugh learns what is expected of him, Arnold's metaphorical baptism in earth becomes literal, as fellow students bury Lamb, an unsporting and cowardly boy, in the earth of the playground. Literally planted in earth, the violent Lamb, who is in fact far from lamblike, may remind us ironically of Rousseau's Émile, flourishing like a flower in a natural environment. In the fallen Eden of Martineau's schoolyard, Nature's education is both harsh and perilous, pitting the strong against the weak, enforcing her lessons with a rough hand: "Only [Lamb's] head appeared above ground. His schoolfellows had put him into a hole they had dug, and had filled it up to his chin, stamping down the earth, so that the boy was perfectly helpless, while wild with rage" (106).

Martineau's portrait of the live burial is instructively ambivalent. Clearly an act of cruelty, even of savagery, the burial in earth is also, in some measure, deserved; further, it possesses an educational value for all the boys involved. Firth, that model of conduct, at first ignores Lamb's cries for help. "It is only Lamb again," he remarks coolly. "You will soon get used to his screaming. He is a very passionate boy" (105).

Lamb's passionate nature—his lack of self-control—is linked in the novel with grave defects of character: cowardice, bullying, dishonesty, untrustworthiness. In *The Crofton Boys*, passionate emotion leads to punishment and public shame, provoking a sort of healthy animal disgust in the other schoolboys.

Lamb's baptism in earth is thus both a punishment dealt by a rough natural justice and a violent warning to reform before it is too late. At the same time, however, rough boy-justice must be tempered by the intervention of more evolved boys like Firth, whose sympathy is finally stirred by Lamb's sufferings. Thus, Firth struggles to dig Lamb out of the earth, but is dragged down in what appears to be a savage ritual:

> [Hugh] saw that Firth was digging, though half-a-dozen boys had thrown themselves on his back, and hung on his arms. He saw that Firth persevered till Lamb had got his right arm out of the ground, and was striking everywhere within reach. Then he saw Firth dragged down and away, while the boys made a circle round Lamb, putting a foot or hand within his reach, and then snatching it away again, till the boy yelled with rage at the mockery. (107)

Hugh proves his mettle by emulating Firth and coming to Lamb's defense. But in his "wild" state (106), Lamb is dangerous; he strikes out at Hugh as well as his attackers. While Lamb's predicament serves as a warning of the rough justice that may be meted out to Hugh if he fails to improve, Lamb himself exemplifies uncivilized, passionate boy-nature. The struggle of Hugh and Firth to raise him from the earth, and the violence they face, not only from Lamb's "tormentors" (107), but from Lamb himself, evokes Arnold's "shrink[ing]" from the "ugliness" of the struggle to refine boy-nature in the rough.

If the masters continue to exert their authority during lessons, explaining the mysteries of sums, themes, and Latin verbs, the boys' real learning takes place through the playground's illicit spatial practices. An indifferent student, Hugh learns to write a theme, not in the schoolroom, but rather because he and his new friend Dale:

> often walked up and down the playground for half an hour together, talking the subject [of Dale's current theme] over.... Hugh presently learned the names and the meanings of the different parts of a theme.... Every week, almost every day now, made a great difference in Hugh's school-life. (154–155)

As a result of Hugh's conversations with Dale, he writes a theme that is praised by the headmaster, Mr. Tooke. Typically, in Martineau's picture of school life, masters serve to ratify the attainment of knowledge or ability, but seem to play little role in facilitating its acquisition. In any case, school knowledge always seems a little beside the point. It is an education in character and morality that Hugh needs to acquire, as his mother makes clear when she decides to send him to Crofton:

> "You have faults,—faults which give your father and me great pain; and though you are not cowardly about being hurt in your body, you sadly want courage of a better kind,—courage to mend the weakness of your mind. You are so young that we are sorry for you, and mean to send you where the example of other boys may give you the resolution you want so much." (43)

Unsurprisingly, Hugh's gravest and potentially most tragic lesson begins in the rough-and-tumble moral schoolroom known as the playground. Hugh is at greatest risk for punishment because he no longer inhabits the limbo of the new boy, and yet has not learned the internal discipline of his mentor Firth, who can subdue the animal nature in himself and others. Only half-socialized into the boys' rigid but primitive hierarchy, Hugh protests when the older boys demand that he carry snow to help them build a snowman.

As we might expect, Lamb, the figure of perilously volatile boy-nature, sets off the violence by launching a snowball into Hugh's face. Hugh escapes to the top of the playground wall, where he perches precariously above his antagonists. Unlike Lamb, whose debased animal nature places him literally and metaphorically below the other boys—Hugh and Firth must raise him strenuously out of the earth—Hugh exhibits an apparently "insolent" pride that leads him to assume an inappropriate position above his older classmates (179). As his unsettlingly unsentimental mother remarks soon after Hugh's accident, one of his besetting sins is "vanity" (210). The older boys' violent struggle to topple Hugh from his high perch offers an insight into the leveling nature of the schoolyard. Those who are placed either too low or too high will be brought stringently into line by their fellow students, regardless of the cost. As Hugh crouches on the high wall, his dangling foot is "snatched at by many hands": "At last one hand kept its hold, and plenty more then fastened upon his leg. They pulled; he clung. In another moment, down he came, and the large heavy coping-stone, loosened by the frost, came after him, and fell upon his left foot as he lay" (180). Hugh's smashed foot must be amputated, forcing him to give up his dreams of being a sailor and a wanderer. As his mother instructs him, however, he now has a "new and delicious pleasure, which none but the bitterly disappointed can feel" (199): "There is a great pleasure in the exercise of the body—in making the heart beat, and the limbs

glow in... a game in the playground; but this is nothing to the pleasure... in exercising one's soul in bearing pain" (199–200).

The playground is a school of pain, both moral and physical. Hugh's
maiming, ultimately a "blessing" offered by "Providence" (210), is the
vehicle of a moral and spiritual refinement, a denial of self that makes
"one's heart glow with the hope that one is pleasing God" (200). Hugh's
finest moral act—in his words "the only good thing I ever did for any-
body in my life" (307)—is hiding the identity of the unknown boy who,
in the midst of so much confusion, succeeded in pulling him off the
wall. Much of the drama of the second half of the novel revolves around
Hugh's temptation to reveal his attacker's identity, and his noble refusal
to tell, an act of self-control praised by everyone from his classmates to
his schoolmaster and his mother. Martineau raises the stakes by revealing that young Tooke, the schoolmaster's callow and selfish son, is the
secret assailant. Thus, Hugh holds a weapon, not only against the guilty
culprit, but against the schoolmaster, and in a sense the school itself.
Hugh's refusal to cast blame not only restores peace to the playground;
it preserves the school intact as an institution. At the same time, unsettling doubts about the school linger; if the master has failed to instill
self-discipline in his own son, how fit is he, ultimately, to educate the
sons of others?

Yet another noble act of self-denial, Hugh's resolution "to bear cheerfully every disappointment and trouble caused by this accident, from
the greatest to the least" (229) also helps launch him on his journey
into Christian manhood. During the long and pain-racked night when
Hugh's foot is amputated, he compares himself to two figures he knows
largely from his reading: the savage, who endures primitive acts of torture imposed by the tribe, and the Christian martyr who suffers stoi-
cally. Paradoxically, Hugh gains a brief respite from his own agony by
describing the intricate tortures he has read about in such minute detail
that his uncle, watching by the sickbed, finds himself "quite sick" (189).

An invalid for much of her life, Martineau is adept in delineating
the degrees and nuances of physical pain. Yet in this crucial scene, her
evocation of the opposing figures of the savage and the martyr has
another function beyond exploring the psychology of pain. Throughout
the novel, didactic religious language competes with the imagery of the
savage, which serves as the raw material of Hugh's dreams. Fascinated
by wild nature and "primitive" places and peoples, Hugh dreams of
being an explorer. He spends his happiest hours reading *Robinson Crusoe* (like Rousseau's Émile), playing shipwreck, and copying pictures
of "savage[s]" (111) from books. Yet Hugh is unfit to enter the world he
fantasizes about, in part because of the untamed wildness within his

own nature. At home, for instance, Hugh's life is a perpetual round of scrapes and disasters, in contrast to the well-regulated domestic conduct of his sisters. In Martineau's world of Christian suffering, pain of some sort is a given. What Hugh needs is to move from the pain of the savage, self-inflicted and self-perpetuating, to the resigned endurance and self-discipline of the Christian martyr. Ironically, then, Hugh's maiming, which at first seems to blast his hopes, finally renders him fit for service abroad. Hearing of Hugh's disciplined resignation in the face of his loss, and his "gallant" (333) refusal to reveal his attacker's identity, the father of one of Hugh's classmates educates him for India and a place in the civil service. Hugh makes the connection between his accident and his future quite explicit: "I never should have gone to India if I had not lost my foot; and I think it is well worth losing my foot to go to India" (335).

Choosing forgiveness, keeping the secret of his attacker's identity, Hugh transcends the rough natural justice of the playground and moves on into the beginnings of Christian manhood. At the same time, Hugh's secret also serves to keep "faith with [his] schoolfellows" (247), to preserve intact the playground's closed circle of games and punishments. According to the logic of the school novel, this circumscribed space of primitive struggle and retribution must be protected because immersion in wild, boy-nature eventually produces the disciplined, civilized man. In the simple colonialist terms of the novel's close, Hugh, having mastered the wild nature within, is now ready to face the perils of Nature in a foreign land: "He was at last, on the wide sea, and going to Asia. His secret was his own (though indeed he scarcely remembered that he had any secret), and he could not but be conscious that he went out well prepared for honourable duty" (336). To position Hugh's struggle within the larger context I have been developing, he must first domesticate his own wildness before leaving his home country of England—especially because his task will be to Anglicize colonial subjects of the foreign territory he is about to enter.

Virtually forgotten today, *The Crofton Boys* repays our attention because it illustrates how fervently the popular school novel portrays boyhood recreation as moral re-creation, an ennobling remaking of character, intellect, and soul. At school, play is serious business, in part because it reveals what Thomas Arnold describes as "the nakedness of boy-nature" (Stanley 137), exposed to public view in unguarded moments. Equally important, however, the novel's starkly evocative playground spaces also work against its rhetoric of moral uplift, making school appear too perilous an enterprise for most boys, if not for its sturdy protagonist. In "spaces of representation," as Lefebvre contends, image undermines official rhetoric. While Hugh's parents and schoolmasters represent school in culturally sanctioned terms as a corrective, disciplinary space, the images of torture and maiming that infest the playground open vistas of undisciplined irrationality. Furthermore, a covert rhetoric of domesticity also orchestrates a redemptive counterpoint to institutional agendas. During Hugh's spiritual dark night of the soul following his accident, his mother comes to domesticate the bleak spaces of school, inspiring him to new heights of religious faith and self-denial. Thus, school succeeds with Hugh only because its egregious failures permit his mother to resume his all-important moral education. Ultimately, Hugh is redeemed, not by institutional schooling, but by an uneasy balance of domestic instruction and immersion in the wildness of boy-nature.

While *The Crofton Boys* largely ignores the highly regulated games and honorable fistfights that constitute recreation in its far more famous descendant, *Tom Brown's Schooldays*, it nevertheless already exemplifies the formula that Thomas Hughes would use to such dramatic effect in the later novel. For many readers, *Tom Brown's Schooldays* is a living synecdoche; it stands for the schoolboy novel genre, with its unstable brew of athleticism and spirituality, rugged optimism and sentimentality, its cult of manliness and its complementary cult of tender, eroticized male friendships, personified by Tom's "chum" George Arthur. Patrick Scott (1990) calls it "the prototype of the schoolboy novel" (34), a remark that illustrates the degree to which the work both spawned imitators and erased from popular consciousness the quieter work of such predecessors as Martineau. In an enduring critical debate, *Tom Brown* has been amply discussed—attacked, mocked, defended, and celebrated. As Scott documents, even early reviewers were divided about the work, some believing it would elevate, and other fearing that it might corrupt, the schoolboy mind. Despite Hughes's avowal that he wrote the novel in order to preach to boys, the work has been broadly associated with the Philistine cult of athleticism that gained ground in the second half of the nineteenth century. Surely it seems superfluous to argue that the real action in *Tom Brown* takes place on the playground. Upon Tom's arrival at school, Hughes devotes the bulk of his famous chapter "Rugby and Football," to a detailed explanation of the unique rules of the Rugby game and to a vivid word-painting of Tom's first match. The succeeding chapter describes the postgame euphoria. In contrast, a single paragraph is sufficient to cover Tom's first half-year of lessons in the third form.

At the same time, *Tom Brown* lacks *The Crofton Boys'* polar opposition between playground and schoolroom, in part because its most significant sites—the playground, the chapel, the residential school-house, and the classroom—are linked by and subordinated to the book's dominant metaphor of the battlefield. No sooner has Tom settled in than he and his irreverent cohort East find themselves engaged in a "war with the masters and the [older bullies of] the fifth form" (195). As Tom comes to believe, "the masters' hands were against him and his against them. And he regarded them, as a matter of course, as his natural enemies" (166). Whether in the dormitory, the quadrangle, or the classroom, Tom finds himself fighting those in power, often in the service, he maintains, of those younger and weaker. And as Hughes sermonizes during Tom's famous fight with the bully Slogger Williams, "From the cradle to the grave, fighting, rightly understood, is the busi-ness, the real, highest, honestest business of every son of man.... It is no good for Quakers... to uplift their voices against fighting. Human nature is too strong for them" (282–283). Fighting is naturalized; human nature unproblematically reflects wild nature's long battle of selection and survival. If some of the schoolmasters seem blind to the impor-tance of fighting, the headmaster himself is keenly aware of it. In fact, Arnold's voice is invoked to second the novel's martial vision. During sermons in the chapel, the Doctor's voice rings out as "clear and stirring as the call of the light infantry bugle" (141); it is the "warm living voice of one who was fighting for us and by our sides" (142), proclaiming life "a battlefield... where there are no spectators, but the youngest must take his side, and the stakes are life and death" (143).

If the chapel and the classroom are equally sites of battle, the play-ground's supreme benefit is that it replicates nature's battlefield while confining it within spatial, temporal, and moral limits; in this garden of warfare, Rugby footballers hone their fighting skills within the moral bounds of "fair play." For Hughes, the football match is worth watching precisely because it is a mock battle: "a battle would look much the same to you, except that the boys would be men, and the balls iron; but a battle would be worth your looking at for all that, and so is a football match" (106). Just as Arnold is the "true sort of captain... for a boy's army" (143), so too old Brooke, the student captain of the schoolhouse team, is "a true football king" whose "earnest and careful" face forecasts "the sort of look I hope to see in my general when I go out to fight" (104).

Paradoxically, then, the playing field, the site of recreation, appears not less regulated but more regulated—and certainly more exposed—than the rest of school life. In Martineau's chaotic playground, Lamb can be buried in earth without the masters' knowledge; young Tooke can commit a guilty act that remains unseen. In contrast, Hughes' level playing fields embody the full measure of the transparency that

Spencer locates in the boys' garden. In the classroom, pupils engage in surreptitious spatial practices, hiding their ignorance with cribs and vulgus books; on the playing fields, in contrast, true character is revealed: "as endless as are boys' characters, so are their ways of facing or not facing a scrummage at football" (107). Cowards like Flashman, "the School-house bully" (106), reveal their true natures by skirting a scrummage and then boasting to the football captain of their part in it. "But," Hughes's comradely narrator asserts to Flashman and his ilk, "he knows you, and so do we" (106).

A morally transparent space, the playground allows not just the narrator, but also Thomas Arnold, to exercise an unsettling panoptical vision. Constantly supervising the workings of boy-nature from his window in the "highest round tower" of the schoolhouse (89), Arnold is fully aware of Tom's fight with Slogger Williams for a good half hour before a respected older student puts a stop to it. Similarly, as Tom and his friend East pursue their "old wild out-of-bounds habits" (188), the Doctor's "eye, which was everywhere," is "upon them" (199). Preternaturally aware of the boys' activities and characters, Arnold often withholds that knowledge from them to foster their strengthening illusion of liberty and independence. Although he paints a less certain, and sometimes even a despairing figure, Arnold's biographer Stanley also attributes to him a panoptical vision:

> His quick and far-sighted eye became familiar with the face and manner of every boy in the school. "Do you see," he said to an assistant master who had recently come, "those two boys walking together; I never saw them together before; you should make an especial point of observing the company they keep;—nothing so tells the changes in a boy's character." (132)

Like Rousseau's garden in *Émile,* where nature must be staged to illuminate for the pupil the supreme logic of natural laws, so the playing fields serve to stage mock battles to prepare students for the great fight that is Nature's and God's grand plan for humanity; the will to fight is planted deep, as Hughes's narrator has observed, in human nature. At the same time, the cricket games on *Tom Brown's* level playing fields are, in the words of Tom and his friend George Arthur, "an institution" (354) that teaches "discipline and reliance on one another" in life's enduring battle (355); thus, the games are "the birthright of British boys old and young, as *habeas corpus* and trial by jury are of British men" (355). In Rousseau's idealized garden, property rights bloom. On Rugby's playing fields, British law is born. As in the Rousseauian paradigm, Nature gives birth to the social impulse, which then must restage nature as its own enduring source and justification. Often casually dismissive of the schoolrooms' lessons, Hughes celebrates the more natural lessons on the playing field; yet as in this passage, distinctions between the natural and the institutional repeatedly break down.

In part, the transparency of the level playing field can be seen as natural because it mirrors Hughes's vision of boy-nature as innately frank and honest. As Hughes declares, Tom Brown, the novel's Every-Boy, has "nothing whatever remarkable about him except excess of boyishness; by which I mean animal life in its fullest measure, good nature and honest impulses, hatred of injustice and meanness, and thoughtlessness enough to sink a three-decker" (143). It is to such an audience of "brave gallant boys, who hate easy-chairs" and "only want to have [their] heads set straight, to take the right side" that Hughes addresses his novel (195). Presumably they are at one with Tom Brown and all the "real boys" who rush about "in high spirits" when they return for the new school term, "however fond they may be of home" (215).

George Arthur, however, the spiritualized chum who helps to civilize Tom, is not a "real boy." Shy, timid, and fearful, he cannot at first make friends or even speak up before other pupils. One of Tom's greatest achievements is to help Arthur (like the Velveteen Rabbit of the famous children's story) to become "real," in this case through healthful, natural exercise. Thus, Tom exposes the frail boy, the son of a poor urban clergyman to nature in the form of "Rugby air," "cricket," and "good long walks" (221), as prescribed by the wise Thomas Arnold. Like Jean-Jacques, that assiduous gardener, Tom is "repaid by seeing his little sensitive plant expand... and sun itself in his smiles" (266). Under Tom's captaincy, Arthur becomes a member of the elite "School eleven"—the cricket team that plays in the heroic final match of the penultimate chapter (346). Yet even there we see Tom's nurturing hand at work: "I'm not quite sure [Arthur] ought to be in for his play," Tom acknowledges, "but I couldn't help putting him in. It will do him so much good" (358). Arthur, whose mystical vision on his sickbed ultimately rouses Tom's latent spiritual life, recovers to be at least an honorary "real boy." As he tells Tom, his "constitution" is "quite changed": "I'm fit for anything now.... That's all thanks to you and the games you've made me fond of" (315).

Just as many Victorians yearned nostalgically for a natural education in the Rousseauian and Spencerian tradition, they also fetishized natural landscape gardening as an improvement on the old-fashioned formal garden. In his charmingly testy book, *The Formal Garden in England* (1892), Reginald Blomfield attacks the popular school of natural landscape gardening for claiming that it is "unnatural to lay out a garden in straight lines and regular banks and to clip your hedges" (11). Favoring the formal architectural approach to gardening, Blomfield denounces the arrogance of the natural school: "The landscape gardener appears to suppose that he has a monopoly of nature. Now, what is 'nature' and what is 'natural' in relation to gardens?" (11). The indignant Blomfield asks the telling question to which, in his view, the school of Rousseau might have both too few and too many answers. For educators who draw vitality from the Rousseauian tradition (and Hughes, more than Arnold and certainly more than Martineau, often operates within that broad and not very easily defined territory) nature can be both a recalcitrant raw material and a standard to aspire to, both human and divine, both wildly primitive and supremely rational. It can be variously invoked as norm, guide, and context, a numinous concept, a privileged emptiness waiting to be filled.

Near the end of *Tom Brown*, a sympathetic master confides to Tom the extent to which the headmaster has rearranged the landscape of Rugby. The "island," an area that adjoined the close but was separated from it by ditches, used to be "laid out in small gardens, and cultivated by frost-bitten fags in February and March" (356). The master and Tom jointly deplore the "afternoons spent grubbing in the tough dirt" as well as the fags' habit of "stealing flowers" (356) from local gardens in order to repair their deficient gardening. As the master confides, it was Arnold himself who brought an end to these ignoble customs by giving the "island" to the sixth form for an exercise field and suggesting that they plant "gymnastic poles" where flowers once grew. In the master's words, the change was carried out "so quietly and naturally, putting a good thing in place of a bad" (357), that Tom and his fellow students never knew the reason for it.

According to the kindly master, Thomas Arnold is quietly redesigning the "nature" of Rugby, shifting it away from the functionless ornamental futility of the "girls' garden," as evoked in Spencer's conventional image, and moving it toward Spencer's depiction of the "boys' garden," with its "poles and horizontal bars for gymnastic exercises," inspiring healthy activity and vigorous competition. In fact, one of Arnold's fears when he accepted the Rugby headship was that he might have to surrender his "leaping-pole and gallows," the gymnastic poles that provided the "entire relaxation" (74), which he regarded as necessary to his health and work. "I want absolute play," he declared, "like a boy" (74). Given the gendered images discussed by Spencer, Arnold is correctively re-gendering Rugby, guiding the old school away from emasculated ornamental traditions and in the direction of vigorous, goal-oriented male activity.

While he probably would have little sympathy with the school garden movement, Arnold is nevertheless a domestic gardener who, like Tom himself, hates "grubbing about in the tough dirt." And, as the confiding master reveals, Arnold has time not only to redesign the nature of Rugby, but also the individual nature of even an ordinary boy like Tom Brown. Thus, as the master explains, Arnold himself has placed the pious and domestic George Arthur in Tom's study in order to cultivate Tom's dormant moral impulses. While nurturing Arthur's health, Tom has been unaware that he himself is being cultivated, "so quietly and naturally," by Arnold as well as by Arthur. Like Rousseau's fictional Jean-Jacques, the master whom Rousseau declared himself incapable of being, Hughes's fictional Thomas Arnold is also a shrewd and patient gardener of the spirit.

Although most readers would agree that *Tom Brown's Schooldays* embodies an aggressively institutional agenda—the celebration of Rugby life—the novel, as we will explore further in the following chapter, also records a profound suspicion of school life. Acutely fearful that school can "ruin" a boy as surely as it can save him, Hughes carries on a running commentary about the dangers of school life.[8] A transitional novel, *Tom Brown* also tempers institutionality with a subtle rhetoric of domestic education. For Foucault, all members of a disciplinary bureaucracy are "interchangeable," as surveillance is conducted through numerous disciplinary mechanisms. Segmented, disciplinary space stands in contrast to the spaces of "domestic supervision," typified, for instance, by the master–apprentice relation (*Discipline* 174). In fact, Hughes's portrait of Arnold embodies elements of both institutional and domestic supervision. Although he employs proctors and head boys as intermediaries, and although his sometimes distant supervision exemplifies a panoptic surveillance, Arnold is simply not replaceable. His towering presence dominates every space from the chapel to the playing field, minimizing their differences and paradoxically imbuing them with the intimacy of the master–apprentice relation. Finally, Arnold's character makes Rugby work, redeeming its numerous dangers. Merging elements of the domestic past with the institutionalizing urge, Hughes depicts Arnold as a larger-than-life master teacher in the tradition of Rousseau and Pestalozzi. Further, Hughes is always opening domestic vistas within the institutional landscape of Rugby, as if to reassure his readers. Thus, we are treated to scenes of the dignified Dr. Arnold frolicking and playing with his children, as well as to a redemptive domestic moment when Arthur's mother moves into the school to nurse her feverish son back to health.

268.— DOUBLE CLASS-ROOM, SHEWING DUAL ARRANGEMENT OF DESKS.

FIGURE 1.1 DOUBLE CLASSROOM—SHOWING DUAL ARRANGEMENT OF DESKS (E. R. ROBSON, *SCHOOL ARCHITECTURE*, 1874).

An experienced teacher will have no difficulty in arranging the drill to be employed in connection with the dual system. The scholars on their part will soon learn to move with greater smartness and precision than is readily attainable under the old system. The importance of doing things in a regular and orderly manner cannot be too forcibly impressed. A definite system of drill is therefore essentially necessary. Some teachers prefer to use numbers only, while others incline to a code in which the orders are given by words.

The following suggestion for a code of drill illustrates our meaning. The teacher may give his orders either by words or numbers :—

(1)—" *Return.*"

At the word " Return," the hands should be raised to grasp the slate.

(2)—" *Slates.*"

At the word " Slates," the slate should be smartly lifted and placed in the groove in front of the desk without noise. The hands should then be lowered.

269.—" RETURN."

270.—" SLATES."

If books have been used, as in the case of an arithmetic lesson, the additional command may follow; (1) " *Return*" (2) " *Books.*" At the second word " Books," the books should be placed on the shelf under the desk, and the hands brought back to their original position.

FIGURE 1.2 SCHOOL DRILL: MOVEMENTS 1-2 (E. R. ROBSON, *SCHOOL ARCHITECTURE*, 1874).

(3)—" *Lift* " (or " *Raise* ").

At the word "Lift," the edge of the flap should be grasped.

(4)—" *Desks.* "

At the word "Desks," the flap should be raised quickly but without noise, and the hands dropped.

271. —"LIFT" (OR " RAISE").

272. —"DESKS."

(5)—" *Stand.* "

At the word "Stand," the scholars should rise smartly with arms straight by their sides.

(6)—" *Out.* "

At the word " Out," the scholar at the *right* end of the desk takes one step to the right and a short step to the *front*. At the same moment the scholar at the *left* end of the desk takes a step to the left and a short pace to the *rear*.

273.—" STAND."

274.—" OUT."

The sixth movement leaves the children standing in Indian file down the respective gangways. The command may then be

FIGURE 1.3 SCHOOL DRILL: MOVEMENTS 3-6 (E. R. ROBSON, *SCHOOL ARCHITECTURE*, 1874).

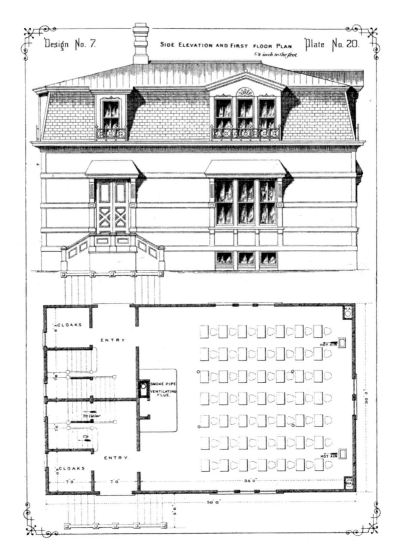

FIGURE 1.4 SCHOOL PLAN INDICATING THE LINEAR ARRANGEMENT OF DESKS (SAMUEL F. EVELETH, *SCHOOL-HOUSE ARCHITECTURE*, 1870).

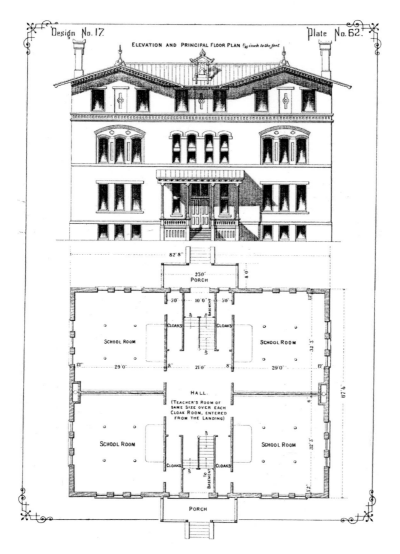

FIGURE 2.1 School Plan Including Space for a Teacher's Room (Samuel F. Eveleth, *SCHOOL-HOUSE ARCHITECTURE*, 1870).

Turning away from the clearly defined, brightly illuminated playgrounds of popular schoolboy fiction, it is worth revisiting Dickens's *bildungsroman, David Copperfield*, for its portrait of an ironized boys' garden. As we saw in the previous chapter, Creakle's academy embodies the Spencerian concept of coercive education within a contrasting pair of schools. Dickens's depiction of the playground at Creakle's school commingles a rhetoric of nature and wildness with the antidomestic rhetoric of institutional education. Arriving at Creakle's academy before the school term starts, David enters the dreary and deserted playground, "a bare gravelled yard, open to all the back of the house and the offices" (78). Utterly level and empty, the playground is a site of unmitigated transparency, enabling passersby to read David's "character" at a glance—because it is "beautifully written" on a pasteboard placard fastened onto the boy's back: "*Take care of him. He bites*" (78). As David laments, "I knew that the servants read it, and the butcher read it, and the baker read it;… everybody… who came to the house… read that I was to be taken care of, for I bit. I recollect that I positively began to have a dread of myself, as a kind of wild boy who did bite" (79). In an agony of shame, David even envisions his future classmates reading the placard; he imagines their very gestures and voices as they intone the warning he carries on his back.

In this absurd but still devastating rendering of panoptical vision, the pain of feeling visible, even to those who are known not to be watching, is both excruciating and utterly unproductive. Although it makes David suffer, the discipline instills no lesson because David has no idea what he is to learn. The wild boy-nature over which Arnold so sincerely grieves, far from a genuine threat, is represented as only a creation of the masters, a bogeyman that finally scares David, its purported embodiment, as much as anyone. Tellingly, David first takes the placard to be a warning about a savage dog, a mythical animal he uneasily searches for, unaware that he is the "savage." In this parodic rendering of the boys' playground, the untamed animal nature within is humorously dismissed as a myth, perpetuated by school functionaries with an economic interest in maintaining their disciplinary institutions.

In contrast to Creakle's playground, the transparent site of an allegedly panoptical control, Dr. Strong's domesticated academy is characterized by the shady garden where the benign and gentle Doctor loves to stroll with his wife. Repeatedly situating the Doctor in a cloistered courtyard that evokes Spencer's girls' garden, the narrative associates him with a feminized domesticity. Through a linguistic misapprehension, David even imagines Dr. Strong as a metaphorical gardener; told that the Doctor is "looking out for Greek roots," David dimly associates this occupation with "a botanical furor on the doctor's part, especially as he always looked at the ground when he walked about" (237). Like Rousseau, then, the Doctor is a gardener—and not of the aggressively masculine Arnoldian type. Yet the Doctor's predilection for his tree-lined garden hints at an ominous undertone, expressing implicit anxieties about the limits of domestic education. Dominated by his masculinized mother-in-law (known as the "Old Soldier"), he risks ceding control of his household (239). His feminization, as he strolls with his wife "in the garden where the peaches were" (239), is typified by the fact that "even the stray rooks and jackdaws" seem "more knowing" in "worldly affairs than he" (238). So often do "vagabond[s]" invade his garden sanctuary "with tales of distress" that the schoolboys themselves feel called upon to "turn them out of the court-yard" (238), rescuing the Doctor before he can offer them supposedly undeserved gifts. In a comic twist on the Doctor's uncertain masculinity, he is suspected of fathering a "beggar-woman's" child (238) when neighbors see the infant wrapped in his gaiters, given to her in a moment of absent-minded benevolence. Yet the image typifies, not a rampant male sexuality, but the radical innocence of a man unaware that his wife's cousin is seeking to seduce her under his own roof.

LOCKED GARDENS: PROPERTY AND THE FEMALE BODY

When David Copperfield asks Agnes Wickfield, "*You* have never been to school, have you?" she replies cheerfully, "Oh yes! Every day" (*Copperfield* 239). As Agnes smilingly explains, however, she goes to school at home, because "Papa couldn't spare me" (229). While the conversation hints at the superiority of domestic education—Agnes is, after all, the supremely wise child who will later become David's spiritual mentor—it also emphasizes the peripherality of the school experience for girls. In school fictions, girls need school only when their families no longer need them, when something is awry in the domestic realm. Turning to images of the girls' school garden, then, we find it so opaque that it is difficult to locate in popular literature. While women writers like Martineau and May were busy writing tales of boys at school, they found little occasion to write of girls' academies. In *The Crofton Boys*, Hugh Proctor's clever and self-disciplined sisters never attend school; they stay contentedly in the domestic sphere, studying with a governess. Portraits of girls' schools are few and far between in popular children's literature until the 1890s, when writers like Evelyn Sharp and Angela Brazil appropriate the schoolboy formula to tales of outdoorsy, tomboyish female pupils. Thus, in Sharp's *The Making of a Schoolgirl* (1897), the heroine agrees with her best chum that "the gymnasium prize was the only one worth having" (77), and regrets her upcoming holidays at home because "I shall miss the gymnasium classes awfully" (76).

For girls who did attend school, however, gardening had been an accepted part of the curriculum at many institutions since the late eighteenth century. As Dorothy Gardiner emphasizes in *English Girlhood at School* (1929), gardening was considered a means of developing feminine domestic traits. Thus, it was an important feminine accomplishment for poor charity scholars as well as pupils at elite fashionable academies:

> The Reverend John Bennett encouraged his readers, by the example of Milton's *Adam and Eve,* to believe that "Attention to a garden is a truly feminine amusement. If you mix it with a taste for botany and a knowledge of plants and flowers you will never be in want of an excellent restorative." The charity scholars at Millenium [*sic*] Hall had each a garden where they might indulge their own fancy, adorning it with beds of flowers, little seats and arbours, and finding in it as much pleasure as other children in sports and games.... In fashionable schools, towards the close of the century, girls were encouraged to possess their own little plots of ground, the healthfulness of the occupation being held to compensate for "a few dagged frocks and dirtied gloves," and likely to lay the foundation of a home-loving character. (357–358)

The training in the girls' gardens described by Gardiner evokes Ruskin's famous distinction between boy- and girl-nature in *Sesame and Lilies* (1865): "there is just this difference between the making of a girl's character and a boy's—you may chisel a boy into shape, as you would a rock.... But you cannot hammer a girl into anything. She grows as a flower does" (124). In Charlotte Brontë's first novel, the widely underestimated *Professor* (1857), the doubly distancing mechanisms of a male narrator coupled with a foreign location permit Brontë to explore more deeply the experience of recoil from "female" nature as embodied in the girls' school garden. As Spencer would four years later, Brontë casts the novel's girls' garden as one-half of a gendered pair. When William Crimsworth takes his first teaching post at M. Pelet's Belgian academy for boys, the new master's austere bedroom is interesting chiefly for its two prominent windows. One allows an unimpeded view of the "boys' playground" (65), a mere "bare gravelled court" (66). The second, intriguingly boarded up because it overlooks the garden of the adjacent "pensionnat de demoiselles" (65), serves as a canvas for Crimsworth's mental pictures of a sheltered and sacrosanct female nature. When he "scrutinize[s]... the nailed boards, hoping... to get a peep at the consecrated ground" of the girls' garden, Crimsworth finds no "chink or crevice" (65):

> it is astonishing how disappointed I felt—I thought it would have been so pleasant to have looked out upon a garden planted with flowers and trees, so amusing to have watched the demoiselles at their play—to have studied female character in a variety of phases, myself the while, sheltered from view by a modest muslin curtain. (69)

Crimsworth aspires to the panoptical vision that is a given in the boys' garden, but forbidden by the enclosures and proprieties—"les convenances" (65)—of the girls' garden. Such proprieties sanction a vision of girls and women as property; like the garden itself, girl-nature must be fenced in by high walls to warn off male trespassers. Working within the novelistic conventions that normalized the male narrator and the male gaze, Currer Bell (Brontë's male pseudonym) appears to relish offering readers a look at men looking at women, or, more accurately, adolescent girls. Crimsworth finds it congenial to look down from a superior vantage point on the mysterious intricacies of girl-nature; naively he anticipates an originary paradise, a domestic green world that promises deliverance from the highly structured routine of the male workaday world: "especially in moments of weariness and low spirits did I look with dissatisfied eyes on that most tantalizing board, longing to tear it away and get a glimpse of the green region which I imagined to lie beyond" (66). Although the shouts of the girls at play suggest that the "lungs of Mdlle. Reuter's girls" (66) are as strong as those of Monsieur Pelet's boys, Crimsworth continues to believe in his illusory pastoral of gendered difference. Ultimately admitted to the girls' garden when he becomes a teacher in the adjacent girls' school, he finds not domestic angels but flawed human beings. Recoiling in horror, he cannot accept this mixed picture of girl-nature and retreats into disgust and contempt for his female charges.[9]

Like so many Victorian school narratives, Brontë's rich studies of school life depict popularly accepted images only to problematize them. *Jane Eyre* presents a haunting image of the girls' garden at the Lowood Charity School, not seen panoptically from above by a male observer, but rather experienced by the girls who walk daily within its walls:

> The garden was a wide enclosure, surrounded with walls so high as to exclude every glimpse of prospect; a covered veranda ran down one side, and broad walks bordered a middle space divided into scores of little beds; these beds were assigned as gardens for the pupils to cultivate, and each bed had an owner. When full of

flowers they would doubtless look pretty; but now, at the latter end of January, all was wintry blight and brown decay. I shuddered as I stood and looked round me: it was an inclement day for out-door exercise; not positively rainy, but darkened by a drizzling yellow fog. (54)

Jane Eyre's first glimpse of the Lowood garden sends an ominous message. Doomed to the drudgery from which Arnold freed the "frost-bitten" student gardeners at Rugby (*Tom Brown* 356), the schoolgirls inhabit a garden that would depress even the optimistic Erasmus Schwab. Like Spencer's repressive "girls' garden," the perilous walled "enclosure" is inexorably shaping the schoolgirls, touching them with its "wintry blight" of feebleness and ill health. While the strongest girls are able to exert themselves in "active play... sundry pale and thin ones herded together for shelter and warmth... and amongst these, as the dense mist penetrated to their shivering frames, I heard frequently the sound of a hollow cough" (54).

As in Spencer's domesticated girls' garden, the Lowood enclosure is "divided" and opaque, cut through by walks to direct the pupils' footsteps, partially hidden by a "covered veranda," and on this occasion at least, "darkened" by an unhealthy "fog." Even worse than Spencer's prim garden, this one excludes any "prospect" of the external world. The walls that supposedly shelter the schoolgirls also keep out not only the outside world, but any vision of themselves participating in that world. As Jane asserts while she stands shivering in the garden, "of the future I could form no conjecture" (54).

If the garden stands as a self-fulfilling prophecy of a contracted future without prospect, it represents the girls' situation in other ways as well. Jane Eyre and David Copperfield are both orphaned children who are exploited by harsh guardians, and have committed remarkably similar offenses. Both children have defended themselves when unjustly attacked, David against the villainous Murdstone, Jane against her cruel cousin John Reed. Yet the names given to their crimes differ. David sees himself convicted of "wildness," quarantined like a mad dog in his graveled yard. Jane, on the other hand, stands accused by her aunt of the stereotypically more "feminine" crime of "deceit" (35). Just as David feels himself becoming, under his pasteboard placard, "the wild boy who did bite," so Jane imagines herself "transformed under [the schoolmaster] Mr. Brocklehurst's eye into an artful obnoxious child" (33).

According to a logic of images that becomes more insistent in Brontë's Belgian novels, the opaque girls' garden, darkened by mist, both shapes and serves as an emblem of the dangers of a posited girl-nature, standing in opposition to the rough frankness of "real boys" like Tom Brown. Or to put it another way, the feminine values enforced at Lowood under Brocklehurst's reign—silence, modesty, humble obedience—have their shadow side: deceit, artfulness, secret pride. No matter how rigorously the girls attempt to conform to his edicts, Brocklehurst paranoically spots a secret girl-nature, a lush "excrescence" welling up under the veil of humility. Thus his horror, on visiting day, at Julia Severn's "mass of curls," despite Miss Temple's explanation that Julia's "hair curls naturally": "Naturally! Yes, but we are not to conform to nature... why that abundance? I have again and again intimated that I desire the hair to be arranged closely, modestly, plainly. Miss Temple, that girl's hair must be cut off entirely;... and I see others who have far too much of the excrescence" (73). In the service of taming nature, Brocklehurst ordains a minor amputation, far less serious than Hugh's in *The Crofton Boys*. Yet Brontë orchestrates the moment so that it still has power to shock. Pruning Julia's curls as he might prune his own garden, Brocklehurst appropriates a wild female nature by rendering it appropriately conventional.

And ironically, Brocklehurst's horror at the "abundance" of female nature is also a self-fulfilling prophecy. When illness arrives with the warmer weather, keeping the cowardly Brocklehurst away from the school, Lowood, perhaps in revenge for Julia Severn's lost curls, "shook loose its tresses; it became all green, all flowery... woodland plants sprung up profusely in its recesses; unnumbered varieties of moss filled its hollows" (89). The girls' garden, once an emblem of mortified nature, revives, subverting dreary restraints and bringing abundance onto the school grounds: "a greenness grew over the brown beds... freshening daily" (88). As Jane digs up woodland flowers to transplant in her space in the Lowood garden, the dividing line between the cultivated garden and wild nature appears permeable. By May, the "garden, too, [like the woodland] glowed with flowers: hollyhocks had sprung up tall as trees, lilies had opened, tulips and roses were in bloom; the borders of the little beds were gay with pink thrift and crimson double-daisies; the sweet briars gave out, morning and evening, their scent of spice and apples" (90). A far cry from Spencer's dull school garden, or from the exquisite cultivated gardens celebrated in Ruskin's idealizations of domesticity, the Lowood garden explodes with hardy hollyhocks and daisies, flowers that thrive in wild nature. During this season of efflorescence and fever, Jane is free to explore her own wild nature on rambles with her "shrewd" and "witty" new friend Mary Ann Wilson, who gives "ample indulgence" to Jane's "faults... never imposing curb or rein on anything... [she] said" (91). The girls transgress conventional boundaries in their speech, just as they violate the walled spaces of the garden by surreptitiously transplanting wildflowers from the woods. Interestingly, the unrestrained and undisciplined Mary Ann has "a turn for narrative" (91). After the silence imposed by the reign of Brocklehurst, the girl's voice flows forth in a discourse that values "entertainment" over moral "improvement," during long "sweet days of liberty" (91). Mary Ann's irregular narratives cast fictive storytelling in opposition to school lessons; similarly, novelists like Brontë and Dickens implicitly cast their own *bildungsromane* as experiential lessons in character formation, emblems of individualized domestic education in conflict with school's regimented pedagogy.

The explosion of growth in the girls' garden, coupled as it is with the fever that burns through the school after neglect and repression, has in it something of excess, and even of moral danger. Finally, Jane cannot feel quite comfortable about her carefree sojourn with the irreverent Mary Ann. In the end, the garden itself seems to recall her from her truancy among the flowers, sending Jane her first inkling of mortality. As Jane lingers in the garden at night, the moon rises "with such majesty in the grave east" that it softens and spiritualizes the wild garden. Jane experiences a vision as unsettling as "formless cloud and vacant depth" (93), which seems a vague call to action. Ultimately, Jane's nighttime vision rouses her to seek out her spiritual mentor Helen Burns, who she learns, is dying of consumption within the school walls.

The mysterious vision in the night-time garden is a rite of passage, as Jane relinquishes the careless happiness of girlhood and begins her transition toward womanhood. But unlike the complementary passage experienced by Hugh and Tom in the boys' garden, Jane's transitional experience is unmediated by the social; this unfolding is staged as immanent in Nature itself—or perhaps more accurately here, Nature *herself.* Jane's old friend the moon (so often a maternal and annunciatory figure who signals impending changes) opens an uncanny and unsocialized way of female knowledge, one that male authority figures like Brocklehurst, St. John Rivers, and even Rochester attempt unsuccessfully to quell.

Repeatedly, not only in *Jane Eyre* but also in *The Professor* and *Villette,* Brontë's depictions of the school garden permit her both to attack stereotypical male conceptions of female nature and also to suggest, paradoxically, that an uncanny, powerful, and even potentially dangerous female nature does exist. The female "abundance" that Brocklehurst fears does indeed manifest itself in the garden; Jane, too, though with a light touch, paints her recoil from its lush excess. Both *The Professor* and *Jane Eyre* question the rigid gender divisions of the girls' garden, shedding light on the means by which patriarchal instruction aims to cultivate and appropriate female nature as domestic property. Yet *The Professor* moves toward erasing the gendered distinctions, while *Jane Eyre* gestures at an unconstrained female nature that appears in elusive and sporadic acts of defiance. Brontë's last school narrative, *Villette*, continues to problematize issues surrounding the cultivation of female nature. Its mysterious and many-faceted school garden has been the subject of extensive analysis, but that novel, which has less to tell us about changing definitions of childhood, lies outside the scope of this study.[10]

NATURE AND PROPERTY IN WONDERLAND

The haunting image of the enclosed garden, in which female child-nature supposedly finds its analogue, emerges vividly in a very different novel with another often defiant female protagonist—the children's classic, Lewis Carroll's *Alice's Adventures in Wonderland* (1865). It is hardly necessary to belabor the argument that *Alice* is, in an important sense, a school novel. Throughout her journey in Wonderland, Alice frequently meditates on, recites, or attempts to instruct others in the lessons she learns at her day school. Animals and mysteriously animate playing cards pose as teachers or superior fellow students. While the Mock Turtle and the Gryphon explain to her the "different branches of Arithmetic—Ambition, Distraction, Uglification, and Derision" (93), belittling her inferior education, the self-consciously sagacious Caterpillar requires her to repeat "You are old, Father William" (50), and then intones in schoolmasterly fashion: "That is not said right.… It is wrong from beginning to end" (53).

The book's concluding trial of the Knave of Hearts has the tone of a class gone wrong, as the jury scribble desperately on their slates, the Queen hurls an inkstand at Bill the lizard when he stops writing, and the cross-examinations turn into pointless and incoherent oral examinations (115). The final piece of evidence is a poem, which the King painstakingly and nonsensically explicates, despite Alice's assertion that "*I* don't believe there's an atom of meaning in it" (114). Alice's recognition that the schoolmasterly officials are in fact mere playing cards, and that she is outgrowing them at a ferocious rate, becoming too large for the schoolroom-courtroom, leads to the wonderfully anarchic ending, in which the giant child makes a mockery of the discourse of adult authority, shown to be as arbitrary and trivial as a game of cards.

Pleasant as the moment is, it is clear that Alice has already internalized the discourse of adult and school authority. As we learn at the beginning of the novel, "this curious child was very fond of pretending to be two people":

> She generally gave herself very good advice (though she very sel-
> dom followed it), and sometimes she scolded herself so severely as
> to bring tears into her eyes; and once she remembered trying to
> box her own ears for having cheated herself in a game of croquet
> she was playing against herself. (25)

Alice's attempts at self-reform are not only painful, but often futile. Their very fruitlessness renders them self-perpetuating, theoretically at least, unending. Alice's brief moments of self-mastery are often suc-ceeded by the loss of coherence, individuality, and selfhood. "But it's no use now," Alice despairingly admits, as she finds herself shrinking for the second time outside the entrance to Wonderland's locked garden: "Why, there's hardly enough of me left to make one respectable person" (25). Alice repeatedly tests her memory for sums and recitations to prove that, in the midst of her disorientation, she is still Alice. Clearly, school is a world she carries within her on her journey into Wonderland.

One of the novel's many plot lines is a quest narrative. Alice strives to reach Wonderland's locked garden, is distracted by a series of absurd and ambiguous lessons, and finally enters the garden to learn that it is not what it seems. Pristine and lovely, the locked garden initially evokes an idyllic pastoral privacy, which Alice yearns to enter, partly because of its allure as mysterious and impenetrable territory. In nine-teenth-century children's literature, the garden serves as a ready image of innocent childhood imagination, the realm of poetry and dreams. Secreted under the earth, at the end of a perilous dark tunnel, this min-iature locked garden also evokes, in an undertone, the mysteries of the female body and female nature.

Alice's attempts to enter the pristine garden lead to a number of con-tortions and self-distortions, changes of size and shape. She drinks a cordial to become small enough to enter, then finds herself too small to reach the key on its glass table. She eats a cake to become larger, then waves the White Rabbit's magic fan to become small again. While the garden at the end of the tunnel may evoke erotic associations, the plot also leads us on to other, perhaps richer, implications. Carried away on the salty ocean of the tears she wept as a giant girl, the new miniature Alice loses sight of the idealized garden. Her self re-creations are futile; when, later in the tale, she suddenly finds herself in the garden, she now recognizes its natural beauty as an illusion, an artifice. The paradisal garden is in fact the property of the domineering Queen, who threat-ens all and sundry with executions and amputations. The incompetent gardeners who planted a white rose bush "by mistake" (778), are engaged in splashing it with red paint. Painted by its workmen like the stage set for a pastoral, the garden evokes nature, secrecy, and privacy only to "erase" them. Once again, nature is converted into property, defined by the wishes of the Queen. Simultaneously, the once mysterious garden shows itself as unnatural, a poor, cobbled-together piece of work. Alice's first reaction to the White Rabbit's bustling journey into Wonderland is, paradoxically, that "it all seemed quite natural" (19). Near the end of the tale, however, after she has left the illusory garden for her unsettling educational debates with the Mock Turtle and the Gryphon, she sits "with her face in her hands, wondering if anything would *ever* happen in a natural way again" (101).

If Wonderland's garden first evokes, and then revokes, the sheltered privacy and impermeability of Spencer's girls' garden, it is also the site of the energetic and raucous games of Spencer's boys' garden. Yet the Wonderland version of croquet is perhaps too "natural." Equipped with "live hedgehogs" for croquet balls and flamingoes for mallets (81), the players refuse to take turns, "quarreling all the while, and fighting for the hedgehogs" (82). The antithesis of the rigorous fair play enforced on Tom Brown's playing field, the game degenerates into chaos as the animals run away and the irritable Queen places players under sentence of execution "for having missed their turns" (84).

Wonderland's unspoiled garden thus reveals itself as an unsettling combination of artifice and "natural" chaos. In a text where school seems eternally embedded in Alice's dream and Alice's conscious-ness, the garden's associations with freedom, privacy, and spontane-ity only serve to foreground opposite qualities: erratic adult authority, unjust scrutiny, and absurd and arbitrary rules and regulations. Just as in Rousseau's garden, "nature" and "child-nature" are constructed by adults. Yet nearly a century later, the construction is blatantly appar-ent, revealing its frayed edges and dripping paint. Alice's repetitive size changes parody disciplinary attempts to reshape child-nature, while also calling into question the possibility of a coherent identity. And yet at the same time, Carroll's novel plays with the notion that if child-nature exists, it expresses itself most saliently in a subversive energy, a fluid and improvisatory play. In this seminal story, childhood can be defined, if at all, only in contrast to the disciplinary mechanisms typi-fied by the world of school and schooling, only as the ever-changing garden outside the institutional walls.

Nineteenth-century depictions of nature at school embody a con-stellation of recurring assumptions about gender and property. As the Rousseauian vision of education according to natural principles increasingly influenced nineteenth-century educators, it breathed new life into the ancient metaphor of the teacher as domestic gardener; the school garden's supposedly natural recreations could typify moral re-creation in institutions as diverse as Tom Brown's public school and the Lowood charity school for girls. A moralized and domesticated nature is invoked as an inspiring guide, elevating students beyond worldly social arrangements even as it sets the pattern for an improved, more natural sense of community. In contrast, undomesticated nature is dangerous, erupting in the tortures imposed by bullies, a disruptive premature sexuality in adolescent girls, and the reckless selfishness that ignores or openly defies adult precepts.

The conversion of nature into property makes the garden a safe territory even as it serves to domesticate child-nature, helping it "grow," in the words of the priggish Dormouse "at a reasonable pace... not in [Alice's] ridiculous fashion" (106). At the same time, of course, the concept of gendered nature enforces growth in the proper direction. Boys master an inner wilderness in preparation for the mastery of chaotic raw nature and the claiming of property in the external world. The transparency of the boys' playing field assists them into the public domain, inviting, even requiring them to exhibit their abilities and characters, the supposedly authentic directions of their individual natures. In the girls' garden, on the other hand, young ladies learn to tend themselves as property, to cultivate either virtue or the appearance of virtue, to veil nature in an opacity suitable to the private sphere. This paradigm, a simple framework that can lend itself in the literature of education to elaborate variations, need not presuppose an innate or unitary nongendered human nature that is then modified. Rather, nature as a force in education is a useful and often contradictory concept for nineteenth-century educators, implying as it does a reassuring link between individual experience and an overarching order. Exploring the imaginative literature of the mid-century, however, reveals how tenuous the link was, leading to so many refashionings and qualifications. A complex and ambiguous space, the school garden nevertheless emphasizes the power of domesticated nature to correct institutionality.

4

THE VIEW FROM THE SICKROOM WINDOW
Zymosis, Brain Fever, and the Dangers of Institutional Education

Arthur laid his thin white hand, on which the blue veins stood out so plainly, on Tom's great brown fist... and then looked out of the window again, as if he couldn't bear to lose a minute of the sunset.

—Thomas Hughes, *Tom Brown's Schooldays*

Oh! could he but have seen... the slight spare boy above, watching the waves and clouds at twilight, with his earnest eyes, and breasting the window of his solitary cage when birds flew by, as if he would have emulated them, and soared away!

—Charles Dickens, *Dombey and Son*

With regard to the health of houses where there is a sick person, it often happens that the sick room is made a ventilating shaft for the rest of the house.

—Florence Nightingale, *Notes on Nursing*

In his *Idea of a University* (1852), John Henry Newman twice compares university education to the curative work of a hospital. Carlyle's *Sartor Resartus* (1836), in contrast, contends that university life fosters a diseased sensibility. Lamenting his expensive "Miseducation," Towgood, Teufelsdrockh's English friend, suggests that its cost could just as well be applied "to endow a considerable Hospital of Incurables" (90).

But as Teufelsdrockh's framing narrative clearly implies, the university itself *is* a house of incurables because its students are "blown out into a state of windy argumentativeness" that ends in "sick, impotent Scepticism" (87) and "fever-paroxysms of Doubt" (89). A similar ambiguity characterizes the elementary and secondary schools of fictive school narratives: Are these schools curative hospitals or hospitals of incurables? Are they healing institutions, ameliorating social and moral ills, or are they rather breeding grounds for a feverish intellectual activity that induces moral and physical disease?

During an era when, in Thomas Huxley's words, education was increasingly viewed as the "great panacea" that would cure all social ills, a concomitant anxiety about the spread of institutionalized education reveals itself in the fictive illnesses that proliferate within so many novels of educational experience. In Dickens's *Nicholas Nickleby* (1838–1839), Smike is mentally stunted and physically enfeebled by his cruel treatment at Dotheboys Hall, dying years later of the constitutional wounds inflicted there. In Harriet Martineau's *The Crofton Boys* (1841), the reckless Hugh Proctor undergoes an amputation as a result of a grave injury on his school's unsupervised playground. The constitutionally weak Paul Dombey wastes away at Mrs. Pipchin's unpleasant and unhealthy school, and continues his inexorable progress toward death under Dr. Blimber's system of "cram" (*Dombey and Son,* 1846–1848). Toots, his fellow victim at Blimber's academy, succumbs to intellectual vacancy after his premature and overly rigorous studies. In Brontë's *Jane Eyre* (1847), Helen Burns escapes Lowood's oppressive institutional regimen only by dying in Jane's arms. E. J. May's Louis Mortimer, the ethereal hero of *Dashwood Priory, or Mortimer's College Life* (1855) "falls insensible on the floor" (77) at his secondary school, invaliding himself by excessive study at his tutor's urging. When his cousin Vernon Digby drives himself too hard at Cambridge, both boys must submit themselves to a lengthy rest cure.[1] Tom Brown bravely staggers to the "sick-room" after being forcibly burned by Flashman and his fellow bullies. His frail friend George Arthur suffers a more serious illness, nearly dying in a school epidemic to which his studious habits may have made him particularly vulnerable.

Diverse as they are, the wounds and illnesses just cataloged shine a glaring light on the various and particularized dangers embodied in each pupil's fictive school, from abusive physical conditions or lack of supervision, to the pressures imposed by hard-driving, ambitious schoolmasters. Unsurprisingly, the most harrowing fictive illnesses and injuries occur at boarding schools, which exercise such comprehensive control over children's physical, emotional, and intellectual development. Both boarding schools and day schools could, of course, be dangerous places. In *Notes on Nursing* (1859), Florence Nightingale implies that every teacher should also be a skilled nurse because of the frequency of school illnesses. "How many of children's epidemics," Nightingale laments, "originate" in "all [the] national and other schools throughout the kingdom" (114). While the enfeebled fictive schoolchildren just enumerated are drawn from the middle and upper-middle classes, Nightingale rightly emphasizes that the largely lower-middle-class and working-class children of the early national schools were also in jeopardy. Similarly, parish school logs paint a grim picture of cold, damp, and unhealthy schoolrooms, and the contagious fevers they incubated, affecting both working-class schoolchildren and their teachers.[2]

If schools posed a particular threat to health, this was only partly because they brought so many children together in crowded conditions; in Florence Nightingale's view, children "are much more susceptible than grown people to all noxious influences" (106). Nightingale's assertion reflects contemporary statistics. The lives of children, especially poor children, were often short. As Eric Hopkins writes in *Childhood Transformed* (1994), "In 1843, the average yearly deaths under ten in London were about 25,000" (114). Beyond this, however, Nightingale's vision of the hypersensitive child evokes the iconographic image that also serves the writers of school narratives: the child's sensitive body as the testing ground for the health or toxicity of the institutions and social arrangements controlled and monitored by adults. Thus, in the novels of the 1830s, 1840s, and 1850s, the bodies of injured, enfeebled, or dying children serve as iconic emblems of contemporary concerns about consigning the domestic work of child raising to institutions, which, for better or worse, would forever shape their inmates.

THE ICONOGRAPHY OF ILLNESS: READING THE SIGNS OF THE CHILD'S JEOPARDIZED BODY

Nicholas Nickleby's initiation into the schoolroom at Dotheboys Hall introduces him, along with the novel's readers, to a gallery of children's diseased and deformed bodies:

Pale and haggard faces, lank and bony figures, children with the countenances of old men, deformities with irons upon their limbs, boys of stunted growth, and others whose long meagre legs would hardly bear their stooping bodies, all crowded on the view together; there were the bleared eye, the hare-lip, the crooked foot, and every ugliness or distortion that told of unnatural aversion conceived by parents for their offspring, or of young lives which, from the earliest dawn of infancy, had been one horrible endurance of cruelty and neglect.... there was childhood with the light of its eye quenched, its beauty gone, and its helplessness alone remaining. (88)

As the language of the passage emphasizes, we are to read this panorama of diseased bodies both viscerally and iconographically. As we respond to the immediate pathos of the children's physical plight, we are also to see their bodies as emblems of adult abuses and failed domestic and institutional arrangements. Thus, the schoolchildren's ruined bodies crowd into our view in order to tell their tales of domestic and school exploitation. Although physical handicaps such as harelips and crooked feet are evidenced as potential causes for the parents' unnatural aversion, such deformities are catalogued as tragic abstractions, divorced from the children's bodies, while childhood itself is held to have a normative beauty that has been eradicated solely by adult abuse. Repeatedly, the novel juxtaposes the quasi-domestic and parental rhetoric of the school's headmaster, Wackford Squeers, with images of starved and diseased children. Readers are invited to contemplate the "unhealthy-looking boy, with warts all over his hands" (93), or the "lame" and "attenuated" figure of Smike, dressed inappropriately in a small boy's tattered clothes (79). Beyond any verbal denunciation framed by the narrator or by the title character (a disillusioned teacher at Squeers's school), the ultimate condemnation of Squeers and his schooling is simply the repeated image of the child's suffering body. Long after he escapes from Dotheboys Hall, Smike's body retains the stigmata of his school experience, fully revealing itself, late in the novel, in the pathetic scene that portrays Smike, despite his years, as a "dying boy" (763).

While the loving detail lavished on Smike's wounded and enfeebled body is typical of nineteenth-century sickbed and deathbed scenes, the school narrative imbues such portrayals with a heightened poignancy and a highly focused indignation against those adult dispensations of power that allegedly attack and destroy the child's health. If novels tend to image the deaths of sympathetic characters as indices of generalized social failure—Stephen Blackpool dies because he refuses to accept a brutalizing industrial society—the death of a child at school can serve as a dramatic indictment not only of schoolmasters and parents, but also of a society that tolerates lethal schools like Dotheboys Hall and Lowood Institution. The deaths of Smike and Helen Burns, which resonated so famously beyond the pages of their respective novels, destroyed the reputations of actual, historical schools. Dickens's novel, of course, not only precipitated immediate and specific changes in the Yorkshire schools, but also fostered a generalized reassessment of the possibilities and obligations of school life. In numerous other novels as well, the figure of the diseased pupil performs a similar, if less dramatic, form of cultural work, sometimes undermining the agenda of a specific type of education, sometimes suggesting more modest educational problems to be overcome, and occasionally calling into question the value of any and all institutionalized education.

In school narratives, the child's diseased body exemplifies its own characteristic iconography. Unlike the vague crowd of deformed school-boys at Dotheboys Hall, the sick children who occupy center stage in their respective novels not only retain their normative beauty, but are also etherealized, as their illnesses develop, into a rarer, stranger loveliness. Thus, the dying Helen Burns possesses, in moments of intellectual excitement, an elusive and "singular" beauty that the healthy Jane cannot equal (*Jane Eyre* 85). Similarly, the convalescent George Arthur exudes an unearthly, angelic grace, compared to his sturdy friend Tom Brown (*Tom Brown* 307). Louis Mortimer, who falls ill at Dr. Wilkinson's school, exemplifies the rarefied traits that typify the sensitive, diseased schoolboy: a "thin white face," "sunken eyes," and "long white fingers" (*Dashwood Priory* 80). His consumptive cousin, Vernon Digby, appears even more handsome as he sickens, given an illusory vitality by his flashing "lustrous" eye and "hectic" color (*Dashwood* 104). The constitutionally feeble Paul Dombey, who becomes terminally ill at school, is similarly "a pretty little fellow" with "something wan and wistful in his small face" (*Dombey* 91). Even Smike, who enters the scene with some of the grotesque traits typical of the pupils at Dotheboys Hall, is progressively etherealized by the end of the novel, becoming a figure with a "pale face" and a "placid smile" (*Nicholas Nickleby* 782) who dies in a garden dreaming of other ghostly and paradisal gardens.

While the enfeebled child's rarefied beauty signals a lost or jeopardized potential, the fictive invalid also glows with a spiritualized sunset radiance that hints at the proximity of death. Such diseased schoolchildren seem to gravitate toward windows, which bathe them in a mysterious light. Thus, the most consistent iconographic element of the school sickroom is not the medicine bottle but the luminous window, which promises escape from the school's stifling institutionality and the constraining architecture of the mortal body. Paul Dombey experiences his most vivid existence as he peers out of windows at the schools of Mrs. Pipchin and Dr. Blimber. After a school illness, the frail Louis Mortimer begins his recovery in a domesticated school sickroom under the redemptive sign of the window: "Mrs. Wilkinson [the schoolmaster's wife] was sitting by him, and caring most tenderly for all his possible wants. He lay very quietly, gazing out of the window, almost too weak to wonder how he came there" (*Dashwood* 78). In *Tom Brown's Schooldays*, the spiritualized George Arthur exemplifies the iconography of schoolboy illnesses in its most flamboyant form:

> It was evening when the housekeeper summoned [Tom Brown] to the sick-room. Arthur was lying on the sofa by the open window, through which the rays of the western sun stole gently, lighting up his white face and golden hair. Tom remembered a German picture of an angel which he knew; often had he thought how transparent and golden and spirit-like it was; and he shuddered to think how like it Arthur looked, and felt a shock as if his blood had all stopped short, as he realized how near the other world his friend must have been to look like that. Never till that moment had he felt how his little chum had twined himself round his heartstrings; and as he stole gently across the room and knelt down, and put his arm round Arthur's head on the pillow, felt ashamed and half-angry at his own red and brown face, and the bounding sense of health and power which filled every fibre of his body, and made every movement of mere living a joy to him. (*Tom Brown* 307–308)

Arthur's mysterious and terrifying beauty serves as a *memento mori*, inviting Tom to imagine the "strange unknown places" (309) where Arthur's mind wanders during his illness. Further, Arthur's transformation by the refining fire of fever also privileges his repudiation of the abuses of ordinary school life. Expressing a widely held view, Florence Nightingale's *Notes on Nursing* maintains that disease is always a "reparative" process (1). Fictive school illnesses frequently draw on such assumptions, transposing them into the moral realm. In this sense, Arthur's illness is a corrective for the school as a whole, calling Tom and his classmates back to a higher code of conduct; thus, as a result of a heavenly vision on the brink of death, the feverish and inspired Arthur urges Tom, somewhat anticlimactically, to abjure cribs and vulgate books.

Staring out of the sickroom window "as if he couldn't bear to lose a moment of the sunset" (308), Arthur watches the birds soaring, just as Dickens's dying Paul Dombey loves to do. Glimpsing the celestial vista beyond the limited precincts of school, Arthur, again like Paul, is capable of offering a critique of school's deforming customs and customary deformations. Evoking a dyad of loss and possibility, the limitations of the diseased body and the redemptive vistas of the window stage a moral picture that calls readers to reenvision the flawed actualities of school life.

At the same time, this easily read image reveals more ambivalent undertones that emerge when it is contextualized in the narrative syntax of the school novel. First, as I explore in the following section of this chapter, the emphatic presence of the window also evokes the zymotic model of disease, in which illness can frequently be cured by an influx of new air. Because zymosis, in practice, thrives on an identification between illness and the site of illness, the presence of zymotic rhetoric in school novels suggests a deep-seated contagion or corruption that may work against the possibility of cure. Further, Arthur's glamorized and eroticized frail body, when contrasted with Tom's shame about his own "health and power," emphasizes an inverse relation in numerous school narratives between spiritual or intellectual development and healthy growth. This tension, explored in the last section of this chapter, reflects societal assumptions about education's deleterious effects on the child's growing body. Thus, while the rhetoric of zymosis, as it operates in a number of school novels, implicitly links the child's jeopardized body with the fictive setting of the school, assumptions about growth and development forge connections between the body's narrative of growth and the momentum of the fictive narrative unfolding in the school novel.

THE BODY IN THE SCHOOL SICKROOM: ZYMOSIS AND THE SYNTAX OF DISEASE

In *The Birth of the Clinic* (1963), Michel Foucault examines three "spatializations" of disease that characterize medical thought during the latter half of the eighteenth century. In its "primary spatialization," disease exists as a category within "classificatory thought." Its rationalized space is thus the two-dimensional one of the classificatory conceptual "grid." Here, disease serves as a generalized and coherent concept, such as "pleurisy" or "apoplexy," with a characteristic development and symptoms. As an essentialized element within the grid, each disease is clearly comprehensible, visible in all its aspects. Yet disease in this space is also oddly limited and self-contained since, to be read and treated by practitioners, it must be rendered present in its secondary spatialization, the three-dimensional space of the patient's body, which hides the disease concept even as it visibly embodies it in often esoteric or confusing symptoms. Clarity and comprehensiveness are lost in the opacity of the body, which manifests some symptoms as it refuses others. The tertiary spatialization of disease signifies "all the gestures by which, in a given society, a disease is circumscribed, medically invested, isolated, divided up into closed, privileged regions, or distributed throughout cure centers, arranged in the most favorable way" (16). While this tertiary realm of disease is no more "derivative" than the other spaces addressed, it is "to a greater extent than the other forms of spatialization... the locus of various dialectics: heterogeneous figures, time lags, political struggles, demands and utopias, economic constraints, social confrontations" (16).

Foucault's map of disease spatializations is specific to a brief era in eighteenth-century French medicine. The bulk of his analysis, in fact, traces the intellectual transactions whereby such a rigid schema is undermined (though not necessarily erased), by means of complex interactions between concepts of the body and illness. Nevertheless, Foucault's depiction of the tertiary spatialization of disease—as a set of arrangements that situate various social and political dialectics—remains enduringly relevant, and serves as an apt description of the sickroom in a diverse array of English school narratives. Further, Foucault's portrayal of *body* and *sickroom* as spatializations linked within, or by means of, a particularized dynamic of disease usefully reminds us of the myriad ways in which the two sites may interact to shape each other.

Mid-century English depictions of fictive sickrooms offer a rich field for the various social confrontations denominated by Foucault because the sickroom, like the schoolroom, was undergoing a contested process of professionalization and sequestration. In her fascinating work *The Sickroom in Victorian Fiction* (1994), Miriam Bailin suggests that Charlotte Brontë's *Shirley* (1849) draws a firm line between domestic and professional nursing; while familial "nurses" transform the domestic sickroom into a redemptive and consoling community of two, hired nurses like *Shirley's* Mrs. Horsfal, (or for that matter Grace Poole in *Jane Eyre*) are associated with incarceration and abuse.[3] Yet in the 1850s, the decade of Shirley's publication, Florence Nightingale and others were working to raise the status of the professionally trained (and paid) nurse, making *her* the standard for all nursing in and out of the home. In *Notes on Nursing*, Nightingale favorably contrasts the professionally sanitized and monitored environment of the hospital with dangerously unsanitary domestic sickrooms. Similarly, Anna Jameson, writing in 1855, lambastes England for being so far behind the Continent in the training of nurses. From this perspective, *Shirley's* appalling Mrs. Horsfal fails her patient not because she has no domestic or familial relation to him, but rather because she lacks professional training.

Thus, Anna Jameson does not regard Brontë's novel as hostile to professional nurses; instead, she quotes extensively from it, citing Caroline Helstone's meditation on women's need for useful work in order to justify training women for the nursing profession.[4]

At the same time, however, both Nightingale and Jameson express ambivalence about a thorough professionalization of nursing and medical care. During the long and mysterious illness that followed her legendary efforts in the Crimea, Nightingale herself chose to be nursed by friends and family members such as her Aunt Mai in her own domestic sickroom. Both Nightingale and Jameson also envision the ideal nurse as professionally trained but nevertheless neither independent nor professional in the generally accepted sense. Rather, the nurse should be a nunlike figure, a sister of mercy, whose conduct is rigorously monitored and whose life is one of womanly devotion and self-sacrifice. Thus, even as the sickroom is being reenvisioned as a more public, professionalized, and regulated space, it clearly encounters the same ambivalence that we have previously located in similar depictions of an emerging school space.

Understandably, then, in novels of education, the school sickroom is a particularly fraught and conflicted space; as it houses and struggles to resolve the vital conflict within the patient's diseased body, it also foregrounds the domestic and institutional hybridity that permeates the school as a whole. If the prime conflict within the societal tertiary spatialization is that between domestic and institutional means of cure, the conflict foregrounded by the fictive disease is frequently depicted as a struggle between the growing body and the developing mind. Because school, with its institutional and professionalizing agenda, has overdeveloped the mind, only a redemptive domestic space can restore the body once illness strikes. As Jack Zipes contends, parents, and adults in general, "engage social and political forces on the battlefield of children's bodies and minds." Ironically, however, like the headmaster Thomas Arnold lamenting the dangers of school, adults find themselves expressing misgivings about the disciplinary methods and structures that they themselves have helped to create: "We desperately want to save our children from the future we have planned for them" (*Sticks and Stones* xii). Embodying adult ambivalence, school fictions cast the child invalid's body as a battleground on which institutional and domestic ideologies contend, sometimes with hopeful, and sometimes with deadly results. The school sickroom represents a last chance for parents and schoolmasters to collaborate to save children from the very curricula that they have instituted.

Bailin emphasizes the unspecified nature of fictive illnesses, regarding novelists' resort to such vague diseases as an artistic license to focus on the curative and reassuring nature of the sickroom: "the conditions of illness remain reassuringly vague, merely the occasion for the benefits they elicit and the desires they legitimate" (7). While Bailin is undoubtedly correct, the vague and fluid portrait of disease that she identifies enjoyed a wider cultural play than she indicates here; it extended beyond the parameters of the novel and into the realm of popular medical literature. Arguably, the contemporary zymotic model of disease, which opposed emerging germ theory, not only enabled such a reassuringly vague vision of illness, but also, to a degree, entailed it.

In her *Notes on Nursing*, Florence Nightingale articulates the widespread and well-established zymotic view that illness is the result of *effluvia*, an organic residue of all living things, which lethally collects in the close and cramped spaces of houses, hospitals, and schools. Thus, it is no less accurate to speak of a "diseased house" than a "diseased patient," and may in fact be a more precise statement of the problem. Nightingale devotes a chapter to the "Health of Houses," including a jeremiad against the ill-constructed, unsanitary houses that cause whole "families [to] die off" (17). The great evil at the heart of the ill-constructed or poorly managed house is the "foul air" (21) that stagnates in its dark, cramped, and ill-ventilated rooms: "Once insure that the air in a house is stagnant," Nightingale warns, "and sickness is sure to follow" (17).

According to Eric Hopkins (1994), "it was not until the 1860s... that the transmission of disease by germs became understood, it being thought that illness could be caught through mysterious miasmas" (115). Before that time, zymosis could accommodate the phenomenon of contagion in two ways. Contagion could be viewed generally as the effect of noxious exhalations of the patient's body. Or it could be seen, as it was by Nightingale, as a phenomenon more apparent than real, the product of an unhealthy atmosphere that exercised a similarly toxic influence on all its inmates. In its famous depiction of fever at school, Brontë's *Jane Eyre* implicitly invokes a zymotic model of contagion. The fever at Lowood results, in large part, from the unhealthy air of its location because the "forest-dell, where Lowood lay, was the cradle of fog and fog-bred pestilence" (89). Similarly, as disease festers in the crowded school buildings, its "rooms and passages" fill with "the effluvia of mortality" (90).

Thus, according to the zymotic model of illness, which Nightingale so enthusiastically endorses, the work of healing is to cure, through sanitary measures, not only the patient himself but the space around him. Nightingale endorses a stringent system of ventilation, dependent on perpetually open windows, chimney flues, and strategically closed doors, as well as the use of Dr. Angus Smith's "air test," which measures the level of "organic matter" in the air.[5] Curing an unhealthy house is largely a work of aerating it, of introducing fresh air in order to purify its stagnant atmosphere.

Paradoxically, then, and in contrast to the basic assumptions of germ theory, the sickroom, properly ventilated and sanitized, may in fact be the healthiest room in an unhealthy house. As Nightingale laments, "With regard to the health of houses where there is a sick person, it often happens that the sick room is made a ventilating shaft for the rest of the house" (22). Full of the unhealthy effluvia of crowded and bustling life, the house releases its toxins into the healthy, airy sickroom, with its purer atmosphere and mandatory open windows. The sickroom door must be closed, Nightingale argues, not to spare the house from its contagion, but rather to maintain its own purity within an unhealthy house.

Widespread concerns about the proper ventilation of houses took on a heightened intensity when schools were being discussed, as testified by numerous texts on school ventilation from the latter half of the nineteenth century to the beginning of the twentieth.[6] In his *School Architecture*, E. R. Robson, the official architect for the London board schools, affirms: "If the freshness and purity of the air breathed by older persons has an important bearing on health… how much more in the case of a child kept long in a schoolroom with many others" (265). Because human exhalations were held to be particularly harmful, experts attempted to quantify insofar as possible, exact amounts of the "foul gases, animal exhalations, and the impurities mingled with air by the process of respiration" (261). Robson quotes a German authority who argues that "each body emits, in the process of breathing two-thirds of a cubic foot… of carbonic acid gas every hour" (265–266). One American, writing soon after the turn of the century, warns: "Children in the primary school classes need at least two thousand cubic feet of fresh air each hour, [while] those in the upper grades" need at least "two thousand five hundred cubic feet" (Dresslar 136). Particularly strong in Germany, France, and England, the movement for open-air schools attempted to document that children instructed out of doors, even in winter, gained weight and showed a higher rate of hemoglobin in their blood (178). Open air schools were thought to be especially helpful for tubercular children, a fact that has particular bearing on school narratives because so many attribute at least some consumptive symptoms to the diseased school child.

While it faded gradually throughout the latter half of the century, the zymotic model of disease continued to undermine the notion that diseases could be classified and categorized as distinct entities. In the words of Florence Nightingale, "Diseases are not individuals arranged in classes, like cats and dogs, but conditions growing out of one another." For Nightingale, diseases are not "separate entities, which *must* exist." Rather they partake of both spontaneous generation and a mysterious mutability that allows one type of disease to transform itself into another. "I have seen," Nightingale writes, "diseases begin, grow up, and pass into one another." Rather than entities, then, diseases are "conditions." Nightingale clearly associates the fear of infection with "ignorant women," while the increasing influence of medical theories of contagion is attributed by implication to wrongheaded "scientific men." Instead, as zymosis explains, diseases are simply the body's flexible and various response to diverse "poisons" and unhealthy conditions, whether bad air, dust, cold, damp, or mental and bodily strain. "For diseases," Nightingale concludes, "as all experience shows, are adjectives, not noun substantives."[7]

It is not my contention, of course, that mid-century novelists, and writers of school novels in particular, were all avid devotees of zymosis. Rather, as a gripping cultural image, the restorative sickroom—poised so movingly between life and death, loss and restitution, terror and hope—carried within it conservative iconic elements, aspects that typified and named it. Even after the triumph of germ theory, writers continued to offer readers the icon of the zymotic sickroom, in which disease is portrayed not as a contagious entity capable of classification, but rather as an elusive "coloration" taken by the overstrained body. In the 1840s and 1850s, of course, images of the zymotic sickroom still carried medical sanction.

Thus, the zymotic paradigm of disease has particular bearing on interactions between institutional and domestic space. As the school novel ignores precise classifications and categories of disease, emphasizing instead the etiology of the unhealthy house, disease moves from one three-dimensional space to another, by means of the body's illuminating manifestations. One diseased locus is healed by another curative space, as the *unhealthy school* is correctively replaced by the sanitary *domesticated sickroom*. Each space is a mirror image—an inverted emblem—of the other. Both the locus of similar dialectics, school and sickroom mimic each other, as both practice on the pupil's mind and body, in shifting and overlapping realms of institutional and domestic space. Foregrounding the struggle between these realms, the sickroom paradoxically brings them together, or to rephrase the matter, it attempts to cure such a spatial disjunction with a new spatial harmony. In the syntax of the school story, illness is the "adjective" that literally modifies or alters a "noun substantive" that is conceived as both the student/patient's body and the school space that contains it.

In Martineau's *The Crofton Boys*, Hugh Proctor is "cured" of both a physical wound and a moral flaw—his reckless impulsiveness—by the amputation of his injured foot, carried out in the school sickroom. But as the physician performs his grim operation, Hugh's mother enters the sickroom to nurse her son, both physically and morally, back to health. Her moral injunctions thus complete the cure begun by the school's physician, reconfiguring the sickroom as a forced harmony of domestic and institutional space. Subsequently, Hugh's sojourn in the school sickroom is followed by a retreat to the domestic sickroom of his uncle's house, where he is nursed and cheered by his visiting sister before he can return, renewed and strengthened, to school.

In *Tom Brown's Schooldays*, George Arthur's illness follows a similar pattern. Arthur's "quiet and loving" mother (321) takes up residence in the school sickroom in order to calm and soothe her son, who in contrast to Hugh, suffers not from an excess of animal spirits, but rather from a dangerous sensitivity associated with his premature spiritual and intellectual development. Entering the sickroom with a candle to find her son engaged in an intensely spiritual conversation with Tom Brown, she warns him away from further excitement: "My dearest boy, you feel a little feverish again. Why didn't you have lights? You've talked too much, and excited yourself in the dark" (320). Driving away the terrifying darkness that we will see enclosing Paul Dombey, who has no mother to nurse him, Arthur's mother, like Hugh's, domesticates the school sickroom before carrying her son home for the lengthy rest cure that will enable him to return, physically renewed, to school. Casting his sickness in zymotic terms, Arthur himself describes the process: "I shall most likely have to go home for a change of air to get well" (311).

Of necessity, then, the school sickroom achieves a shifting and precarious harmony of institutional and domestic space, dialectically regulating the claims of mind and body, school and home, adult agendas and childish capabilities. In contrast, the flaws of the failed school sickroom are encapsulated in Smike's skeleton description of a schoolboy's death at Dotheboys Hall: "I was with him at night, and when it was all silent he cried no more for friends he wished to come and sit with him, but began to see faces round his bed that came from home; he said they smiled, and talked to him; and he died at last lifting his head to kiss them" (*Nicholas Nickleby* 97). As the dying boy embraces the familial phantoms he has conjured, his sickroom's failure to reintegrate domestic space is glaringly illuminated. The school sickrooms in *Dombey and Son* and *Jane Eyre* similarly fail to reintegrate the domestic and institutional projects—or perhaps more accurately, they move toward such an integration too late. Paul Dombey and Helen Burns function as narrative scapegoats whose destruction elevates, and in part cures, those around them. Paul humanizes the Blimbers, while the dying Helen instructs and inspires Jane with her domesticated vision of heaven.

Similarly, as we shall see, Paul's illness allows Blimber's academy to temporarily reformulate itself as a familial group, while the death of Helen, along with the illness of her fellow students, reveals the unhealthiness of Lowood and spurs its restoration to "health" under more domestic management. The prelude to such a restoration, of course, is the terrifying conversion of Lowood into a fever hospital, a narrative turn that aligns Brocklehurstian institutionality with Carlyle's house of "incurables." Tellingly, the corrective domestication of school space that results from the school illnesses of Paul Dombey and Helen Burns leaves them isolated from family ties. Paul's school sickroom, where the unpleasant teacher Mrs. Pipchin presides as nurse, never opens to include his maternal sister Florence, who passionately avows her desire to nurse her brother, and finally assumes the role too late when her brother returns home to die. Similarly, Helen's remarried father, who seems at times as distant as the heavenly father she longs to embrace, never appears to succor her. Without a renegotiation of the provinces of school and home, no cure is possible for the diseased child.

The lesson is clear, and recapitulates, in symbolic form, the paradigm of zymosis. The recovery of sick pupils like Hugh and Arthur suggests that their schools are largely healthy and sound, though perhaps in need of some minor adjustments. Arthur's illness is particularly interesting in this regard because it exemplifies a mutual transaction between school and sickroom. While Arthur's sickroom vision purifies and ultimately strengthens school morality, inspiring a new, more rigorous moral code, Arthur's frail constitution has also been strengthened by the demands of school life. As he exults to his friend Tom, "our old medical man… said my constitution was quite changed, and that I'm fit for anything now. If it hadn't I couldn't have stood three days of this illness. That's all thanks to you, and the games you've made me fond of" (*Tom Brown's Schooldays* 315). As we have seen in previous chapters, the standardized methods of the new regulated school and the domestic instruction practiced at home have an inverse and compensatory relation, antidoting and correcting each other. Similarly, the natural physical education of the schoolyard, with its rough games and free play, strengthens the body, antidoting the intellectual overstimulation that subtly corrupts schoolchildren's constitutions and results in sequestration in the sickroom. Thus, Arthur's illness ultimately strengthens the school, as school life has already strengthened his constitution. In contrast to Brocklehurst's Lowood, Thomas Hughes's fictive Rugby ultimately fulfills Newman's idealistic vision of an educational institution as a curative hospital. In this context, the school sickroom may be seen as both a last resort and a final opportunity to regulate the conflicting claims that have caused the child's body, as well as the collective community of the school, to fall ill. Popular schoolboy novels such as *Tom Brown* are, of course, particularly committed to alleviating societal concerns with such reassuring reconciliations.

In stark contrast to the cures achieved at Crofton and Rugby, the deaths of Paul Dombey, Helen Burns, and the unnamed boy in Smike's harrowing story confirm that their schools are indeed "sick," are in fact unhealthy houses in Nightingale's sense. While *Nicholas Nickleby* and *Jane Eyre* suggest that specific educational abuses can be eradicated, the first by wholeheartedly punishing Squeers and the second by providing a corrected version of Lowood, *Dombey and Son*, as we shall see, conducts an all-out attack on institutional education, portraying, in its lethal impact on Paul's frail body, a materialistic society's self-deception about its educational goals and methods. Similarly, E. J. May's *Dashwood Priory* suggests that while institutional education may be a necessary evil, it must nevertheless be regarded with extreme suspicion as a dangerous threat to children's growth and health.

THE BODY AND NARRATIVE: PARABLES OF DEVELOPMENT AND GROWTH

While schools could be considered dangerous places for a variety of reasons, Herbert Spencer eloquently expresses his era's widespread concerns about the mental and physical strain produced specifically by "undue study" at school. In *Education: Intellectual, Moral and Physical* (1861), Spencer "factually" delineates many of the negative outcomes of education that also fill the pages of school novels:

> Go where you will, and before long there come under your notice cases of children, or youths, of either sex, more or less injured by undue study. Here, to recover from a state of debility thus produced, a year's rustication has been found necessary. There you find a chronic congestion of the brain, that has already lasted many months, and threatens to last much longer. Now you hear of a fever that resulted from the over-excitement in some way

brought on at school. And, again, the instance is that of a youth who has already had once to desist from his studies, and who, since he has returned to them, is frequently taken out of his class in a fainting fit. We state facts. (*Education* 261)

To be sure, Spencer's observations evoke a long tradition of suspicions provoked by education's dangerous "overstimulation" of the brain. In 1621, Robert Burton not only delighted in depicting the many forms of melancholy madness that tormented "sedentary, solitary" scholars as a result of "overmuch study" (260); he also complained that "tyrannical, impatient, hare-brain Schoolmasters, dry-as-dusts," are "as bad as hangmen and executioners" and "make many children endure a martyrdom" (284–285). More than a century later, Rousseau famously warned the too-ambitious schoolmaster to stay his hand: "Apparent facility of learning," he announced sweepingly in *Émile* (1762) "is the cause of children's ruin" (107). Like many of his contemporaries, however, Spencer is troubled by the allegedly progressive intellectualization of life that Victorians both celebrated and feared as the "march of mind." Thus, he sees the debilities associated with overeducation as a distinctively modern problem, resulting from modernity's "unnatural" educational demands:

Old and young, the pressure of modern life puts [on all age-groups] a still-increasing strain. In all businesses and professions, intenser competition taxes the energies and abilities of every adult.... Fathers... are all the year round obliged to work early and late.... The constitutions, shaken by this long continued over-application, they bequeath to their children. And then these comparatively feeble children, predisposed as they are to break down even under an ordinary strain upon their energies, are required to go through a *curriculum* much more extended than that prescribed for the unenfeebled children of past generations. (*Education* 260–261)

In Spencer's argument, modernity and overeducation are linked with the specter of a "physical degeneracy" (280) that expresses itself in moral and intellectual decay, in "morbid feelings" (272) and "stupidity" (266). A dangerous and volatile "heredity," characteristic of medical and social thought in the latter half of the century,[8] stands at the center of Spencer's portrait of a regressive mental and physical devolution, which ironically seems the inevitable accompaniment of the progressive "march of mind." As civilization enters a highly developed phase in which intellectual activities predominate, the compromised body takes its own revenge; the fathers who have sacrificed their vital powers to mental overstimulation generate an enfeebled progeny. Spencer's concerns about physically impaired fathers have their counterpart in medical warnings about the barrenness of overcivilized women. According to Sally Shuttleworth: "Early nineteenth-century [medical] accounts" contrast "the seeming fertility and lack of labor pains of 'primitive' females" with the infertility and suffering of "their diseased, 'civilized' counterparts.... Woman's 'mission' is to try and suppress all mental life so that the self-regulating processes of her animal economy can proceed in peace."[9]

As Michel Foucault emphasizes in *Madness and Civilization* (1961), the intellectual overstimulation that allegedly triggered mental collapse was increasingly envisioned, in the eighteenth and nineteenth centuries, as a criminal and willful abuse. Those who indulged themselves in the "abuse of things that were not natural, the sedentary life of cities, novel reading, theatergoing, immoderate thirst for knowledge" were responsible for their own sufferings. The "passions and imaginations one had cultivated too complacently—all combined in the irritation of the nerves, finding there both their natural effect and their moral punishment" (157). In keeping with this new moralized reading of mental collapse, Spencer insists, "all breaches of the laws of health are *physical sins*" (*Education* 283), not only against the individual body but also against its future offspring. The excessive intellectual activity that both its perpetrators and victims justify as a rigorous devotion to learning can be both "vicious" and, from the perspective of its effects on future generations, "criminal."[10] The forcing of children's intellects into a premature bloom thus becomes a crime on the part of the too-ambitious schoolmaster, to be treated with a high degree of seriousness in novels of education as well as in nonfictional educational discourse; at the same time, as Burton suggested two centuries earlier, its child-victims are to be seen as martyrs to a morally flawed educational system.

As we have seen in novels of childhood education, the sensitive, spiritualized child is often the first target of the school epidemic; thus, illness can become an indicator of spiritual and intellectual development. Sensitive and diseased children like Paul Dombey, Helen Burns, and George Arthur serve as interpreters and oracles of the moral illnesses and redemptive possibilities of their respective societies. Their very vulnerabilities allow them a diagnostic and revelatory function, granting them, in a qualified sense, the right to speak as moral "physician" as well as patient. Constitutionally frail and physically enfeebled, these wise and haggard children appear to have developed their intellectual and moral powers at the expense of the body. Though they must either die or be strenuously regenerated, they also serve to articulate and define the novel's intellectual and moral world for the more vital but less developed protagonists who ultimately carry a greater promise of growth.

Spencer articulates a similar cultural dilemma by opposing growth and development as specifically distinct concepts, arguing that each serves to enfeeble the other:

> It is a physiological law,... that there is an antagonism between growth and development. By growth, as used in this antithetical sense, is to be understood increase of size; by development, increase of structure. And the law is, that great activity in either of these processes involves retardation or arrest of the other. (271)

Spencer grounds his argument in specific instances drawn from his understanding of the natural sciences of his day. While a caterpillar grows quickly, he argues, it makes no development in structural complexity. Once in its chrysalis form, it shows a remarkable development in structural complexity, but no growth in size. The human brain is governed by the same law; excessive study in youth, Spencer speculates, stimulates a structural development that ultimately impairs overall brain growth. Spencer's "physiological law" extends metaphorically into the realm of intellectual and moral life. An overly complex sensibility, particularly when developed too young, impedes growth toward maturity and an independent adult life.

In a similar way, school novels set up oppositions between the premature development of a complex sensibility and the vital energy needed for growth. While Jane Eyre has the greater potential for growth—and while Brontë's novel endorses growth by focusing on her—Helen Burns clearly has the advantage in her development in the intellectual and moral realm. Arguably, then, the novel makes use of Helen's development to foster Jane's growth, as Helen's uncanny adult wisdom tempers Jane's impetuous energies. In the same vein, though with more positive results, George Arthur's spiritual development refines Tom Brown's extreme vitality and is correctively tempered by Tom's rich potential for growth. The tension between development and growth energizes and shapes the school story, fostering an ambivalence that idealizes the seductions of overeducation, while it wards off or contains the attendant brain fever, mental collapse, or physical degeneracy that may jeopardize growth toward a mature independence.

While novelistic depictions of school illnesses clearly serve varied purposes and evoke a rich range of emotional tones, some common denominators emerge. As we have seen, even school novels like *Tom*

Brown's Schooldays, which seem to celebrate their particular brand of schooling, often reveal and strive to alleviate fears about overeducation, and institutional education in general, through their depictions of school illnesses and the school sickroom. E. J. May's *Dashwood Priory, or Mortimer's College Life* and Dickens's *Dombey and Son* ring fascinating, if somewhat ominous, variations on the school parable of development and growth, illustrating how precarious and elusive the balance between Spencer's oppositional polarities can become. Today relatively forgotten, *Dashwood Priory* vividly dramatizes the dangerous lure of a highly intellectual school regimen; the narrative saves one of its two intellectually driven protagonists from death-by-learning, while the other tragically succumbs. Like a number of school novels, May's tale risks romanticizing the morbidly developed, etherealized characters who suffer the results of their own mental overstimulation, then draws back to affirm the more "wholesome" pleasures of growth. *Dombey and Son* delineates two negative and complementary consequences of undue study emphasized in both non-fictional and fictive educational discourse: (1) physical wasting and eventual death, and (2) mental wasting and the death of the mind. The first danger is exemplified in the case of the frail, physically doomed Paul Dombey, who suffers from a precocious mental development; the second is illustrated by his fellow student, Toots, who degenerates into imbecility after excessive study, while remaining physically healthy and therefore capable of growth.

Just as Hugh Proctor, *The Crofton Boys'* hardy and reckless protagonist, prefigures the famous hero of *Tom Brown's Schooldays*, so E. J. May's Louis Mortimer is a literary precursor of Tom Brown's spiritualized and frail friend George Arthur, whose gentle example subtly elevates the moral tone of his raucous schoolfellows. George Arthur's brief illness seems little more than the occasion for his dream vision of Heaven, which regenerates his friend Tom, saving him from the use of vulgates and cribs; in contrast, Louis's illness is far more extensively treated. Along with the wasting consumption of his cousin Vernon Digby, Louis's debilitating disease constitutes a major lynchpin of the novel's plot of *bildung* as spiritual development. Even more than *Tom Brown's Schooldays*, May's evangelical novel is designed to instruct and regenerate its readers, just as Louis, the pious Methodist schoolboy, regenerates and instructs his classmates. Like Thomas Hughes, May occasionally interrupts her narrative to preach to readers, to remind them of truths they may have forgotten, or to underline some moral lesson that the narrative has just dramatized. Like George Arthur's fever, Louis's wasting illness leads the sufferer to new spiritual revelations, and also confirms his sterling worth to his sometimes skeptical fellow students.

Louis's disease incorporates elements of the zymotic model because it makes visible the toxic atmosphere that has remained latent in Dr. Wilkinson's unhealthy house. As May writes, Louis's rigorous studies are "too much for his strength." His "unceasing routine at last brought its attendant train of weariness, languor, violent headaches, and sleepless nights" (*Dashwood Priory* 75). Louis's overstrained nerves manifest themselves in a series of fainting spells and "fits," temporarily alleviated by exposure to a pure outdoor air. Experiencing his first spell of faintness as he reads over his assigned translation of Sophocles, Louis declares desperately, "Air,—I want air." He does indeed revive in the "open air," and a school friend underlines the lesson. Emphasizing that Louis needs more of "Heaven's breezes" (76), Louis's classmate associates the fresh outdoor atmosphere with both the natural world and the spiritual realm, in contrast to the unnatural demands of the schoolroom. Although the determined Louis apparently recovers enough to submit himself once again to the rigors of schoolwork, his reentrance into the schoolroom proves lethal. When he attempts to read, "the same misty swimming of the head" returns, and he falls "insensible on the floor," only reviving when he is carried to the "open window" (77).

Louis's dramatic collapse in the schoolroom inspires his schoolmaster to recognize his own implicit culpability for his pupil's mental overstrain: "Poor fellow!" Wilkinson laments. "I ought to have guarded against this; he is quite overdone" (77). Louis's cure is effected by a withdrawal from the schoolroom's unhealthy atmosphere, his exposure to invigorating outdoor air, and his re-situation in a realm of domestic space. As a visiting physician explains to the pale and prostrated boy "You must put by Latin and Greek.... I shall order the very acceptable prescription of home for you" (79). Removed first to Wilkinson's drawing room, Louis experiences another fit so extreme that the doctor fears for his life. Louis must be further isolated within a domesticated sickroom, "a light and prettily furnished room on a cheerful side of the [schoolmaster's] house, away from all noise.... His weakness was so excessive that a sudden noise would bring on a fainting fit" (79). When his parents arrive to further domesticate Louis's sickroom, the news is "almost too much for him" (80). He improves slightly, however, after his parents remove him to pleasant lodgings where he can receive "daily airings" (80). Ultimately, Louis's cure is completed during his months in a cottage in Torquay, where he is wheeled in a bath chair to breathe in the invigorating sea air.

Like the tubercular convalescents who allegedly progressed better in open-air schools, Louis is rescued, ultimately, by his withdrawal from what Robson would later describe as a "vitiated or overheated" school "atmosphere" that negatively "affects the whole" of "general health" (266). Freed from Dr. Wilkinson's academy, Louis thrives, both literally and metaphorically, physically and morally, on a more sustaining air unpolluted by the intellectual hothouse. Thus, according to the logic of May's narrative, Louis's prudent parents save his life, not only by promptly removing him from school, but by forestalling his return there. Although, after months of convalescence, Louis is pronounced fit to return either "to home or school, whenever he pleased" (99–100), his parents choose to bring him home. As May emphasizes, "School was not to be thought of again" (100). Louis now studies at home with his brother Neville, whose domestic education has rendered him "quite [Louis's] equal" (104). School's dangerous demands are in fact easily dispensed with. As May informs us approvingly: "Louis's own studies were now very easy. Mr. Mortimer was not ambitious for any of his children, and only desired that Louis should be sufficiently prepared for the ministry of the Church" (104).

Louis's sensible parents, who value a "natural" and "spiritual" development (the two terms are largely equated in May's narrative, while supposedly unnatural societal demands are linked with an anti-spiritual outlook) stand in contrast to the parents of his cousin Vernon Digby, who foolishly urge their son to excel in intellectual pursuits unsuited to his frail constitution. After falling ill as a result of his impulsive tendency to push himself too hard both physically and mentally, Vernon also retreats to Torquay, where he, Louis, and their mothers enjoy a domestic idyll in the valley of the shadow. With his greater spiritual wisdom, Louis meekly submits himself to a life of physical and intellectual passivity; in contrast, the ambitious Vernon, intellectually "superior" to Louis (88), chafes at his confinement to the domestic sickroom and exults in his prospective intellectual triumphs at school. Louis solicitously wonders, "Do you not, dear Vernon, make a god of intellectual enjoyment?" (90). While Louis basks in "heaven's breezes" and submits the means of his cure to nature and God, Vernon reveals his distorted perspective by envisioning heaven as merely a "wide expanse of immeasurable thought" (88).

While Louis retires to his home to complete his moderate studies, the overambitious Vernon insists on returning to Cambridge too soon, where he attains "the summit of his collegiate desires, being proclaimed senior wrangler, first gold medallist, and first Smith's prize-man" (101–102). Although the ceremony at which Vernon receives his gold medal is "a grand scene" that inspires him with "visions of future greatness" (105), May emphasizes that it is, tragically, simply the climax of Vernon's intellectual fever: "His strength was unequal to the ordeal imposed on his excitable frame. He did not know it himself"(105). While his proud parents fail to see "the hectic spot" on his cheek and the feverish "fire of his lustrous gray eyes" (104), Vernon has been effectually doomed by his return to Cambridge, just as Louis earlier brought on a life-threatening fit by returning too soon to Dr. Wilkinson's schoolroom. In a scene heavy with irony, Vernon arrives at his family's house for a coming-of-age party that in fact signals only the coming of death. His overhopeful grandfather comforts himself that Vernon will triumph over the dangers of intellectual "precocity": "he was never forced, sir.... The danger, sir, is forcing the intellect" (108). Soon after the old man's pronouncement, Vernon's illness escalates; he coughs blood and retreats, too late, to a sickroom he will never leave.

The strikingly similar etiology and development of Louis's and Vernon's diseases (both cases involve consumptive symptoms) along with their glaringly different outcomes, dramatizes the dangers of school's intellectual demands. Vernon, far more than the subdued Louis, is an eloquent, brilliant, and charismatic figure; arguably, by sacrificing this seductive embodiment of precocious intellectual development, just on the verge of his coming of age, the narrative clears a field for Louis's healthy growth. Pursuing a more moderate course of studies at Oxford, Louis eventually obtains a parish and plans marriage. Dedicated to improving and instructing the poorer members of his flock, Louis now "establishe[s] a kind of little lecture or schoolroom in each court where a vacant room could be found, and endeavour[s] to rouse the poor ignorant miserable ones to something better" (343). For May, the schoolroom now takes its proper place as a locus of moral uplift and traditional class paternalism rather than as an unhealthy and unsettling breeding ground for feverish intellectual exercises.

It is interesting that a writer so deeply suspicious of school life should have devoted herself, as May did, to the school novel.[11] Like Martineau in *The Crofton Boys*, she seems to have found the schoolboy's progress toward maturity an apt embodiment of the Christian soul's struggle toward a spiritual union with God. From this perspective, trial-by-school is perhaps a necessary evil, and depictions of institutionalized education's flaws and dangers take on a vital and compelling energy. In May's moralized pageant of growth, Vernon's seductive intellectual development is a more advanced case of the disease that infects Louis, imperiling his life, before he is blessedly healed. Yet strikingly, the devout May employs an anti-educational rhetoric similar to that of Herbert Spencer, the freethinking disciple of evolutionary progress. Different as they are, both writers participate in the widespread reaction against institutionalized education and its growing dominance over domestic and quasi-domestic arrangements.

May's depiction of Louis's cure conventionally valorizes the schoolboy's growth over his development. In contrast, Dickens's *Dombey and Son* depicts schools that problematize and compromise both of the Spencerian polarities, offering us not only Paul Dombey's precocious and doomed development, but also his classmate Toots's mindless and perhaps equally unsatisfactory growth. True, Toots does survive as an endearing eccentric to be rewarded eventually by a consolatory marriage to the sharp-tongued but motherly Susan Nipper. Nevertheless, the portrait of school life is a bleak one, evoking Carlyle's "Hospital of Incurables" (*Sartor Resartus* 90), who are made ill by their allegedly ameliorative institution.

As the dying Paul Dombey leaves the educational forcing house known as Dr. Blimber's academy, he moves from a brilliantly lighted interior scene, almost garishly luminous, into the darkness of a waiting coach. Leaving behind a vulnerable visibility, he embarks on a trajectory toward a vanishing point cloaked in distance and darkness. Inside the school, Paul is the object of all eyes. As his teachers and fellow pupils shout their goodbyes, their faces appear:

> all piled and heaped up, as faces are at crowded theatres. They swam before him… like faces in an agitated glass…. From that time, whenever he thought of Doctor Blimber's, it came back to him as he had seen it in this last view; and it never seemed to be a real place again, but always a dream, full of eyes. (204)

The hungry eyes that gaze on Paul as he makes his final exit from Blimber's "theatre" are plausibly read not only as a consoling dream of community, embodying the familial love that Paul had longed for throughout his stay at school, but also as a nightmare of vigilant expectation, never fulfilled; for the members of Blimber's family are always watching Paul, marveling at his oddness, and striving strenuously to "bring him quickly forward" to a destination he never achieves (146). In the logic of Dickens's mixed, or doubled, image, Paul's extreme visibility evokes both his desire and its terrible consummation, his willingness to give himself to the school's agenda, and its hungry appropriation of his body and will to its own ends.

But Dickens chooses not to end the scene on this resonant note, attaching to it one final unexpected moment, staged as an epilogue and an anticlimax:

> This was not quite the last of Doctor Blimber's, however. There was something else. There was Mr. Toots. Who, unexpectedly letting down one of the coach-windows, and looking in, said, with a most egregious chuckle, "Is Dombey there?" and immediately put it up again, without waiting for an answer. Nor was this quite the last of Mr. Toots, even; for before the coachman could drive off, he as suddenly let down the other window, and looking in with a precisely similar chuckle, said in a precisely similar tone of voice, "Is Dombey there?" and disappeared precisely as before. (204)

Toots's repeated question—"Is Dombey there?"—sends both Paul and Florence into hilarious, and perhaps slightly hysterical, laughter. Yet Toots's clownish question is, of course, prophetic. Unlike the other members of Blimber's establishment, Toots glimpses what has become the central fact of Paul's existence at school—his progressive disappearance. As the school's lighted interior becomes a "dream of eyes" that cannot see, the vacant-eyed Toots penetrates the reality of Paul's enshrouding darkness with an absurd question and a bleak "egregious" chuckle. Because of his coercive education, the once promising Toots is now a hollow man; as Dickens emphasizes, his now extinguished "ideas" lack even the qualified existence of "ghosts" (166), imbuing his feeble presence with a phantomlike sense of loss. The scene evokes the strange communion that binds Paul and the hulking, broad-shouldered Toots. Throughout Paul's stay at Blimber's, his fragmented conversations with Toots—masterpieces of disjunction and incoherence, litanies of odd questions and stranger answers—typify their shared, if unspoken, victimhood. Their communication is less a matter of words than of gestural and formal acknowledgments of a shared plight, an intimacy of phantoms.

Like a number of good-hearted, intellectually damaged Dickensian characters, Toots succumbs to mental vacancy as a result of the suffering and strain caused by cruel adult caretakers. *Nicholas Nickleby's* Smike, the victim of long years of abuse at school, suffers from an "addled brain" and at nineteen, puzzles over a page of text that "a child of nine" could master (143–144). *Little Dorrit's* Maggie and David Copperfield's Mr. Dick have the minds of children, at least partly as a result of fevers associated with physical suffering and prolonged mental and emotional strain. Across the Atlantic, Alcott's *Little Men* (1871) portrays a similar figure, the tragic schoolboy Billy Ward. Once "an unusually intelligent boy," he has been prematurely schooled by his ambitious father, expected to "absorb knowledge as a Strasburg goose does the food crammed down its throat" (23). His father's intellectual forcing results in a fever that nearly kills Billy and also destroys his intellect. Like Billy's, Toots's mental collapse is triggered, not just by generalized emotional abuse, but rather by the intellectual pressure of the school forcing house. When paired with Paul, his eerily apt complement and fellow victim, the sometimes comic Toots becomes part of a more sweeping educational critique.

Both Paul and Toots are casualties of the educational forcing house according to the weaknesses of their constitutions; Paul is burdened with an "old" mind (or, as the Blimbers insist, an "old-fashioned mind") in a stunted body, while Toots houses a child's mind in the healthy body of a man. Two extreme consequences of overeducation, Paul's morbid development and Toots's mindless growth collide in an educational standstill. Blimber unwittingly announces his pedagogical failures when he identifies Paul and Toots as his school's "Alpha and Omega," its "beginning" and "end" (147). To find a young male protagonist capable of carrying on the novelistic work of *bildung* (Florence, like so many of Dickens's child-heroines, is exempt from *bildung* since she is born with a full complement of womanly virtues), readers must look beyond the precincts of school to the energetic Walter Gay, who learns his lessons about life in his uncle's shop, Mr. Dombey's office, and on the streets of London.

In the words of Herbert Spencer, "a forced development of intelligence in childhood entails disastrous results—either physical feebleness, or ultimate stupidity, or early death" (*Education* 266). *Dombey and Son* enacts these diverse consequences, assigning physical feebleness and early death to the precocious Paul Dombey, and "ultimate stupidity," or a forced imbecility, to the physically vital but mentally ruined Toots. In their drastically different ways, both boys expose the perverted school regimen of Dr. Blimber, who perpetrates his Spencerian sins against the body not through Squeers's malice, but rather out of a combination of ineptitude and ambition.

Repeatedly, Blimber's school is depicted as an unacknowledged sickroom, an unhealthy house where no cure can be attempted because the disease flourishes, unrecognized, in the school's toxic atmosphere. The schoolroom, when Paul enters it for the first time, houses "eight young gentlemen in various stages of mental prostration" (153). Two "very feverish" pupils grapple with mathematical problems, while another has sunk into "a state of stupefaction" accompanied by characteristic symptoms; the boy's body is "flabby and quite cold" (153). Similarly, the pupils who share Paul's bedroom exhibit the mental distress and intellectual overstimulation that presage school illness. One babbles Latin and Greek in his sleep, while another is "ridden by his lesson as a nightmare" (159). In the ironic imagery of disease that permeates Paul's introduction to the school, even the unimpressionable Mr. Dombey falls under the Blimbers' spell because a "learned enthusiasm is very contagious" (147).

The antagonism between Blimber's academy and the body is comically demonstrated in a dinner-table scene that punctuates a Blimberian disquisition on Roman imperial banquets with the incoherent sounds of the student Johnson choking at table:

> "And one dish," pursued Doctor Blimber… "called, from its enormous dimensions, the Shield of Minerva, and made, among other costly ingredients, of the brains of pheasants—"
>
> "Ow, ow, ow!" (from Johnson).
>
> "Woodcocks."
>
> "Ow ow, ow!" (157).

The pupil's wordless cacophony finally drowns out Blimber's catalog of alimentary abstractions, with its telling depiction of feasting on "brains." The aptly named Feeder, Blimber's assistant, furthers the scene's function as a pageant of illness, expressing his fear that Johnson will "burst some vessel" (157) and die of "apoplexy" (158). This absurd scene first slyly converts Blimber's living quarters into a vast, contagious sickroom, and then comically exorcises the specter of disease as the butler and Blimber's assistant attend to the illness that the Doctor so sublimely ignores.

If Doctor Blimber's academy is implicitly portrayed as a chaotic sickroom, it is overtly metaphorized as an educational "hot house" (141), which forces its young plants into an unnatural and premature bloom. It is no accident that Paul dreams of escaping with his sister Florence to some "beautiful gardens" (160) because Blimber's hot house "forcing system" (143) stands in opposition to the unforced, natural growth of the Rousseauian garden, frequently portrayed, as we have seen in a previous chapter, as the schoolroom's healing corrective. In Dickens's *David Copperfield*, Doctor Strong's schoolroom, which offers a domestic and supposedly natural education, overlooks the serene spaces of an old garden. In Doctor Blimber's unnatural metaphorical garden, on the other hand, "the boys blew before their time. Mental green-peas were produced at Christmas." As Dickens further emphasizes, "There was not the right taste about the premature productions, and they didn't keep well" (141). More than the sickly bodies of the other pupils, Toots's grotesquely overgrown form—his nose is "swollen" and his head "excessively large" (141)—typifies the results of the hot house system:

"he suddenly left off blowing one day, and remained in the establishment as a mere stalk" (142).

While both Paul and Toots languish in Blimber's forcing house, Paul's weak constitution is also explicitly a casualty of his domestic losses. Deprived first of his mother, then of his nurse Polly, and finally of the companionship of his sister Florence, he seeks maternal surrogates in such unsatisfactory substitutes as Mrs. Pipchin, Miss Blimber, and Mrs. Blimber. Before attending Blimber's academy, Paul lives with the witchlike Mrs. Pipchin, who conducts classes in her home. Like Creakle in *David Copperfield*, Mrs. Pipchin evokes the image of domestic education only to violate its code. Scrupulously protective of her own domestic comforts, she deprives her pupils of affection and sustenance. Deteriorating at Mrs. Pipchin's antidomestic school, Paul declines even more rapidly under Blimber's classical curriculum, as Dickens notes almost in passing: "Such spirits as he had in the outset, Paul soon lost of course" (166).

By the time the latent sickness at Blimber's has been acknowledged—manifested in the conversion of Paul's bedroom into a sickroom, stocked with such typical articles as a curative "jelly" and a mysterious medicine bottle that appears "magically" (191)—no remedy is possible, only diagnosis. A visiting apothecary announces Paul's "want of vital power" and his "great constitutional weakness" (190). Ironically, however, Paul's constitutional decline signals a shift in emotional tone, freeing him and others to enjoy the subtly altered school. Liberated from lessons, Paul now experiences Blimber's as a "house" rather than a "school," sounding with preemptive nostalgia the mysteries of its domesticity; thus he pays "little visits" to his cohorts in the schoolroom, each of the Blimbers, and even to the dog (194). Paul is now "free of the whole house" (194) in two senses: He can explore it at will, and he is in the process of parting from it. Now the good genie of Blimber's academy, Paul humanizes it as he finds lost books for his schoolfellows and straightens Cornelia Blimber's untidy desk. Paul even sits at the feet of the learned Doctor while he reads, in an image that oddly anticipates Annie Strong's humanizing attendance on her equally abstracted and scholarly husband, the benign Doctor of *David Copperfield*.

Paul's illness not only softens the harsh school regimen but also introduces a holiday atmosphere into the academy as he anticipates the annual party that becomes, in part, his farewell celebration. For Paul, the festive gathering shines a beneficent and humanizing light on all its inmates, rendering the foolish Mrs. Blimber "lovely" (196)—in Paul's eyes at least—and inspiring the normally subdued Mr. Feeder to dance with uncharacteristic abandon, as if to incite the music to "wild tunes"

(200). Even the rigorous Cornelia Blimber, whose tutoring has sapped Paul's vital energy, is moved to acknowledge him as her "favourite pupil" (203), granting him her equivalent of the privileged and familial inclusion that he has longed for.

Miriam Bailin argues that the Victorian sickroom, in its idealized aspect, carries the promise of utopian transformations; as it integrates nurse and patient into its "consoling community," it converts bodily illness into a means of "substantiating a stable, unified self and a reassuring relation to others—a relation which explicitly evokes the attachment of parent and child" (6). In its reestablishment of a community of nurturing relations, the fictive sickroom, Bailin suggests, can serve as a "cure" for both narrative impasse and the recalcitrant stasis of isolated characters unable to move toward resolution of their fictive conflicts.

In the case of Paul Dombey, the relational dynamic so deftly described by Bailin serves to transform school space, by means of the sickroom, into a particular subset of domestic space. Once he is diagnosed as a sick child who must be nurtured, Paul's illness relieves, at least temporarily, the dangerous pressure and unhealthy atmosphere of the school's forcing house, allowing its latent disease to manifest itself and move toward the process of cure. For readers of the novel, Paul's illness first allows them to witness and condemn the coercive mechanisms of the educational forcing house, and then encourages them to forgive its adult managers and practitioners, as they are reincorporated into the human family by the redemptive aspects of that illness. By allowing even the grotesque Mrs. Pipchin, Paul's former teacher, to serve as a nurse at Paul's bedside, the novel suggests that the educational system and its assumptions, rather than specific individuals, are to blame. Thus, the narrative depiction of Paul's illness allows Dickens to invoke the moral guilt that characterizes Spencer's "physical sins," and yet forestall its application to the Blimbers, their assistants, and the pupils' complicit parents, in order to evoke a systemic disease that infects not only the pupil-victims but also its adult monitors and administrators.

Like May's novel, *Dombey and Son* incorporates elements of zymosis into its narrative of illness, but with an additional complication. As Florence Nightingale warns, according to the zymotic model of disease, the curative sickroom, redolent of a purer and fresher air than that of the unhealthy house in which it is situated, can end by ventilating the house rather than curing the patient. By converting Paul's room into a sickroom, Dickens's narrative "ventilates" and freshens Blimber's unhealthy house, with its intellectually overheated atmosphere, rendered metaphorically toxic by the "high and false... temperature at which the Doctor kept his hothouse" (166). Nightingale's *Notes on*

Nursing particularly deplores the dangerous "hot-house" heat of sickrooms with closed windows (7). In both Nightingale's monitory work and *Dombey*, the unnatural growth of the hot house is implicitly perceived as a state of dis-ease and dis-equilibrium, resulting from a lack of healthful ventilation.

As noted above, in the iconography of the sickroom, the window signals redemption or transition by means of a consoling and enlivening vista of the outside world; further, as I have suggested, the zymotic model of illness, with its emphasis on curative infusions of a purer air, in a sense literalizes this moral and psychological dimension of recovery, embodying it in the recuperative mechanisms of the body. Nightingale can wax romantic as she describes her patients' love of windows, exemplifying their physical and mental craving for a freshened outdoor atmosphere, as well as an escape from the tedium of the sickroom. In a note headed "Desperate desire in the sick to see out of window," she describes the case of a heroic nurse who injured herself carrying her paralyzed and dying patient across the room so that he could "see out."[12]

Along with his fellow invalids Louis Mortimer and George Arthur, Paul Dombey experiences a "desperate desire to see out of" the "window"; similarly, his health fluctuates along with his exposure to the healing outdoor air. In Mrs. Pipchin's dangerously stuffy school, his physical decline accelerates: "In the winter time the air couldn't be got out… and in the summer time it couldn't be got in…. It was not, naturally, a fresh-smelling house; and… the window of the front parlour… was never opened" (99). Although Paul improves when he takes the air by the sea and feels "the wind blowing on his face" (108), once in Blimber's "great hothouse" (141), he suffers his first major attack, and revives in part because "the window was [now] open" (189). At Blimber's, Paul is repeatedly depicted "looking through the window of his little bedroom" (167) watching for glimpses of Florence or listening for the sound of "the wind" on "a beautiful night" (167). Yet although Paul steals "up to his window every evening to look out" (168), he remains imprisoned, "breasting the window of his solitary cage when birds flew by, as if he would have emulated them, and soared away!" (168). Though diseased in a different sense, and though his illness is never acknowledged by Blimber, the blighted Toots is also depicted "looking at the gas-lighted world over the little iron bars in the left hand corner window… like a greatly overgrown cherub who had sat up aloft much too long" (142).

Thus, Dr. Blimber's school enters the narrative as an unacknowledged sickroom or, in Nightingale's sense, an "unhealthy house" infected by a stagnant atmosphere; the recognition of Paul's sickness, however, signals a shift in emotional tone, initiating a temporary release from the forcing system. In Nightingale's image, the sickroom ventilates the house, resulting in the patient's death, but allowing us to reenvision the house in humanized terms, as embodying a set of forgivable and redeemable domestic relations. Finally, the sickroom's release from the level of metaphor into the realm of literal fact serves as a cathartic experience both for the school and for readers. Paul's loss signals the possibility of redemption for the school's human community.

Yet this qualified redemption exists, not in the precincts of school space, but rather through the redefinition of "school" as "home." The novel, in fact, carries on a widespread attack on the whole spectrum of English education. The "charitable Grinders" who forcibly educate the impoverished Polly Toodles's son end by corrupting the boy's character and blighting his future; the public school experience, as described by Major Bagstock, is an equally horrific sketch of the ritual that would later be commemorated in *Tom Brown*: "We put each other to the torture there, Sir. We roasted the new fellows at a slow fire, and hung 'em out of a three pair of stairs window" (126–127). On all levels, institutional education is a process of physical and mental deformation—an assault on the child's body—that not only enfeebles the children on whom it practices but also corrupts its adult practitioners. Parents and teachers, as well as all the pupils at both Mrs. Pipchin's and Dr. Blimber's schools, are subtly tainted, although the vitally wounded Paul and Toots typify the most extreme injuries.

As discussed in previous chapters, the traditional *bildungsroman* allies itself with individual growth of an allegedly organic and non-schematic kind—a growth frequently invoked to attack the supposedly formulaic lessons of school. *Dombey and Son*, which incorporates elements of *bildung* into its depictions of Paul, Florence, and Walter, pursues a similar strategy. Following Spencer's paradigm, the subset of the *bildungsroman* known as the school narrative is willing to jettison development in favor of growth, yet it permits itself a longing backward glance at those child victims of mental and spiritual overdevelopment who sacrifice growth to self-knowledge. Such wise children occupy an ambiguous position within the school novel; although the narrative frequently must abandon them in favor of the dynamic principle of growth, they serve as conduits for the values and insights that the more hardy protagonists must eventually attain. Strikingly, such figures may also give voice to the particular kind of thinking—the exhaustive analysis of character and motive—that the novel itself strives to emulate. Thus, Paul Dombey exhibits an uncanny understanding of motive and character, along with a profound sensitivity to image, metaphor, and the poetic dimension of language. By sacrificing their frail bodies as inevitable narrative losses, Paul and his numerous fictive counterparts foster narrative momentum. Thus, while schools and schooling ostensibly destroy Helen Burns, Vernon Digby, and Paul Dombey, on another level their narratives make use of these doomed figures as monitory exempla to reinforce a commitment to both individual growth and narrative development.

Although not all fictive depictions of overeducation rely on sickroom scenes, novelistic portraits of the school sickroom, when they do occur, serve to characterize both the school in general and its degree of danger. In novels of successful education, the sickroom offers neither a thorough domestication of illness nor a retreat to exclusive domesticity, but rather a final, redemptive chance to right the balance between institutional and domestic space, initiating a preliminary sojourn at home and a subsequent return to school. In novels that condemn outright a particular form of school education (works like *Nicholas Nickleby*, *Jane Eyre*, or *Dombey and Son*), no cure is available within the precincts of school; the whole institution is revealed as an unhealthy house, and may become, at least temporarily, a species of sickroom or hospital, a house of incurables. The zymotic model of illness, still prevalent at mid-century, offers a powerful metaphor for the dangers of school life, a trope that evolves out of current medical theory and practice. As Florence Nightingale acknowledges in *Notes on Nursing*, even the rigorously regulated sanitary sickroom of the hospital had its own particular institutional disease, *pyaemia* or hospital infection, thought to be brought on by the crowding together of so many bodies, all exchanging noxious exhalations. Thus, institutionality, which casts itself as sanitary and corrective, carries with it its own inherent form of corruption. Fictive schools risk developing a lethal and particularized brand of pyaemia, one that may undermine not only the health of individual children, but also, as numerous school narratives suggest, the social present and society's future.

CONCLUSION

George Eliot's *Mill on the Floss* (1860) celebrates a rare anarchic moment in the schoolroom. Boarding with the middle-class clergyman Mr. Stelling, Tom Tulliver struggles dispiritedly with his Latin grammar, subjected to a classical education that clashes with his practical, active temperament. During a visit from his sister Maggie, Tom exults in the schoolmaster's absence. The children become bored and frolic around Stelling's lectern on which the heavy grammar book rests. The unusual presence of a girl in the schoolroom spurs Tom to show off, casting off his customary listlessness. Racing in subversive circles around the empty space where the schoolmaster usually stands, the children inadvertently topple the reading desk. As it crashes to the ground, its resonant boom echoes through the characteristic silence of the schoolroom:

> Away they jumped with more and more vigour, till Maggie's hair flew from behind her ears, and twirled about like an animated mop. But the revolutions round the table became more and more irregular in their sweep, till at last reaching Mr Stelling's reading-stand, they sent it thundering down with its heavy lexicons to the floor. (128)

In Eliot's artfully wrought description, the children's "revolutions round the table" manifest an impulse toward "revolution" that has been brewing in Tom's spirit ever since his arrival. Their crazy circles, evermore "irregular in their sweep," defy the linear grooves, the mechanical "straight line" in which Stelling's mind has been "trained" to move (147). Similarly, as they send Mr. Stelling's reading-stand "thundering down" from its eminence, they challenge the authority of his booming voice, which Eliot slyly suggests, sounds to Tom like "supernal thunder" when it actually rings as hollow as the thunderous noise of "well-rolled barrels" (118). Thus, the children's brief revolution in the schoolroom hints not only at Tom's secret angers, but also at the ease with which

Stelling's authoritative facade can be toppled. Maggie's loose mop of hair emphasizes her gender, as does the wild dance that the girl and boy perform together around Stelling's citadel of learning.

As we have seen, a similar anarchic moment occurs when Alice grows too large for the hybrid courtroom/schoolroom in Wonderland and scatters the King, Queen, and their court, emblems of adult authority now miniaturized and reduced to mere playing cards. Dickens stages his own demolition of the schoolroom in *Great Expectations* (1860–1861). Bored and rebellious in the blatantly commercial dame school held in the shabby shop of "Mr. Wopsle's great-aunt" (68), the students revolt as the teacher dozes. They enter into their own "competitive examination on the subject of boots, with the view of ascertaining who could tread the hardest upon whose toes" (68). Similarly, Farrar's *Eric* (1858) depicts its repressed schoolboys breaking loose in the secret spaces of the nighttime dormitory. Exuberantly, they jump and bound, play leapfrog and stage wild theatricals; one schoolboy compares them to "dancing hippopotami" (109). As the impulses of the body reassert themselves in the disciplinary spaces of all four schools, institutional space is transformed. Lecterns fall, books crash to the floor, benches topple, and shouts fill the impersonal silence.

Diverse as they are, these narratives linger delightedly on moments when schoolchildren break out of their disciplinary constraints, engage in wild impromptu dances, and metaphorically "deconstruct" school. Even when the lectern is righted and the children's voices hushed, such short-lived moments resonate and echo in later scenes, hinting that the supposedly impermeable spaces of school are more vulnerable than they seem. The docile bodies of Foucauldian disciplinarity continue to carry their subversive potential. Discipline must not only be enforced but reinforced. Learning to think and move in train leaves open the possibility of train wrecks and erratic journeys. A cultural space constructed by means of spatial practices can, theoretically at least, be shaken by a single resistant bodily gesture. Thus, the Victorian novel's answer to the institutionalization of life typified by school restraint is finally the *energeia* of the child's recalcitrant body. In this sense, the "demolition" of school and the celebration of chaotic childhood energies express a crucial impulse at the heart of Victorian school narratives. In fact, mid-century novelists fight a rearguard action against the institutionalized lessons and standards they so often stage as antithetical to novelistic ways of seeing and knowing; specifically, novelists associate their art with the erratic and errant trajectories of narrative in contrast to the hierarchies of the new pedagogy's classificatory "grid" (Foucault, *Discipline* 145).

At the same time it must be acknowledged that as fictions provide alternative spaces to the schoolroom—including the teacher's room, the garden, and the sickroom—these adjacent settings also illustrate the partitioning into useful sites that Foucault sees as typical of modern institutional space. For all its resistant physicality, the child's body becomes inflected by its locale, and by that locale's spatial practices. Similarly, the child's training instills a self-control that accepts and expects separate sites for work and play, for collective effort and solitude, for affection and loss. Written for leisure moments in a society that increasingly measures and segments time and space, novels inevitably help to further the spatial partitioning that many of them implicitly oppose.

Strikingly, with the establishment of the system of national schools by the end of the century, much of the energy leaches out of the school narrative. The dream of a common education for all had been implemented, and although it was altering society in numerous ways, it was far from the panacea that some reformers had anticipated. Instead, it brought new problems, including concerns about overly standardized, limited curricula and poorly trained teachers. In general, these concerns tended to be strategic rather than broadly philosophical. Determining the future of education was now the province of trained professionals and educational experts rather than novelists and journalists such as Dickens.

Fiction of the late nineteenth and early twentieth centuries responds to these changes in diverse and intriguing ways. First, the popular school novel experiences a late and sentimental flowering. In their monitory parables of schoolboy experience, Martineau and May challenged the conventions and lessons of the schools they depicted. *Tom Brown* certainly romanticized aspects of Rugby life, but it had also questioned established traditions in the context of a militant Christianity. Later school fictions recycle the conventions of earlier novels, spicing them with a prospective nostalgia, depicting the tradition-hallowed school experience as a series of golden days soon to be lost. This sentimentalization of the school story is most noticeable in the new genre of schoolgirl fiction.

Earlier, women writers focused on the rigors of schoolboy life; now, as private schools for girls emerged, modeled in part on the old public school plan, writers like L. T. Meade situate girls within the province of the old schoolboy narrative in works such as *Betty: A Schoolgirl* (1894), *The Darling of the School* (1915), and *The School Favourite* (1908). One of the most original and amusing of the schoolgirl novels, Evelyn Sharp's *The Making of a Schoolgirl* (1897) aims to extend public school conventions to a new race of schoolgirls who affect a hardened nonchalance evocative of schoolboy cynicism; the schoolgirls engage in feuds, rivalries, and passionate school friendships, and favor gymnasium classes over domestic pursuits. A feminist and proponent of women's education, Sharp nevertheless takes care to emphasize that intellectual development will not defeminize women or make them unsuitable for heterosexual relations. At the end of the novel, when the protagonist Becky brings a friend home for the holidays, the girls' friendship takes second place, as each chum pairs off with a suitable boy. Sharp's work is, as Beverly Lyon Clark argues, an unfairly neglected classic.[1] Nevertheless, it fails to raise the larger and unsettling questions freely explored by Hughes and Martineau. Unlike Hughes's *Tom Brown*, widely read by, and reviewed for, an adult audience, the admittedly charming *Making of a Schoolgirl* deliberately eschews the fictive mainstream. As it is more skillfully marketed to its target audience of young readers, school fiction is increasingly ghetto-ized.

At the same time, literary depictions of school life continue, but to a different end. James Joyce's *Portrait of the Artist as a Young Man* (1916) breaks new ground for the school narrative, showing the resilience and flexibility of the literary school story, while also testifying to its limitations. Stephen Dedalus's boarding school comprehends vivid depictions of the school sites already explored: a rough-and-tumble playground punctuated by the "thud of the footballers" where boys vie for supremacy, and character is revealed;[2] a sickroom where Stephen spends time gazing out the window like his frail and sensitive literary precursors, George Arthur and Paul Dombey;[3] and a repressive classroom where Stephen is beaten by the prefect of studies for breaking his glasses: "Get at your work, all of you," the prefect "crie[s]" after the beating, just as Creakle once shouted, "Now get to work, every boy" (*Portrait*, 89). The novel even includes an initially terrifying but ultimately redemptive visit to the rector's private room, which evokes the benevolent paradigm of domestic education; like the nurturing Miss Temple remedying the abuses of Scatcherd and Brocklehurst in her private parlor, the "kind-looking" rector (73) smiles and shakes Stephen's hand, assuring him that the authoritarian prefect will not be allowed to punish him again. Depicting the supposedly coercive transactions of Irish Catholic society, *Portrait* can be seen as the last school novel to embody a nineteenth-century tradition of social and political critique. Brilliantly original and innovative, *Portrait* nevertheless has a retrospective quality, harkening back to earlier school fictions while also ironizing their generic tropes and motifs. Moving away from the traditional *bildungsroman* as well as from the concept of the individual self as a clearly defined, self-contained entity, literary modernism also sheds the nine-

teenth-century fascination with school as a center of character formation and vital social reform.

While school scenes continue to be significant elements in children's
fiction and novels of development on both sides of the Atlantic, they
generally lack the reformist edge of their Victorian forebears. The popular Harry Potter series, a recent permutation of the long tradition of
boarding school stories, has developed into a cultural phenomenon at a
time when the school narrative has lost most of its impetus for political
and social reform.[4] Like *Portrait*, the Harry Potter novels recapitulate
the major sites of school narratives: a series of often coercive classrooms,
a teacher's room that houses a phoenix, a playground reenvisioned as
a field for aerial contests on brooms, and an infirmary where injured
pupils can grow new bones. Preserving the archaic relics of the public
school story, the museumlike Hogwarts academy is a cabinet of wonders to which time has added a gloss of quaintness, a patina of mystery.
In contrast to the contentious, cranky, and supremely earnest school
narratives of the Victorian era, Rowling's fantasy eschews our major
cultural debates, apparently endorsing a public school morality that is
already, in major respects, a nostalgic dream of the past. In Rowling's
narrative, it takes magic to revivify the school story once again, placing
it, at least fleetingly, at the center of popular culture.

In sum, school fictions no longer suggest that settling the "problem"
of school once and for all will revitalize our society and renew our
experience of what it means to be human. The dream of universal education—the "great change" that Robson celebrated so wholeheartedly—
has been achieved, leaving skepticism and disillusionment in its wake.
And yet, even if we look askance at the Victorians' astounding capacity for hope, their belief that they could reshape society by means of a
finely calibrated educational system, their efforts and concerns nevertheless remain enduringly relevant. The contradictions implicit in our
drive toward the oppositional goals of institutionality and domesticity,
social cohesion and individual possibility, standardization and playful
improvisation, continue to beset our educational discourse in profound
ways on both sides of the Atlantic.

ENDNOTES

INTRODUCTION

1. See George Eliot, *The George Eliot Letters*. Ed. Gordon S. Haight. 6 vols. (New Haven: Yale University Press, 1970), vol. 6, 47.

2. An avid reader of Rousseau's works, Pestalozzi not only named his son Jean-Jacques, but also modeled his early training on that of Émile. Pestalozzi's writings mingle a talent for fictive narrative with luminous evocations of an educational ideal. His influential Rousseauian pedagogy was further propagated by the dynamic Friedrich Froebel (1782–1852), whose German *kindergarten* movement was brought to England in the early 1800s by devoted disciples. A master teacher who visited Pestalozzi's famous model school at Yverdon and published the influential and Rousseauian *Autobiography*, Froebel followed both Rousseau and Pestalozzi in advocating a natural and experiential education. Both Pestalozzi and Froebel gave greater specificity to Rousseau's myth of an idealized domestic education that served to redeem both teacher and pupil.

3. Victorian novelists also produced vivid depictions of additional sites related to the institutionalized schoolroom. From *Eric* and *Tom Brown's Schooldays* to Dickens's *David Copperfield*, the often chaotic and erotically charged dormitory plays a crucial role in school narratives. My work deals with this site only allusively because depictions of it only rarely involve the direct supervision of adults; instead, the space normally serves as an outlet for repressed violent and sexual impulses when the schoolmaster is absent.

4. In *The Production of Space*, Lefebvre contrasts official *representations of space*, which carry the sanction of government authority or political and social elites, with the so-called *spaces of representation* generated through image and metaphor in the work of artists and writers. Incorporating symbolic and emotionally charged elements, such spaces of representation are more apt to embody the "clandestine or underground side of social life" (33).

5. Supporters of Carus Wilson, the school's founder, denounced Brontë's supposedly libelous attack on the institution.
6. Katharine Capshaw Smith, *Children's Literature of the Harlem Renaissance* (Bloomingdale: Indiana University Press, 2004), xix.
7. Litvak's analysis of Brontë's *Villette* is of particular interest because it links the pedagogical performances of Lucy Snowe and Paul Emmanuel with the extravagant theatricality of the actress Vashti. Emphasizing the performative and theatrical dimensions of a culture of surveillance, which stages privacy as surely as it orchestrates performances in the public realm, Litvak deconstructs oppositions between public and private, teacher and pupil, inspector and inspected, emphasizing the internalization of mechanisms of surveillance.
8. Arnold laments the fact that student teachers he has observed use their lessons to show off their knowledge rather than to develop their "faculty of teaching" (Arnold, *Reports* 281).

CHAPTER 1

1. See "Docile Bodies," Foucault, *Discipline and Punish*, 135–169.
2. Founded in 1808 as the Society for Promoting the Lancastrian System of Education for the Poor, the organization was renamed the British and Foreign School Society in 1814.
3. See Binns, *A Century of Education*, 18.
4. See Ellis, *Educating Our Masters*, 22–23.
5. Advocates of a new system of national schools saw in it the promise of liberating pupils from the ignorance and incompetence of poorly trained masters, from the oppressive authoritarianism of church control in the case of parish schools, and from sectarian squabbling between Anglican and dissenting educational organizations. At the same time, the vaunted "independence" of a new nonsectarian and professionalized school space masked its opposite—an interdependent bureaucracy, enforcing its own shifting and arbitrary standards and fostering an expansion of government power.
6. To twentieth-century eyes, such quasi-domestic schools appear distinctly different from the home education offered by tutors and governesses. To Victorian observers, however, an unbroken continuum existed between the schoolroom in a private family house and the schoolroom in a private schoolmaster's house. Such schoolrooms were not only judged by the same standards, but might well be presided over by the same master or mistress in a different incarnation. Thus, professionally but not personally, it is unremarkable when Jane Eyre moves from teaching at Lowood to teaching in a private schoolroom at Thornfield. The influential Friedrich Froebel, whose doctrine of natural education helped to shape early childhood instruction in England, made a simi-

lar move when he temporarily gave up teaching in the German school system to serve as a private tutor to two promising students. Similarly, in *Education: Intellectual, Moral, and Physical* (1861), Herbert Spencer freely intersperses educational examples drawn from home and school without pausing to foreground, or even to remark on, their difference.

7. "In practice," according to Ellis, "this standard [a given amount of space allotted to each schoolchild] was not insisted upon" (68).

8. See Mary Poovey, *Uneven Developments: The Ideological Work of Gender in Mid-Victorian England* (Chicago: University of Chicago Press, 1988).

9. As Malcolm Seaborne notes in his introduction to Robson's work, "Nonconformists in the earlier part of Victoria's reign had rarely chosen Gothic for their schools" (Robson, *School Architecture*, 20).

10. The National Society (founded 1811) advocated and fostered the education of children in Anglican schools, while the British and Foreign School Society (founded 1808) derived from the work of the Quaker Joseph Lancaster. Aiming to be nonsectarian in its religious teachings, it consequently attracted numerous dissenters of a variety of persuasions.

11. See Catherine Gallagher and Stephen Greenblatt, *Practicing New Historicism* (Chicago: University of Chicago Press, 2000), 17, 16.

12. Donald Nicholson-Smith's otherwise fine translation of *The Production of Space* (Cambridge, MA: Blackwell, 1991) unfortunately blurs Lefebvre's lucid contrast between "representations of space" and "spaces of representation" when he translates the latter term more concisely as "representational spaces." Lefebvre's parallel syntax emphasizes the parallel and complementary functions of his terms.

13. *Philosophical Essays Preliminary Dissertation* xlviii, quoted in James Mill, *Analysis of the Phenomena of the Human Mind*, epigraph on frontispiece, np.

14. Born in Scotland and educated at the University of Edinburgh, James Mill avidly attended the lectures of Dugald Stewart, whose encyclopedic studies of the mind's processes drew on and popularized the work of his distinguished mentor Thomas Reid. While Mill's *Analysis* provides exhaustive examples and explanations of the principles of association, it also presents them in a radically reductive form. Having little patience with the fine distinctions of Locke and Hume, Mill frequently reasons them away, constructing a clear, simple and mechanistic model of the human mind and its processes.

15. *Concerning Human Understanding*, Book 3, chap. 7, sec. 2: 472.

16. John Stuart Mill's preface to the 1869 edition of *Analysis of the Phenomena of the Human Mind* traces a genealogy that emphasizes Locke, Reid, Hartley, and others, downplaying his father's debt to Hume. Yet Locke is most concerned with the dangers of random associations, fearing that "the confusions of two different Ideas" by means of customary

associations inculcates "False Views" (*Concerning Human Understanding*, Book 2, chap. 13, sec. 18: 401). In fact, James Mill himself cites Hume as the first clear articulator of the principles of association.

17. By Mill's day, Hume's theories had been filtered through the treatises of the later Scottish empiricists, who offered a more systematic but less dynamic presentation of them. Thus, James Mill's desire to expand and codify Hume's theory of mental associations is in keeping with the current climate of thought. Doubt is built into Hume's system; Mill's apparent aim is to eliminate doubt, filling in the blank spaces, and banishing all traces of mystery. If Hume, in his brilliant and daring *Treatise of Human Nature* (1739–1740), frequently gives the impression of a man willfully carrying a flickering candle flame through epistemological darkness, Mill appears more like a man seated in a well-lit library, thoroughly stocked with helpful and illuminating volumes. In place of Hume's mesmerizing vision of mental flux, Mill finds an unproblematic mental territory in need of mapping and classification. For Mill, the mind is a container and thoughts are simply its contents; Mill wishes to illuminate both the container and the contained.

18. In the process of restructuring Hume's principles, Mill radically redefines them: "Mr. Hume," he explains, "said that our ideas are associated according to three principles: Contiguity in time and place, Causation, and Resemblance." Mill goes on to reduce "Causation" to "Contiguity," because cause and effect are supposedly contiguous in time. Mill involves himself in a tangle of logical contradictions here. For one thing, he dismisses any conception of a latent cause, one that does not appear in close proximity to its effect: "Causation, the second of Mr. Hume's principles is the same with contiguity in time, or the order of succession." Even more problematically, Mill identifies "Resemblance" with "Contiguity" of place because things that look alike supposedly occur in like places or in close proximity. Thus, flowers are thought to resemble each other largely because they grow in similar conditions, in gardens or fields, and so forth (vol. I, chap. III, sec. 11, 106–110).

19. "From this observation," Mill contends, "we may refer resemblance to the law of frequency, of which it seems to form only a particular case" (106–111). Resemblance is now seen as an aspect of frequency, which Mill has already identified with contiguity of place because "frequency" for Mill simply refers to multiple instances of a single object contiguously, that is, in a single location.

20. Mill's arguments rely on a hidden analogy between space and time, a tendency to read them as similar extensivities. For Mill, the linking principles of association not only animate the train of thought, as they do for Hume, rather they are identical with the train. Succession is what motivates succession. Contiguity is the first principle of a train that is conceived as a series of contiguities. John Stuart Mill found his father's

equation of resemblance and contiguity "perhaps the least successful attempt at a generalization and simplification of the laws of mental phenomena to be found in the work" (*Analysis* 111, note).

21. According to Jenny Bourne Taylor (*In the Secret Theatre of Home*, 1988): "In Carpenter's psychology, (as in Bain's and Spencer's) associationist methods directly feed into and are modified by a linear, progressivist evolutionism" (60).

22. As an active participant in the intellectual life of Edinburgh, Currie was perhaps more likely than his English colleagues to be in touch with the seminal thought of the Scottish empiricists. Admittedly, too, Scotland was often considered to be educationally in advance of England, achieving universal education long before the latter country. On the other hand, Currie's handbook for teachers, *The Principles and Practice of Common School Education* (1862), was also published and read in England. The work nevertheless draws on a lifetime of educational training and practice, and therefore has relevance to earlier educational developments.

23. As Philip Collins emphasizes in *Dickens and Education*, "Mr. Gradgrind's questions are a parody of the object-lesson" (134) as it was increasingly practiced in so many nineteenth-century English classrooms. Once an emblem of experiential learning, entailing the bringing of actual objects into the classroom, Pestalozzi's "original idea" had become, Collins argues, "perverted—as appears in [one teacher's]... instruction, 'Produce, draw, or imagine a cat'. Too often the children did not have in front of them the 'object' under discussion" (155). Herbert Spencer, although a proponent of object lessons, worried about their abuse by poor teachers, arguing that the "system of object lessons" was "well-conceived but ill-conducted" (*Education* 106); because his plans are often "vitiated" (118) by those who try to implement them, Spencer argues, the "realization of the Pestalozzian idea remains to be achieved" (119).

24. "I am trying to psychologize the instruction of mankind," Pestalozzi wrote in his famous essay "The Method" (*How Gertrude Teaches* 315). Studying the so-called natural development of the human mind, Pestalozzi tried to duplicate or facilitate nature's methods in the classroom. For numerous English observers, the centerpiece and paradigmatic model of the famed method was the object lesson. The term, indeed, came to stand metonymically for the whole of Pestalozzi's complex curriculum. In the object lesson, students learned not from recitation, reading, or rote memorization, but rather by studying and exploring the manifold objects of the world, often with minimal instruction from their teacher. Clearly, object lessons had particular application in the natural sciences; the implications of the method, however, went far beyond any particular discipline. For object lessons emphasized not only the importance of developing observational powers, but also the primacy of the child's subjective realm in forging connections between observed objects and

concepts. In England, as the vogue for object lessons led teachers like Currie to implement them in a more standardized form, the object lesson degenerated into a routine lecture on an object, requiring only minimal participation from students.

25. *Concerning Human Understanding*, Book 2, chap. 33, sec. 6: 396.

CHAPTER 2

1. Rousseau contrasts the education of the "citizen," designed to serve the state or the social power structure, with the clearly preferred education suitable to the "man" in his natural state (*Émile* 41). In this tradition, Froebel and Pestalozzi orchestrate similar oppositions between natural and artificial means of education. Similarly, Herbert Spencer delineates an opposition, central to his thought, between "coercive" and a supposedly noncoercive education. For Spencer, the "coercive" and authoritarian "physical-force system" of education must be replaced by a "non-coercive treatment" that "appeals to the higher feelings" and fosters "the culture of the sympathies" (*Social Statics* 166–171).

2. Although E. R. Robson, appointed the official architect of the London School Board in 1872, assumes the teacher's "private rooms" (220) to be part of the typical school plan in his seminal *School Architecture* (1874), he generally opposes attaching the teacher's living quarters to the school building: "There must be no internal communication between the house and the school" (221–22). In part this is because such "internal communication" risks inciting the teacher "to forget the difference between work and leisure" (221). In contrast to Robson's standardizing approach to school space, the blurring of such distinctions is, of course, an article of faith for advocates of domestic education.

3. In a similar way, the idealized depictions of family life in a range of Victorian fictions, such as Dickens's *Our Mutual Friend* (1865–1866) and Brontë's *The Professor*, implicitly attack the harsh transactions of the commercial marketplace.

4. See, for instance, Mary Poovey, *The Proper Lady and the Woman Writer: Ideology as Style in the Works of Mary Wollstonecraft, Mary Shelley, and Jane Austen* (Chicago: University of Chicago Press, 1984); Gayatri Chakravorty Spivak, "Three Women's Texts and a Critique of Imperialism," in *Feminisms: An Anthology of Literary Theory and Criticism*, eds. Robyn R. Warhol and Diane Price Herndl (New Brunswick, NJ: Rutgers University Press, 1991), 896–912; and Jeffrey Cass, "The Contestatory Gothic in Mary Shelley's *Frankenstein* and J. W. Polidori's *Ernestus Berchtold*: The Spectre of a Colonialist Paradigm." *JAISA: The Journal of the Association for the Interdisciplinary Study of the Arts 1*, No. 2 (Spring 1996): 33–41.

5. Speaking of the English prejudice in favor of "[w]arming by open fires" Robson asserts, "part of this may be due to the poetry of long association with the hearth and home." Robson himself endorses both "the undoubtedly cheerful appearance of the blazing grate" and "its tendency to promote ventilation" (*School Architecture* 272).

6. In *Our Mutual Friend*, Lizzie Hexam narrates entertaining domestic fictions for her younger brother Charlie, educating him in her own generous and hopeful vision of life as they sit by the fireside. In contrast, the national schools educate Charlie in a rigid and unbending view of class and upward mobility; in consequence, the snobbish Charlie becomes ashamed of his wise but illiterate sister.

7. Quotations are from the following edition: Rousseau, Jean Jacques. *Émile or On Education*, trans. Allan Bloom (New York: Basic, 1979).

8. See Martini's "*Bildungsroman*—Term and Theory," in Hardin, *Reflection and Action*.

9. Wilhelm Dilthey, *Poetry and Experience. Selected Works*, eds. Rudolf A. Makkeel and Frithjof Rodi (Princeton, NJ: Princeton University Press, 1985) 5: 335.

10. In *Plots of Englightenment*, for instance, Richard Barney deemphasizes the impact of Rousseau on English eighteenth-century fiction. Examining in detail the educational writings of Locke, Fénelon, Mary Astell, and others, Barney argues that the dramatic structure of lessons in educational discourse impacts on the narrative structure of concomitant fictions. Thus, Robinson Crusoe's adventures mirror the pedagogical structuring of experience in patterns of conflict, disorientation, and resolution.

11. A colossal work, *Leonard and Gertrude* took Pestalozzi years to write and revise. First published in the years between 1781 and 1787, the novel was issued in revised editions between 1790 and 1792 and again between 1819 and 1820.

12. With Eurocentric arrogance, Spencer asserts, "As the child's features— flat nose, forward-opening nostrils, large lips, wide-apart eyes, absent frontal sinus, &c.—resemble for a time those of the savage, so, too, do his instincts" (*Education: Intellectual, Moral, and Physical* 206).

13. See Gadd *Victorian Logs*, 1979.

14. David Vincent, "The Domestic and the Official Curriculum in Nineteenth-Century England," in *Opening the Nursery Door: Reading, Writing, and Childhood, 1600–1900*, eds. Mary Hilton, Morag Styles, and Victor Watson (New York: Routledge, 1997), 161–179.

15. Vincent documents the vitality of working-class education outside the classroom, and its ability to teach diverse skills: "The craftsman had a far wider range of skills to impart to his apprentice than the schoolteacher had to his pupil" (169). He cites a stonemason's son who "learned as he grew up to swim and fight, to play the fife, to make potato nets, and peel osiers, to work gainfully in a bookbinder's, an iron foundry, and a car-

penter's" shop (169). In addition, such a domestic education highlighted the teaching of ethics through hard-earned lessons of experience: "Ethics were a family concern" as financially hard-pressed parents "sacrificed food, comfort, and rest for their growing children" (171).

16. *Report of the Commissioners on the State of Popular Education in England, with an Index, 1861*. The Irish University Press Series of British Parliamentary Papers: Education General, vol. 3 (Shannon, Ireland: Irish University Press, 1969), 89.

17. *Poor Man's Guardian*, June 16, 1832. (Previously published in *The Ballot*) Rpt. in *Education, Government, and Society in Nineteenth-Century Britain: Commentaries on the British Parliamentary Papers*, eds. Celina Fox, Richard Johnson, et al. (Shannon, Ireland: Irish University Press, 1977).

18. I draw throughout this discussion on Martini's fine analysis of Morgenstern's thought. As Morgenstern continued to develop his understanding of the concept, Martini suggests, his analyses are less coherent than the definition later codified by Dilthey.

19. *Inlandisches Museum* 1, no. 3, 13, quoted in Martini's essay, "*Bildungsroman*—Term and Theory," included in Hardin, *Reflection and Action: Essays on the* Bildungsroman, 1991.

20. In *Social Statics* (1851), Herbert Spencer contrasts "coercive education" (161) with a humane, supposedly noncoercive approach to child-raising, an opposition that, in many respects, approximates the distinction between domestic and institutional education.

21. In her *Life of Charlotte Brontë* (1857), Elizabeth Gaskell suggests that Patrick Brontë's somewhat unconventional views on child rearing may have been influenced by "the ideas of Rousseau" (107). Evidently, Charlotte Brontë's early educational views were also shaped by those of Rousseau. According to Christine Alexander's *The Early Writings of Charlotte Brontë*, the narrator of "A Fresh Arrival" (1833), an unpublished tale written when Brontë was seventeen, "recommends a Rousseauian education" for a child with a flawed character (107). Brontë advises delaying book learning until the age of twelve, emphasizing instead an active experience of wild nature. Famously, Rousseau had also warned against the training of the intellectual faculties before the age of twelve. Sixteen years later, when Brontë published *Shirley*, she created a romance between *Shirley*, her wealthy heroine, and a sensitive Rousseauian tutor, an affair that echoes aspects of the doomed love affair in Rousseau's influential *Nouvelle Heloïse*. When her friend Caroline Helstone praises Rousseau for "certain divine sparks" that "make my soul glow," but also faults him for "weakness," Shirley defends him. Implicitly she argues that Caroline cannot appreciate Rousseau because she is too much like him. As Shirley asserts, "I daresay I should be more tolerant of a Rousseau than you would, Cary: submissive and contemplative yourself, you like the stern and the practical" (*Shirley* 255).

22. Gaskell's *Life of Charlotte Brontë* treats Brontë's depictions of Lowood largely as a literal record of conditions at Cowan Bridge; Gaskell seems particularly concerned to vindicate Brontë of charges of exaggeration without condemning Carus Wilson, the school's founder. Blaming the bad food on the "careless, dirty, and wasteful cook" (46), for instance, she is driven into somewhat contradictory statements. "It seems strange that Mr Wilson should not have been informed by the teachers of the way in which the food was served up," she opines (47). Yet only a few sentences later, she suggests that they did indeed complain and were ignored: "when he heard of [their complaints], his reply was to the effect that the children were to be trained up to regard other things than dainty pampering of the appetite" (47).

23. Absurd as it is, the ban on supposedly frivolous home decoration aptly evokes the trend that endorsed education for working-class children as a means of reforming the home; children instructed in principles of hygiene and thrift would later apply that knowledge to the efficient management of their own homes.

24. The girlish pupil-teacher Frances Henri in Brontë's *The Professor* combines similar domestic traits with her role as Crimsworth's love interest. In Frances's case, her domestic qualities evoke not only the future home that she and Crimsworth will share, but also the lost home of England, which of course seems more appealing once Crimsworth has left it behind.

25. Helen's previous warnings against bitterness serve Jane well when Miss Temple requires her to narrate her history at the house of her abusive guardian, Mrs. Reed: "mindful of Helen's warnings against the indulgence of resentment," Jane "resolve[s]" to "be most moderate," and "infuse[s] into the narrative far less gall and wormwood than ordinarily" (*Jane Eyre* 82–83). Her fair-mindedness wins Miss Temple's approval.

26. Invoking the word "Barmecide," Jane refers to the last name of a prince in a tale from *The Arabian Nights*, who offers a beggar dishes allegedly heaped with delicious food. In fact, however, the plates are empty. Thus, she emphasizes the fairy-tale quality of her daydreams at Lowood.

27. In both Elizabeth Gaskell's *North and South* and Dickens's *Nicholas Nickleby*, for instance, domestic space surreptitiously expands into the realm of institutionality. *North and South*'s Margaret Hale returns to visit the parish school where she once taught, only to find that it has become an institutional terrain, regularly traversed by school inspectors. Like Currie's students, Margaret's former pupils now practice a system of scientific parsing, a new discipline that only baffles and troubles Margaret. Because of her love and friendship for one of her old students, however, Margaret is able to inject an ephemeral domesticity into the highly supervised classroom, stealing a moment to express her affection by holding the girl's hand. Similarly, in Dickens's *Nicholas Nickleby*, the title character finds himself becoming a surrogate parent for his pupil

Smike at Squeers's jail of a school. Ultimately, Nicholas can facilitate the much abused Smike's escape from his coercive school only by adopting him into a familial relation in his own home.

28. For example, the oppressive Dotheboys Hall in *Nicholas Nickleby* is enmeshed in a web of parodic domestic rhetoric.

29. An early proponent of this view, Badri Raina (*Dickens and the Dialectic of Growth* 1986) takes issue with the work of previous critics such as Francis Needham. Raina argues that David and Uriah Heep are merely "varying formulations of an identical drive" (97); both have embarked single-mindedly "upon a pursuit of the goal that capitalism has set for the ambitious individual"; to this end, David is prepared "to jettison human claims" (100).

30. Wackford Squeers, the cruel headmaster in Dickens's *Nicholas Nickleby*, embodies a similar paradox. He not only keeps school at home, but also employs the rhetoric of domestic education to characterize Dotheboys Hall, his oppressive academy where boys go hungry and suffer repeated beatings.

CHAPTER 3

1. Rousseau links and contrasts the claiming of property through cultivation to the seizing of property by means of the imperialistic project. While the former is valorized over the latter, both are instances of the desire to gain "power" through "captivity":

> It belongs to every age, especially his, to want to create, imitate, produce, give sign of power and captivity. It will not take two experiences of seeing a garden plowed, sowed, sprouting, and growing vegetables for him to want to garden in his turn.... He takes possession of [his garden] by planting a bean in it. And surely this possession is more sacred and more respectable than that taken of South America when Nunez Balboa in the name of the King of Spain planted his standard on the shore of the South Sea. (98)

2. See Rousseau's footnote on p. 100.

3. In Derrida's argument, Roussseau "considers writing as a dangerous means, a menacing aid... an artful ruse to make speech present when it is actually absent" (*Of Grammatology* 144). Like that other dangerous supplement (masturbation), writing initiates a chain of substitutions in which "presence" is deferred and the myth of an originary presence is perpetuated; thus, the "sequence of supplements" forges "an infinite chain, ineluctably multiplying the supplementary mediations that produce the sense of the very thing they defer: the mirage of the thing itself, of immediate presence, or originary perception" (157).

4. Only one of Spencer's many narrative and descriptive passages within a work of philosophical argumentation, this fascinating comparison summons up the richly novelistic educational writings of Rousseau and Pestalozzi.

5. Spencer goes on to answer his rhetorical question: educators fear that physical exercise will develop their female students into unnatural, "masculine" women. Working to allay such fears, he builds an argument in favor of physical education for women.

6. Like Lord Jim, heroes of schoolboy novels often find their ultimate self-definition in imperialist adventures. After school trains them to master their own inner wilderness, they are fit to tame the "wild" nature embodied in the English colonies.

7. See Clark's excellent introduction to Evelyn Sharp's *The Making of a Schoolgirl* (1897), 5.

8. Hughes is particularly fearful of the influence of older boys who may set a dangerous example for their fags and younger followers. Before Tom leaves for Rugby, his father warns him, "If schools are what they were in my time, you'll see a great many cruel blackguard things done" (72). Repeatedly, Tom's moral well-being is jeopardized by the temptations of school. As Tom and his friend East increasingly flout authority, the headmaster fears that they "may do great harm to all the younger boys" (211). Of course, some of Hughes's warnings are oblique, as when he laments the fate of "the miserable little pretty white-handed curly-headed boys, petted and pampered by some of the big fellows, who... did all they could to spoil them for this world and the next" (233). Uncomfortable even with this indirect reference to the sexual aspects of fagging, Hughes expresses regret in a footnote that he cannot strike out the above passage. As he adds, "many boys will know why it is left in" (233, note).

9. Crimsworth's disdain for his female pupils involves many factors, including his wariness about Catholicism and Catholic education, prejudices that his author appears to share. At the same time, Crimsworth's queasy disgust for female sexuality has much to do with his disillusionment.

10. In Brontë's *Villette*, the school garden almost exhibitionistically displays its contrasting identities. The site of a fetishized privacy, it is also revealed as the ultimate site of surveillance, supervised by the vigilant Paul Emmanuel from his chamber window. Promising solitude, it is yet supremely social, the charming background for fêtes and celebrations. Standing in opposition to the rigid etiquette of the classroom, it nevertheless at certain seasons dominates the general school life, even merging seamlessly with school activities and imparting its laxness to familiar routines. For all its air of flowery festival, it is a burial ground in at least two senses, the legendary graveyard of a nun walled up alive for sexual transgressions and also the site where Lucy chooses to entomb one facet

of her secret erotic life, along with her packet of Dr. John's letters. While it invites erotic transgressions, hospitably receiving love letters dropped into its leafy alleys, it also lends itself to erotic mortifications.

CHAPTER 4

1. Some thirty years later, in George Gissing's *A Life's Morning* (1888), the sensitive university student Wilfrid Athel enacted the same pattern, retreating home in nervous prostration after following a too-ambitious course of reading and study.

2. In 1866, John Davies, a parish schoolmaster who himself died two years later of a chronic, unspecified disease, enumerates the dismal record of illnesses prevalent at the Northam School: "April 11: Odiam sent home on acct of measles—Moore sent home on acct of ringworm—Tolman sent home, measles... April 17: A very full school, although many boys were ill. April 25: Three boys sent home very ill... May 2: Many boys at home ill—measles very prevalent" (Gadd 63). In 1876, scarlet fever attacked the families of children who attended the Whitchurch Parish School in Oxfordshire. One logbook record is tersely eloquent about its effects: "July 14: Weather severly [*sic*] Hot teachers & children have not much ener[g]y for their work. Scarlet fever still raging" (Horn 53).

3. According to Bailin, "in Martin Yorke's admittedly exaggerated, but narratively definitive account" of Robert Moore's convalescence in *Shirley*, "Moore [is] 'mewed up, kept in solitary confinement. They mean to make an idiot or a maniac of him'" (67–68).

4. See Jameson's footnote, in *Sisters of Charity* 12–16.

5. See Nightingale's footnote 9 of *Notes on Nursing*.

6. Robson's *School Architecture* (1874) cites numerous earlier works from Germany, France, England and America. See, in particular, Barnard's *School Architecture* (1848), an expansion of his earlier *School-House Architecture* (1842). Later works, such as Dresslar's *School Hygiene* (1913), continue to make the point as emphatically.

7. See Nightingale's lengthy note on page 23 of *Notes on Nursing*.

8. In *Notes on Nursing*, Nightingale laments:

   so often... a great grandmother, who was a tower of physical vigour descend[s] into a grandmother perhaps a little less vigorous but still sound as a bell and healthy to the core, into a mother languid and confined to her carriage and house, and lastly into a daughter sickly and confined to her bed. For, remember, even with a general decrease of mortality you may often find a race thus degenerating and still oftener a family. You may see poor little feeble washed-out rags, children of a noble stock, suffering morally and physically, throughout their useless, degenerate lives, and yet people who are going

to marry and to bring more such into the world, will consult
nothing but their own convenience as to where they are to live,
or how they are to live (22).

Writing at the beginning of the twentieth century in the *Eugenicist Review*, A. A. Tredgold similarly emphasizes the insidiousness of the slow generational process of mental decline. Beginning with mild conditions such as "migraine" or "hysteria," such mental flaws might easily be exacerbated, in successive generations, into "insanity" or "deficiency" (quoted in Jackson, *Borderland of Imbecility* 99).

9. See "Female Circulation" in *Body/Politics* (1990), ed. Mary Jacobus, 59.
10. In *Notes on Nursing*, Florence Nightingale also argues that the repeated violation of the "physical laws" of health may be seen as unwitting crimes. She likens the typical citizen's laxness in combating preventable diseases—diseases metaphorized as the secret "murderers, in the musty unaired rooms" of unhealthy houses—to a newspaper account of a madman who "cut the throat" of a "poor consumptive creature" (7).
11. One of May's better-known works, *Louis's Schooldays* (1850), traces the previous education of the schoolboy hero of *Dashwood Priory, or Mortimer's College Life*.
12. See Nightingale, footnote, 47.

CONCLUSION

1. See Clark's illuminating introduction to the novel.
2. As in *Tom Brown*, the playing field renders boys' characters transparent: "Rody Kickham... would be captain of the third line all the fellows said. Rody Kickham was a decent fellow but Nasty Roche was a stink" (*Portrait* 5).
3. Like his many fictive predecessors, Stephen loves looking out the window while ill at school: "How pale the light was at the window! But that was nice" (31).
4. In *Sticks and Stones: The Troublesome Success of Children's Literature from Slovenly Peter to Harry Potter*, Jack Zipes argues that conventional assumptions and generic plot elements underlie the apparent originality and phenomenal success of the Harry Potter series: "In the case of the Harry Potter books, the phenomenality detracts from their conventionality, and yet their absolute conformance to popular audience expectations is what makes for their phenomenality" (176).

BIBLIOGRAPHY

PRIMARY WORKS

Novels

Alcott, Louisa M. *Little Men: Life at Plumfield with Jo's Boys.* 1871. Boston: Little Brown, 1940.

Brontë, Anne. *Agnes Grey.* 1847. Oxford: Clarendon, 1988.

Brontë, Charlotte. *Jane Eyre.* 1847. Oxford: Clarendon, 1969.

_____. *The Professor.* 1857. Oxford: Clarendon, 1987.

_____. *Shirley.* 1849. Oxford: Clarendon, 1979.

_____. *Villette.* 1853. Oxford: Clarendon, 1984.

Carroll, Lewis. *Alice's Adventures in Wonderland and Through the Looking-Glass.* 1865 and 1872. New York: Penguin/Signet Classic, 1960.

Conrad, Joseph. *Lord Jim.* 1900. Boston: Riverside, 1958.

Dickens, Charles. *Bleak House.* 1852-1853. Oxford: Oxford University Press, 1987.

_____. *A Child's History of England.* 1851-1853. London: Bradbury and Evans, 1852-1854.

_____. *David Copperfield.* 1849–1850. The Oxford Illustrated Dickens. London: Oxford University Press, 1966.

_____. *Dombey and Son.* 1846–1848. The Oxford Illustrated Dickens. Oxford: Oxford University Press, 1987.

_____. *Great Expectations.* 1860–1861. The Oxford Illustrated Dickens. Oxford: Oxford University Press, 1987.

_____. *Hard Times.* 1854. The Oxford Illustrated Dickens. London: Oxford University Press, 1970.

_____. *The Life and Adventures of Martin Chuzzlewit.* 1843–1844. The Oxford Illustrated Dickens. London: Oxford University Press, 1968.

_____. *The Life and Adventures of Nicholas Nickleby.* 1838–1839. The Oxford Illustrated Dickens. London: Oxford University Press, 1950.

_____. *Our Mutual Friend.* 1864–1865. The Oxford Illustrated Dickens. London: Oxford University Press, 1970.

Eliot, George. *The Mill on the Floss.* 1860. Oxford: Clarendon, 1980.

_____. *Felix Holt*. 1866. Oxford: Clarendon, 1980.

_____. *Daniel Deronda*. 1876. Oxford: Clarendon, 1988.

_____. *Middlemarch*. 1871–1872. Oxford: Oxford University Press, 1997.

Farrar, Frederic W. *Eric, or Little by Little. A Tale of Roslyn School*. 1858. New York: Rudd and Carleton, 1859.

Gaskell, Elizabeth. *North and South*. 1854-1855. New York: Penguin Books, 1970. Rpt, 1979.

Gissing, George. *A Life's Morning*. 1888. New York: Harvester Press, 1984.

_____. *The Odd Women*. 1893. New York: New American Library, 1983.

Hardy, Thomas. *Jude the Obscure*. 1894-1895. Boston, MA: Houghton Mifflen, 1965.

Hughes, Thomas. *Tom Brown's Schooldays*. 1857. Oxford: Oxford University Press, 1989.

Joyce, James. *A Portrait of the Artist as a Young Man*. 1916. New York: The Modern Library, 1996.

Martineau, Harriet. *Deerbrook*. 1839. 2 vols. New York: Harper, 1839.

_____. *The Crofton Boys*. 1841. London: Charles Knight and Co., 1841.

May, E. J. *Louis's Schooldays: A Story for Boys*. 1850. New York: Appleton and Co., 1852.

_____. *Dashwood Priory, or Mortimer's College Life*. 1855. New York: Appleton & Co., 1856.

Meade, L. T. *Betty: A Schoolgirl*. 1894. New York: Grosset & Dunlap, 1894.

_____. *The School Favourite*. 1908. London: W. & R. Chambers, 1908.

_____. *The Darling of the School*. 1915. London: W. & R. Chambers, 1915.

Rousseau, Jean-Jacques. *Julie, or the New Heloise*. 1761. *The Collected Writings of Rousseau*, vol. 6. Translated by Philip Stewart and Jean Vache. Hanover, NH: University Press of New England, 1997.

Rowling, J. K. *Harry Potter and the Sorcerer's Stone*. 1997. New York: Scholastic, 1997.

Sharp, Evelyn. *The Making of a Schoolgirl*. 1897. Oxford: Oxford University Press, 1989.

Shelley, Mary. *Frankenstein*. 1816. Oxford World's Classics. Oxford: Oxford University Press, 2001.

Sterne, Lawrence. *The Life and Opinions of Tristram Shandy, Gentleman*. 1759-67. New York: Oxford University Press, Oxford World Classics, 1983.

Trollope, Anthony. *Dr. Wortle's School*. 1880. London: Penguin Classics, 1999.

Nonfiction

Arnold, Matthew. *Culture and Anarchy*. 1869. Cambridge: Cambridge University Press, 1960.

_____. *Discourses in America*. 1885. London: Macmillan, 1896.

_____. *Reports on Elementary Schools, 1852-1882*. 1889. London: Macmillan, 1889.

Barnard, Henry. *School Architecture*. 1848. New York: Teachers College Press, 1970.

Blomfield, Reginald. *The Formal Garden in England*. 1892. London: Macmillan, 1936.

Burton, Robert. *The Anatomy of Melancholy*. 1621. New York: Farrar and Rinehart, 1927.

Carlyle, Thomas. *Sartor Resartus*. 1836. Oxford: Oxford University Press, 1987.

Carpenter, William. *Principles of Mental Physiology, with Their Applications to the Training and Discipline of the Mind, and the Study of Its Morbid Conditions*. 1874. New York: Appleton and Co., 1882.

Coleridge, Derwent. *The Teachers of the People; a Tract for the Time, with an Introductory Address to the Right Honourable Sir John Taylor Coleridge, D.C.L.* London: Rivingtons, 1862.

Currie, James. *The Principles and Practice of Common School Education*. 1862. Cincinnati, OH: Robert Clarke, 1884.

Dresslar, Fletcher B. *School Hygiene*. 1913. (Facsimile Edition) New York: The Macmillan Company, 1998.

The Education Papers: Women's Quest for Equality in Britain, 1850–1912. Edited by Dale Spender. New York: Routledge, 1987.

Eliot, George. *The George Eliot Letters*. Edited by Gordon S. Haight. 6 vols. New Haven, CT: Yale University Press, 1954.

Eveleth, Samuel F. *School-House Architecture*. New York: American News Company, 1870.

Froebel, Friedrich. *Autobiography of Friedrich Froebel*. 1861. Translated by Emilie Michaelis and H. Keatley Moore. Syracuse, NY: C. C. Bardeen, 1889.

Greene, M. Louise. *Among School Gardens*. Philadelphia, PA: Russell Sage Foundation, 1910.

Household Words: A Weekly Journal conducted by Charles Dickens. Formerly *All the Year Round*. Ed. Charles Dickens. London: Bradbury & Evans, 1850-1859.

Hume, David. *A Treatise of Human Nature*. 1739–1740. Vol. 1 of *David Hume: The Philosophical Works*. Edited by Thomas Hill Green and Thomas Hodge Grose. Darmstadt, Germany: Scientia Verlag Aalen, 1964.

Huxley, Thomas Henry. "A Liberal Education; and Where to Find It," 27–53. In *Lay Sermons*. 1870. New York: Appleton and Co., 1870.

———. *Science and Culture*. 1880. London: Macmillan, 1882.

Jameson, Anna. *Sisters of Charity: Catholic and Protestant, Abroad and at Home*. 1855. 2nd Ed., Enlarged, with a new preface. London: Longman, Brown, Green, and Longmans, 1855.

Locke, John. *An Essay Concerning Human Understanding*. 1690. London: Oxford University Press, 1975.

———. *Some Thoughts Concerning Education*. 1693. Oxford: Clarendon, 1989.

Mill, James. *Analysis of the Phenomena of the Human Mind.* 2nd ed. 2 vols., 1869. New York: Augustus M. Kelley, 1967.

_____. *James Mill on Education.* Edited by W. H. Burston. London: Cambridge University Press, 1969.

Mill, John Stuart. *The Autobiography of John Stuart Mill.* 1873. Edited by A. O. J. Cockshut. Halifax: Ryburn, 1992.

Newman, John Henry. *The Idea of a University.* 1852. New Haven, CT: Yale University Press, 1996.

Nightingale, Florence. *Notes on Nursing: What It Is, and What It Is Not.* 1859. New York: Churchill Livingstone, 1980.

Pestalozzi, Johann Heinrich. *How Gertrude Teaches Her Children, an Attempt to Help Mothers to Teach Their Own Children and an Account of the Method.* Translated by Lucy E. Holland and Francis C. Turner. Edited by Ebenezer Cooke. Syracuse, NY: C. W. Bandeen, 1898.

_____. *Pestalozzi's Educational Writings.* Edited by J. A. Green. New York: Longmans, Green, and Company, 1912.

Robson, E. R. *School Architecture.* 1874. Leicester University Press, 1972.

Rousseau, Jean-Jacques. *Émile, or On Education.* 1762. Translated by Allan Bloom. New York: Basic, 1979.

Ruskin, John. *Sesame and Lilies.* 1865. New York: Thomas Y. Crowell and Co., 1891.

_____. *The Crown of Wild Olive.* 1866. Vol. 1 of *Ruskin's Works.* New York: Lovell, Coryell and Co., 1890.

_____. *The Poetry of Architecture.* 1837-1838. Vol. 12 of *Ruskin's Works.* New York: Lovell, Coryell and Co., 1890.

Schwab, Erasmus. *The School Garden: Being a Practical Contribution to the Subject of Education.* 1870. Translated by Mary Tyler Peabody Mann. New York: M. L. Holbrook and Co., 1879.

School Gardens in Europe: Reports from Consuls of the United States, vol. xx. Bureau of Foreign Commerce, Department of State. Washington, DC: Government Printing Office, 1900.

"The Schoolmaster: Essays on Practical Education," from the *Quarterly Journal of Education.* 2 vols. London: Charles Knight, 1836.

Sipe, Susan B. *School Gardening in English Rural Schools and in London.* U.S. Department of Agriculture, Office of Experimental Stations, Bulletin 204. Washington, DC: Government Printing Office, 1909.

Spencer, Herbert. *Education: Intellectual, Moral, and Physical.* 1861. Paterson, NJ: Littlefield Adams, 1963.

_____. *Social Statics: The Conditions Essential to Human Happiness Specified, and the First of Them Developed.* 1851. New York: Robert Schalkenbach Foundation, 1995.

St. John, James Augustus. *The Education of the People.* London: Chapman and Hall, 1858.

Trollope, Anthony. *An Autobiography*. 1883. London: Oxford University Press, 1950.

Wiese, Ludwig Adolf. *German Letters on English Education, Written during an Educational Tour in 1876*. 1876. Translated by Leonhard Schmitz. New York: G. P. Putnam's Sons, 1879.

SECONDARY WORKS

Adrian, Arthur A. *Dickens and the Parent–Child Relationship*. Athens: Ohio University Press, 1984.

Alexander, Christine. *The Early Writings of Charlotte Brontë*. Buffalo, NY: Prometheus Books, 1983.

Allsobrook, David Ian. *Schools for the Shires: The Reform of Middle-Class Education in Mid-Victorian England*. Manchester: Manchester University Press, 1986.

Andrews, Malcolm. *Dickens and the Grown-Up Child*. London: Macmillan, 1994.

Archer, R. L. *Secondary Education in the Nineteenth Century*. Cambridge: Cambridge University Press, 1921.

Armstrong, Frances. *Dickens and the Concept of Home*. Ann Arbor, MI: UMI Research Press, 1990.

Armstrong, Nancy. *Desire and Domestic Fiction: A Political History of the Novel*. New York: Oxford University Press, 1987.

Bachelard, Gaston. *The Poetics of Space*. 1958. Translated by Maria Jolas. New York: Orion, 1964.

Bailin, Miriam. *The Sickroom in Victorian Fiction*. New York: Cambridge University Press, 1994.

Ball, Nancy. *Educating the People*. London: Maurice Temple Smith, 1983.

_____. *Her Majesty's Inspectorate, 1839–1849*. Edinburgh: Oliver and Boyd, 1963.

Banks, Olive. *Parity and Prestige in English Secondary Education*. London: Routledge and Paul, 1955.

Barney, Richard. *Plots of Enlightenment: Education and the Novel in Eighteenth-Century England*. Stanford, CA: Stanford University Press, 1999.

Bashford, Alison. *Purity and Pollution: Gender, Embodiment and Victorian Medicine*. New York: St. Martin's, 1998.

Binns, Henry Bryan. *A Century of Education: Being the Centenary History of the British & Foreign School Society, 1808-1908*. London: Dent, 1908.

Birchenough, C. *History of Elementary Education in England and Wales from 1800 to the Present Day*. Baltimore, MD: Warwick & York, 1914.

Bloom, Harold, ed. *Charles Dickens's Hard Times*. New York: Chelsea, 1987.

Boone, Troy. *Youth of Darkest England: Working-Class Children at the Heart of Victorian Empire*. New York: Routledge, 2005.

Borer, Mary Cathcart. *Willingly to School*. London: Lutterworth, 1976.

Chase, Karen, and Michael Levenson. *The Spectacle of Intimacy: A Public Life for the Victorian Family*. Princeton, NJ: Princeton University Press, 2000.

Certeau, Michel de. *The Practice of Everyday Life*. 1980. Translated by Steven Rendall. Berkeley: University of California Press, 1984.

Charlesworth, Michael, ed. *The English Garden: Literary Sources and Documents*, Vol. iii, *Chronological Overview, 1772–1910*. East Sussex: Helm Information, Ltd., 1993.

Clark, Beverly Lyon. *Regendering the School Story: Sassy Sissies and Tattling Tomboys*. New York: Garland, 1996.

Cohen, Monica F. *Professional Domesticity in the Victorian Novel: Women, Work, and Home*. Cambridge: Cambridge University Press, 1998.

Collins, Philip. *Dickens and Education*. New York: St. Martin's, 1963.

Deane, Bradley. *The Making of the Victorian Novelist: Anxieties of Authorship in the Mass Market*. New York: Routledge, 2003.

Derrida, Jacques. *Of Grammatology*. Translated by Gayatri Spivak. Baltimore, MD: Johns Hopkins University Press, 1974.

Digby, Anne, and Peter Searby. *Children, School and Society in Nineteenth-Century England*. New York: Macmillan, 1981.

Dilthey, William. *Poetry and Experience. Selected Works*. Edited by Rudolf A. Makkreel and Frithjof Rodi. Princeton, NJ: Princeton University Press, 1985.

Eagleton, Terry. *Myths of Power: A Marxist Study of the Brontës*. New York: Macmillan, 1975.

Ellis, Alec. *Educating Our Masters: Influences on the Growth of Literacy in Victorian Working-Class Children*. Aldershot: Gower, 1985.

Emmison, F. G., ed. *Catalogue of Essex Parish Records, 1240–1894*. Chelmsford: Essex County Council, 1966.

Evans, Keith. *The Development and Structure of the English School System*. London: Hodder and Stoughton, 1985.

Felski, Rita. *Doing Time: Feminist Theory and Postmodern Culture*. New York: New York University Press, 2000.

Foucault, Michel. *The Birth of the Clinic: An Archeology of Medical Perception*. 1963. Translated by A. M. Sheridan Smith. New York: Random House, Vintage Books, 1994.

_____. *Discipline and Punish: The Birth of the Prison*. 1975. Translated by Alan Sheridan. New York: Random House, Vintage Books, 1995.

_____. *Madness and Civilization: A History of Civilization in the Age of Reason*. 1961. Translated by Richard Howard. New York: Random House, 1965.

Gadd, E. W. *Victorian Logs*. Studley: K. A. F. Brewin, 1979.

Gallagher, Catherine, and Stephen Greenblatt. *Practicing New Historicism*. Chicago, IL: University of Chicago Press, 2000.

Gardiner, Dorothy. *English Girlhood at School: A Study of Women's Education through Twelve Centuries*. London: Oxford, 1929.

Gardner, Phil. *The Lost Elementary Schools of Victorian England*. London: Croom Helm, 1984.

Garforth, F. W. *John Stuart Mill's Theory of Education*. New York: Harper and Row, 1979.

Gaskell, Elizabeth. *The Life of Charlotte Brontë*. 1857. London: J. M. Dent, 1997.

Gezari, Janet. *Charlotte Brontë and Defensive Conduct: The Author and the Body at Risk*. Philadelphia: University of Pennsylvania Press, 1992.

Gordon, Lyndall. *Charlotte Brontë: A Passionate Life*. New York: Norton, 1994.

Green, J. A. *The Educational Ideas of Pestalozzi*. London: W. B. Clive, University Tutorial Press, 1911.

Green, Laura Morgan. *Educating Women: Cultural Conflict and Victorian Literature*. Athens: Ohio University Press, 2001.

Habermas, Jürgen. *The Structural Transformation of the Public Sphere: An Inquiry into a Category of Bourgeois Society*. 1962. Translated by Thomas Burger. Cambridge, MA: MIT, 1989.

Hainton, Raymonde, and Godfrey Hainton. *The Unknown Coleridge: The Life and Times of Derwent Coleridge 1800–1883*. London: Janus, 1996.

Hardin, James N. *Reflection and Action: Essays on the* Bildungsroman. Columbia: University of South Carolina Press, 1991.

Harrison, John F. C., ed. *Utopianism and Education: Robert Owen and the Owenites*. Classics in Education 37. New York: Teachers College, Columbia University, 1968.

Hilton, Mary, Morag Styles, and Victor Watson, eds. *Opening the Nursery Door: Reading, Writing, and Childhood, 1600–1900*. New York: Routledge, 1997. — REQUEST

Honey, John Raymond de Symons. *Tom Brown's Universe: The Development of the Victorian Public School*. London: Millington, 1977.

Hopkins, Eric. *Childhood Transformed: Working-Class Children in Nineteenth-Century England*. Manchester: Manchester University Press, 1994.

Horn, Pamela, ed. *Village Education in Nineteenth-Century Oxfordshire: The Whitchurch School Log Book and Other Documents*. Oxford: Oxfordshire Record Society, 1978.

Hurt, J. S. *Elementary Schooling and the Working Classes, 1860–1918*. London: Routledge and Keegan Paul, 1979.

Hutchins, B. L. and A. Harrison. *A History of Factory Legislation*. 1903. New York: Augustus Kelly, 1966.

Jacobus, Mary. "The Buried Letter: Feminism and Romanticism in *Villette*," 42–60. In *Women Writing and Writing About Women*. Edited by Mary Jacobus. London: Croom Helm, 1979.

Jacobus, Mary, Evelyn Fox Keller, and Sally Shuttleworth, eds. *Body/Politics: Women and the Discourses of Science*. New York: Routledge, 1990.

Jackson, Mark. *The Borderland of Imbecility: Medicine, Society, and the Fabrication of the Feeble Mind in Late Victorian and Edwardian England*. New York: Manchester University Press, 2000.

Jennings, Ruth. *Lofty Aims and Lowly Duties: Three Victorian Schoolmasters*. Sheffield: Sheffield Academic Press, 1994.

Jordan, Thomas E. *Victorian Childhood: Themes and Variation*. Albany: State University of New York Press, 1987.

Kane, Penny. *Victorian Families in Fact and Fiction*. London: Macmillan, 1995.

Keen, Suzanne. *Victorian Renovations of the Novel: Narrative Annexes and the Boundaries of Representation*. Cambridge: Cambridge University Press, 1998.

Kelly, Richard. *Lewis Carroll*. Boston, MA: Twayne, 1977.

Kincaid, James R. *Child Loving: The Erotic Child and Victorian Culture*. New York: Routledge, 1992.

Kirkpatrick, Robert J. *Bullies, Beaks, and Flannelled Fools: An Annotated Bibliography of Boys' School Fiction, 1772–1990*. London: E. B. Reproductions, 1990.

Lawrence, Evelyn, ed. *Froebel and English Education*. New York: Schocken Books, 1969.

Leavis, F. R. *The Great Tradition*. 1948. New York: New York University Press, 1964.

Lefebvre, Henri. *The Production of Space*. 1974. Translated by Donald Nicholson-Smith. Cambridge, MA: Blackwell, 1991.

Litvak, Joseph. *Caught in the Act: Theatricality in the 19th Century English Novel*. Berkeley: University of California Press, 1992.

Magnet, Myron. *Dickens and the Social Order*. Philadelphia: University of Pennsylvania Press, 1985.

McGavran, James Holt, ed. *Romanticism and Children's Literature in Nineteenth-Century England*. Athens, GA: University of Georgia Press, 1991.

Moglen, Helene. *Charlotte Brontë: The Self Conceived*. New York: Norton, 1976.

Montague, C. J. *Sixty Years in Waifdom, or The Ragged School Movement in English History*. 1904. Montclair, NJ: Patterson Smith, 1970.

Musgrave, P. W. *From Brown to Bunter: The Life and Death of the School Story*. London: Routledge and Kegan Paul, 1985.

Myers, William. *The Teaching of George Eliot*. Bath: Leicester University Press, 1984.

Nelson, Claudia. *Boys Will Be Girls*. New Brunswick, NJ: Rutgers University Press, 1991.

Nestor, Pauline, ed. *Villette: Contemporary Critical Essays*. London: Macmillan, 1992.

Pedersen, Joyce Senders. *The Reform of Girls' Secondary and Higher Education in Victorian England: A Study of Elites and Educational Change*. New York: Garland, 1987.

Peterson, M. Jeanne. "The Victorian Governess: Status Incongruence in Family and Society," 3–19. In *Suffer and Be Still: Women in the Victorian Age.* Edited by Martha Vicinus. Bloomington: Indiana University Press, 1973.

Poovey, Mary. *The Proper Lady and the Woman Writer: Ideology as Style in the Works of Mary Wollstonecraft, Mary Shelley, and Jane Austen.* Chicago: University of Chicago Press, 1984.

_____. *Uneven Developments: The Ideological Work of Gender in Mid-Victorian England.* Chicago, IL: University of Chicago Press, 1988.

Purvis, June. *Hard Lessons: The Lives and Education of Working-Class Women in Nineteenth-Century England.* Cambridge: Polity, 1989.

_____. *A History of Women's Education in England.* Philadelphia, PA: Open University Press, 1991.

Quigly, Isabel. *The Heirs of Tom Brown: The English School Story.* London: Chatto and Windus, 1982.

Raina, Badri. *Dickens and the Dialectic of Growth.* Madison: University of Wisconsin Press, 1986.

Reichertz, Ronald. *The Making of the Alice Books: Lewis Carroll's Uses of Earlier Children's Literature.* Montreal: McGill-Queen's University Press, 1997.

Richards, Jeffrey. *Happiest Days: The Public Schools in English Fiction.* Manchester: Manchester University Press, 1988.

Sadoff, Dianne F. *Monsters of Affection: Dickens, Eliot, and Brontë on Fatherhood.* Baltimore, MD: Johns Hopkins University Press, 1982.

Sanders, Valerie. *Reason over Passion: Harriet Martineau and the Victorian Novel.* New York: St. Martin's, 1986.

Sandiford, Peter. *The Training of Teachers in England and Wales.* New York: Columbia University Teachers College, 1910.

Scott, Patrick, and Pauline Fletcher, ed. *Culture and Education in Victorian England.* Lewisburg, PA: Bucknell University Press, 1990.

Shuttleworth, Sally Kay. "The Surveillance of a 'Sleepless Eye': The Constitution of Neurosis in *Villette*," 313–335. In *One Culture: Essays in Science and Literature.* Edited by George Levine. Madison, Wisconsin: University of Wisconsin Press, 1987.

Silber, Kate. *Pestalozzi: The Man and His Work.* New York: Schocken Books, 1973.

Simon, Brian, and Ian Bradley, eds. *The Victorian Public School: Studies in the Development of an Educational Institution.* Dublin: Gill and Macmillan, 1975.

Stanley, Arthur Penrhyn. *The Life and Correspondence of Thomas Arnold, D.D., Late Head-Master of Rugby School, and Regius Professor of Modern History in the University of Oxford.* 1844. London: B. Fellowes, 1846.

Sutherland, Gillian. *Policy-Making in Elementary Education, 1870–1895.* Oxford: Oxford University Press, 1973.

Taylor, Jenny Bourne. *In the Secret Theatre of Home: Wilkie Collins, Sensation Narrative, and Nineteenth-Century Psychology.* London: Routledge, 1988.

Vincent, David. "The Domestic and the Official Curriculum in Nineteenth-Century England." In *Opening the Nursery Door: Reading, Writing, and Childhood, 1600–1900.* Edited by Mary Hilton, Morag Styles, and Victor Watson. New York: Routledge, 1997.

Warhol, Robin R., and Diane Price Herndl, eds. *Feminisms: An Anthology of Literary Theory and Criticism.* New Brunswick, NJ: Rutgers University Press, 1991.

Williams, Raymond. *Culture and Society 1780–1959.* New York: Columbia University Press, 1960.

Zipes, Jack. *Happily Ever After: Fairy Tales, Children, and the Culture Industry.* New York: Routledge, 1997.

_____. *Sticks and Stones: The Troublesome Success of Children's Literature from Slovenly Peter to Harry Potter.* New York: Routledge, 2001.

INDEX